ARTHUR SCHOPENHAUER

ARTHUR SCHOPENHAUER
PHILOSOPHER OF PESSIMISM

BY

FREDERICK COPLESTON, S.J.

*Professor Emeritus of History of Philosophy
in the University of London*

SEARCH PRESS LONDON

BARNES & NOBLE BOOKS NEW YORK
(a division of Harper & Row Publishers, Inc.)

SEARCH PRESS LIMITED
2–10 Jerdan Place, London SW6 5PT
First published, 1946
© Frederick Copleston, 1946, 1975
ISBN 0 85532 354 X

Published in the USA 1975 by
Harper & Row Publishers, Inc.
BARNES & NOBLE IMPORT DIVISION
ISBN 0 06 491281 7

REPRODUCED AND PRINTED BY PHOTOLITHOGRAPHY AND BOUND IN
GREAT BRITAIN AT THE PITMAN PRESS, BATH

CONTENTS

PREFACE TO THE SECOND EDITION

THIS BOOK was first published some thirty years ago. Mr Patrick Gardiner's excellent Penguin Book on Schopenhauer appeared in 1963. So did the two chapters on Schopenhauer in the seventh volume (*Fichte to Nietzsche*) of my *History of Philosophy* (a fact which explains the absence in my bibliography of any reference to Mr Gardiner's book). There is not however very much in English on this subject; and there seems to be a certain demand for the reprinting of my 1944 work. If I were now setting out to write a book on Schopenhauer, the result would doubtless be rather different from my actual publication. But the 1944 book embodied a distinctive approach and point of view; and this fact constitutes a reason for reprinting it in its original form. I do not think that a policy of tinkering here and there with the text would be a satisfactory procedure; and I have neither the time nor the inclination to produce a new work.

Schopenhauer has a widely ranging and impressive vision of the universe and of human life. One conspicuous feature of it is the prominence given to what we may describe as the dark aspects of the world and of man's life and history. This feature, Schopenhauer's vivid realization and portrayal of the prevalence of suffering and evil, might be expected to commend his thought to those who feel impatient at the way in which some philosophers have treated the theme in a remarkably cavalier manner. Schopenhauer doubtless tries to explain; but he does not try to explain away. Another main feature of his philosophy is the metaphysical significance which it ascribes to the fine arts, and to music in particular, and the role which they are represented as playing in human life. And though the way in which philosophers such as Schelling, Hegel and Schopenhauer incorporate aesthetics into a general metaphysical vision and subordinate it to the demands of an overall pattern doubtless seems to a good many minds to be thoroughly misguided, there are others to whom Schopenhauer's ideas about art and the artist might be expected to appeal. A third salient feature is the philosopher's interest in oriental religion, in Hinduism and Buddhism. By modern standards he was far from being an expert in this field; but the use which he made of themes taken from oriental thought might be expected to attract some of those in the modern world who look to the wisdom of the East for a way of salvation. Finally, Schopenhauer had a wide knowledge of literature and could write not only intelligibly but well, salting his philosophical works and essays both with wit and with amusingly pungent remarks about institutions and persons, especially about his rivals in the philosophical field. As far as literary style goes, Schopenhauer might well be thought more likely to attract readers than most other German philosophers, apart of course from Nietzsche.

Though however one can think of reasons why the philosophy of Schopenhauer should attract the attention of various classes of people, it could hardly be said to have enjoyed any lasting popular success. In the last years of his life Schopenhauer did indeed become famous; and he was for a time one of the more respected metaphysical philosophers. But it would be rash to claim that he is much read nowadays. It is natural to ascribe this eclipse to the fact that nineteenth-century idealism was succeeded by other lines of thought and to a prevailing mistrust of overall world-views and metaphysical systems. Though however these are doubtless influential factors, they do not seem to provide a complete explanation. For Hegel, one of Schopenhauer's main objects of outspoken disapproval, can hardly be said to have been forgotten, certainly not if we bear in mind recent philosophical literature in countries other than our own. It is reasonable to argue that we have to take into consideration features peculiar to Schopenhauer's thought. For example, when speaking of the debate between materialism and theism William James remarks that theism guarantees an ideal order which will be permanently preserved; and it is arguable that part of the attraction of both theistic and idealist world-views lies in their representations of history, cosmic and human, as a teleological process, a movement towards an ideal goal. With Schopenhauer however it is a question of the individual seeing through the veil of Maya and turning away from this world towards what can be described, from the phenomenal point of view at any rate, as ' nothingness ', the negation of the will to live. This is not an idea which is likely to appeal to those who are attracted, for instance, by the thought of Teilhard de Chardin. It is of course much more likely to appeal to those who feel drawn towards the Hindu religious philosophy of Brahman or to Buddhism. But most of these are probably more interested in practices such as ' transcendental meditation ' than in struggling with a nineteenth-century thinker who tries to exhibit his philosophy as a development of the thought of Kant. Besides, Schopenhauer would be a rather indirect way of approaching oriental religious philosophy. Again, while the writings of Schopenhauer may attract those who feel that opting out is a desirable policy, those who are interested in social reform and in working for a more just society are unlikely to feel much enthusiasm for the thought of someone who had no use for the revolutionary movements of his time and who regarded the function of the State as being simply that of preserving order and protecting property. To read Hegel simply in function of Marx is of course a very one-sided procedure. At the same time Hegel lays great emphasis on social-political life; and this emphasis is conspicuously lacking in the case of Schopenhauer. The latter may have excelled at depicting some of the horrors of human existence and history; but the policy of turning away towards the attainment of Nirvana is not calculated to attract those who feel the need for more positive action in this world and believe that sympathy or compassion based on a metaphysical view of the phenomenal character of this world of multiplicity is not enough.

It would indeed be an exaggeration if one were to say or imply that the philosophy of Schopenhauer has fallen into complete neglect. But it seems true to say that the interest which it has won in recent years has tended to arise in an indirect manner, that is to say by way of the thought of other writers. To take an obvious example, students of Nietzsche are naturally stimulated to acquire some knowledge of the philosopher who at one time exercised a powerful attraction on Nietzsche's mind and whom Nietzsche never ceased to admire despite his insistence on the need for substituting a yea-saying attitude to life for a no-saying or negating attitude. Again, interest in the music and ideas of Richard Wagner naturally prompts one to seek some acquaintance with the thought of Schopenhauer. And similar remarks can be made in regard to those who make any extended study of literary figures such as Thomas Mann. Another example would be investigation into the early influences on Wittgenstein's mind, which demands some knowledge of Schopenhauer's thought. Further, quite apart from cases of direct influence on other philosophers and writers, Schopenhauer's philosophy can excite the interest of those who look for anticipations of themes treated by writers who do not appear to have been directly influenced by the

German thinker. For instance, Bergson's theory of the basic vital role of the intellect reminds one forcibly of Schopenhauer's idea of the practical function of perception and intelligence, though there is no evidence that the former borrowed his ideas from the latter. Again, though Freud certainly did not derive his theories from Schopenhauer, there is a good deal in the philosopher's thought which can be regarded as an anticipation of Freudian themes.

These remarks are not of course intended as an assessment of the value of Schopenhauer's philosophy. If it has suffered an eclipse, this does not necessarily show that it deserved to be forgotten. And if in recent years it has generally been approached in the indirect ways referred to above, this does not prove that it has no intrinsic claims to be studied for its own sake. A good deal depends however on our estimate of Schopenhauer's overall vision of reality. To be sure, there are a good many individual lines of thought which may seem to merit attention. In some cases however these are presented in the writings of other philosophers too. If, for instance, we isolate Schopenhauer's theory of character-determinism from its general context and consider it by itself, it has an evident affinity with a line of thought expounded by J. S. Mill. Again, there is an evident affinity between some of his ideas and those of Henri Bergson. The overall vision of reality however, the philosophical system as a whole, is certainly not to be found in the writings of Bergson, and still less in those of J. S. Mill. Whether or not one mistrusts world-views, it is with reference to his own vision of reality that Schopenhauer has to be judged.

This consideration gives rise of course to the question whether there are any criteria for assessing the merits and demerits of such world-views. No doubt there are. There are internal criteria, such as intelligibility and coherence. And when it is a question of comparing different world-views, we can ask, for example, whether one world-view emphasizes a particular aspect of the world or of human life at the expense of other aspects which receive more adequate treatment in another philosophy. Further, unless we propose to treat metaphysical systems simply as though they were analogous to pictures or poems or symphonies, we can examine and assess the argument by which a given philosopher claims to establish his views. To be sure, a person who accepts a world-view may do so because it seems to him to ' click ', to represent the universe as it is or to explain certain features of the world or of human life or history, when explanation means seeing something in the light of an overall pattern. He may not bother much, if at all, about particular arguments. Further, if someone is convinced that the basic and valuable element in a metaphysical system is simply the general vision and that the arguments advanced to support it are of minor importance, he is likely to find any detailed examination of such arguments a tiresome procedure, an activity pursued by pedants who are unable to appreciate the significant element in the philosophy in question and concentrate instead on niggling criticism. Though however this attitude is understandable and expresses a judgment of value with which one can sympathize, the fact remains that if a philosopher offers arguments to prove or support certain positions, it is perfectly reasonable to examine their nature and function and to assess their merits or demerits as arguments. To recognize this fact it is not necessary to go to the extreme of maintaining that the sole job of a philosopher is to pursue critical evaluation of other philosophers' arguments. We are not confined to a choice between claiming that philosophy consists simply in argumentation and in critical evaluation of arguments and claiming that all that counts is impressionistic vision.

It would obviously be inappropriate to use a preface as a place in which to embark on a systematic application of stated criteria of judgment to a philosophy which had not yet been even outlined. If however a book is being reprinted after a considerable interval of time, and the author chooses to add a new preface, he is entitled to make comments in it about his own treatment of the theme. So I propose to make a few brief remarks about my handling of Schopenhauer's philosophy.

The book is written from a Christian point of view, a point of view which is not Schopenhauer's. It may therefore appear that criticism is external, in the sense that Schopenhauer's philosophy is compared with Christian belief and rejected when it conflicts with such belief. And it is undeniable that there is some ground for this impression. The concluding pages of the book show clearly enough that the author assumes the truth of Christianity and judges Schopenhauer's world-picture in accordance with this assumption. At the same time in the course of the book the philosopher is frequently criticized on the ground of incoherence, in the sense of incompatibility between different elements of or positions in his overall world-view. Such criticism may tend to take the form of a somewhat tiresome sniping at frequent intervals; but it is internal, and it is, I think, often justified. Schopenhauer is not incoherent in the sense of being unintelligible. On the contrary, it is because he is intelligible that we are able to detect inconsistencies. There is of course nothing to be surprised at if there are some inconsistencies in any intellectual construction which aims at giving an overall picture of reality. If a philosopher confines his attention to one particular clearly defined and easily manageable theme, he may be able to avoid inconsistency. If however he extends the range of his reflection to cover the universe, the risk of overlooking inconsistencies is obviously increased. At the same time we may well feel that it is preferable that some philosophers should incur the risk than that no philosopher should do so. The intellectual heritage of mankind would be very much poorer if there had been no thinkers prepared to take the risks involved in the construction of overall world-views. Apart however from the risks run in common by the authors of metaphysical systems, there is a special feature of Schopenhauer's thought which provides occasion for criticism on the score of inconsistency. He was an admirer of Kant, and his theory of the world as 'idea', as phenomenal, is based on a development of Kantian themes. He then proceeds to claim knowledge of the nature of what appears, of the thing-in-itself; and it is doubtful whether his metaphysics of the Will can be harmonized successfully with his use of Kantian themes. In a sense he uses Kant to go beyond Kant. And though he may regard himself as Kant's true successor, it is by no means everybody who would accept this view of the matter.

It is however understandable if some readers grow impatient when an eminent philosopher is criticized on the ground of inconsistencies in his thought. For one thing, even if two positions are incompatible or at least difficult to harmonize, this does not show which of them is right. Indeed, if they are not simply contradictory, neither of them may be right. Or each may contain an element of truth. For another thing, the game of detecting inconsistencies tends to divert attention from the philosopher's overall vision and thus to appear as the niggling criticism of a small mind. Thus in Schopenhauer's case there may well be some difficulty in harmonizing the doctrine expounded in the first book of his *magnum opus* with his meta-physics of the Will; and Kant would presumably think that the difficulty was insuperable. But this does not alter the fact that the metaphysics of the Will expresses an original and striking vision of reality. It cannot be refuted simply by observing that it does not fit in with other elements of Schopenhauer's thought. For it might be in itself a perfectly reasonable way of seeing the world. Moreover, it might be possible to restate Schopenhauer's philosophy in such a way that the Kantian elements which barred the way to metaphysics would be eliminated. At any rate it cannot simply be taken for granted that this possibility is excluded.

In Schopenhauer's opinion the genuine or true philosopher is the thinker whose problems arise out of reflection on the world itself, whereas the ' false ' philosopher inherits his problems from the writings of his predecessors, from books. This point of view may indeed have been proposed in a pole-mical spirit and have involved injustice to the contemporary thinkers of whom Schopenhauer disapproved. For example, inquiry into the development of Hegel's thought shows clearly enough that to a very considerable extent his problems arose out of reflection on the world about him, the cultural situation. Some of Hegel's problems can indeed be seen as arising in the context of post-Kantian philosophy and in dialogue with other philosophers; but, as has already been noted, Schopenhauer himself treated questions which he regarded as arising out of the critical philosophy of Kant. At the same time he undoubt-edly looked directly at the world about him, human and non-human; and he did not allow his vision to be obscured by theories which glossed over what presented itself to his gaze. He may indeed exaggerate the shadows; and some of his ideas, such as his analysis of happiness as ' negative ', seem to me untenable. But, as I have suggested at the end of the first chapter on Schopenhauer in the seventh volume of my *History of Philosophy*, it is precisely because of its one-sidedness that his picture of the world can serve ' as an effective counter-balance or antithesis to a system such as that of Hegel in which attention is so focused on the triumphant march of Reason through his-tory that the evil and suffering in the world are obscured from view by high-sounding phrases '.

Recognition of the evil and suffering in the world is not however the same thing as doing metaphysics. And it is tempting to assume that Schopenhauer proposes his metaphysical theory of the one Will, manifesting itself in all phenomena, as an explanatory hypothesis, intended, that is to say, to explain the restless and unceasing striving after self-perpetuation, even at the expense of other persons or things, which the philosopher finds in all things. The examples of this striving which Schopenhauer finds in the inorganic, organic and human spheres can then be regarded as designed to serve as empirical confirmation of the hypothesis.

In point of fact Schopenhauer does not propose his theory of the one Will as an hypothesis designed to explain the evil and suffering in the world. He maintains that access to the thing-in-itself is provided through inner consciousness, in which one becomes aware that bodily action is simply objectified will. And he argues that the thing-in-itself must be one unique reality inasmuch as multiplicity belongs to the phenomenal sphere. In other words, Schopenhauer first tries to establish that our world is phenomenal and then, despite Kant, claims that we can have access to the thing-in-itself which, as underlying and manifesting itself in phenomena, must be one reality. We can thus regard the copious examples of restless striving, of egoism and of strife as designed more to show the nature of the one Will to live than to prove its existence, though Schopenhauer doubtless thought of them as also pointing to the existence of the underlying reality which he described as Will. The examples however are clearly not so much logical demonstrations as persuasive arguments designed to show that a metaphysical theory of the ultimate reality is exemplified on the phenomenal or empirical level. If I were now writing a book on Schopenhauer, I would plan to devote more space to analyzing the kinds of arguments which he employs. But this might of course result in a duller book, at any rate for those who are primarily concerned with his general view of reality and with his aesthetic and ethical doctrines.

Schopenhauer's ethics is of course an integral part of a general philosophy. It is not simply an afterthought, as it were, an addition prompted by reflection on Hindu and Buddhist themes and, to a lesser extent, on Christianity. It cannot of course be regarded as logically deducible from Schopenhauer's metaphysics, if this is interpreted as being purely descriptive. But I do not think that his theory of the Will is purely descriptive, in the sense of being free from all judgments of value.

For he tends to speak of the Will in terms which imply that it is evil in itself. In any case it is the source of all evil, and subservience or slavery to the Will is represented as the root of all phenomenal evil and suffering. In this case of course it follows that the desirable line of conduct is to turn away from the Will; and as the Will is described as the Will to live, this means turning away from life towards the absence of all striving and desire, towards Nirvana. A partial and temporary emancipation is achieved through aesthetic contemplation, but a lasting peace can be won only through the transcending of the ego. Given Schopenhauer's description of the metaphenomenal Will, peace could not be won through absorption into it. He does indeed admit that the ultimate reality might conceivably have attributes which are unknown to us. But, as manifested in phenomena, the Will is itself the source of all evil and suffering. Hence, as far as we can see, liberation from the servitude to the Will can be achieved only through entry into nothingness, the total extinction of the personality.

We may well ask of course how the Will in its finite manifestation can turn against itself in self-loathing and achieve extinction. There are other awkward questions too which can be put to Schopenhauer in regard both to his aesthetics and to his ethics. To a good many readers however such questions appear tiresome. They are more likely to be concerned with the question whether the policy of turning away from life in asceticism and mortification is a desirable one. If it is judged undesirable, it is presumably because man is thought of as having a moral vocation in this world, directed, for instance, towards the development of a better society. But on Schopenhauer's premisses this view would hardly make sense. If we believe simply that the world and human history are ' meaningless ', in the sense that they have no goal or end determined independently of human choice, we can perfectly well maintain that man shows his peculiar dignity in striving after the realization of moral ideals in a meaningless world. But if empirical reality is necessarily riddled with evil and suffering and if life is inevitably a source of evil and strife, the sensible policy would seem to be that of turning away from life   In other words, reflection on Schopenhauer's ethics turns our attention back to his theory of reality, his metaphysics. It is not simply a case of absence of ' meaning ', as in the thought of Albert Camus. It is a case of a metaphysical source of evil, which constitutes the ' inside ', so to speak, of the phenomenal world. And a turning away from this world and from life to Nirvana is thus the only reasonable course of action, on the assumption that its possibility is consistent with Schopenhauer's premisses.

It is not my intention to suggest that the way of life (or, if preferred, way out of life) commended by Schopenhauer is non-detachable from his metaphysics. If, as I have suggested, his metaphysics includes basic judgments of value or at any rate provides grounds for making certain determinate value-judgments, the connexion between it and the philosopher's ethics is obviously made closer than it would be if the ethics were simply something added on under the influence of oriental thought. At the same time the ethics is detachable in the sense that it would be possible to commend the policy of overcoming self-centredness and mortifying desire without mentioning the metaphysics of the one Will, just as it would be possible to commend Stoic ideals of conduct without mentioning the Stoic metaphysics or to expound the Epicurean ethics without saying anything about the theory of atoms which Epicurus took over from the Greek atomists. If however it is a question of turning away from life, it is only natural to ask, to what is one directed or exhorted to turn instead? Is it to union with the Absolute or to nothingness? Of course, if union with the Absolute is regarded as involving absorption in the One and if nothingness is interpreted as the extinction of individual consciousness and personality, it is obviously arguable that the two come ultimately to the same thing, and that it really makes no difference whether one talks about Union with the Absolute or Brahman or what not or whether one talks about nothingness. My point however is simply that reflection on the policy of turning away from life and the world leads naturally to questions about the nature of reality. Besides, Schopenhauer would clearly wish to support his ethical ideas by referring to metaphysical themes. For example, the ideal of sympathy is supported by the doctrine that individuation is phenomenal, belonging to the veil of Maya, so that other people's sufferings are also one's own. Again, the ideal of holiness, attained through asceticism and holiness, is supported by Schopenhauer's view of the nature of the Will.

Supporting moral judgments by means of factual assertions is obviously a common practice. If we say that Tom is a good man and someone asks us why we think so, we may mention actions which Tom has done or various features of his conduct or his habitual disposition to act in certain ways. It is possible of course that we might be appealing simply to linguistic convention. That is to say, when we say that Tom is good, it is possible at any rate that we mean simply that Tom is the sort of man who is conventionally described as good, and that we support this statement by referring to lines of conduct which are conventionally thought to exemplify the concept of goodness. But let us suppose that when we say that Tom is good, we do not simply mean that the word ' good ' is so used in ordinary language as to apply to Tom. This may well be implied; but let us suppose that we are also sincerely describing Tom as being good and that we are using the word to commend or praise Tom. In this case, when we refer to facts, such as Tom consistently acting in certain ways, we are not simply mentioning facts: we are also saying, implicitly at least, that these ways of acting are themselves good. We express a moral attitude towards them. In other words, though we do make factual assertions, judgments of value are implied. And it seems to me that when Schopenhauer supports his ethical teaching by means of metaphysical theories, judgments of value are implied which make the connexion reasonable. For example, when he describes the empirical world as phenomenal, as belonging to the sphere of Maya, he implies that penetration of the veil of Maya is a good thing, a commendable policy. It would be possible for someone to maintain that it would be much better to remain in the sphere of ' illusion ' than to attempt to penetrate beyond into a region which, from our point of view at any rate, is the sphere of nothingness. Given however the judgment that penetration of the veil of Maya is a worthy and desirable end, all that remains is the question what this means in practice and what is involved in regard to conduct. We then get Schopenhauer's ethics with its theory of degrees of penetration. There is the level of justice at which a man penetrates the veil of Maya to the extent that he does not assert his own interests or rights to the exclusion of those of other people. There is the level of sympathy or love at which a man sees through, as it were, the appearance of plurality to the extent that he understands that all are ultimately one and that the sufferings of others are also one's own. And there is finally the level of holiness at which the will in its phenomenal manifestation turns against the Will to live which constitutes the ' inside ' of all empirical reality.

As has been already remarked, it is difficult to see how the Will in its phenomenal manifestation can turn against itself, even if Schopenhauer thinks that this is made possible by the development of reason which comes to transcend its biological functions, the slavery of the Will, and is thus able to achieve an objective understanding of reality. Such difficulties apart however, we can see how Schopenhauer's metaphysics and ethics are closely interlocked in one world-view. There is indeed the basic difficulty to which attention has already been drawn. As Schopenhauer starts from a modification or development of the critical philosophy of Kant, does he not at the outset bar the way to knowledge of the thing-in-itself? Schopenhauer is not blind to this difficulty, and he tries to cope with it, though with disputable success. At the same time there can be little doubt that he presents a striking and intelligible world-view. To use a Nietzschean phrase, Schopenhauer is a ' yea-sayer ' to the extent that he paints a picture of the world and of human life and history as he believes that they really are and not as they have been presented by those who refuse to look the facts in the face but prefer to gloss them over in the name of preconceived theories or beliefs. But inasmuch as he turns against reality as he sees it and expounds a way out of life, he is obviously a ' no-sayer '; and it was as such that Nietzsche came to see him. However striking it may be, Schopenhauer's total world-view is likely therefore to have only a limited appeal. For while there are doubtless many people who say No to the world as it is, in regard to this or that feature of, say, human society, they generally accompany this No by saying Yes to some ideal which they believe or hope to be realizable in this world. To utter a comprehensive No in regard to reality and to look on extinction and nothingness as constituting a desirable goal is a procedure which appeals to a much fewer number of people. Not of course that this proves Schopenhauer to be wrong. He would simply comment that he was always well aware that the vast majority of people were caught in the veil of Maya and clung to life, and that holiness, as he saw it, was rare.

The construction of world-views has been attacked from various angles. A stock criticism is that world-views are inevitably impressionistic in character and that the philosopher, being intent on producing a comprehensive synthesis, tends to lump together questions which should be treated separately, to slur over distinctions which should be made, and to pay far too little attention to his arguments. In other words, the development of world-views can hardly be regarded as scientific philosophy. From another angle, the construction of world-views has been criticized on the ground that it is not genuine metaphysics, when metaphysics is taken to involve a reductive process of working back to some unquestionable starting-point, followed by a process of logical deduction. For such critics the so-called transcendental method is essential to genuine metaphysics. Philosophers who construct world-views are thought of as making assumptions which should be subjected to critical questioning. If the philosopher proceeds in an inductive manner, such assumptions are unavoidable. A number of presuppositions are accepted uncritically as a point of departure.

There is clearly a good deal which can be said in favour of the first line of criticism. If however it is suggested, as it once was, that philosophers could really get somewhere and achieve results by considering separately and successively clearly defined small questions (small in comparison with questions about the nature of reality as a whole), the objection arises that philosophical problems tend to interlock and that the laboratory technique also has its drawbacks and its unexamined presuppositions. There is doubtless a middle way between setting out to construct an overall synthesis and trying to break up traditional problems into separate questions which can be solved successively once and for all. But it is not surprising if scientific philosophy tends to become pure logic, something which, it can be argued, is a distinct discipline which should not be labelled ' philosophy '.

As for the second line of criticism mentioned above, talk about genuine metaphysics seems to express a value-judgment which need not necessarily be accepted. It may indeed be claimed that the transcendental method is the only one which leaves no uncriticized assumptions and which leads to assured results. But it is at any rate questionable whether there can be a presuppositionless philosophy; and it is perhaps not quite so clear as the transcendental Thomists seem to think that one can successfully adopt a method taken from Kant and post-Kantian idealism to produce the Thomist metaphysical rabbits out of a reconstituted hat.

These remarks are not intended to imply that all philosophers ought to set about producing world-views, that each should

construct a system. In my opinion this would be a silly suggestion. All I claim is that it is a natural tendency to seek after
an overall view or synthesis, and that there are cases of original
thinkers, gifted with a power of imaginative vision, who are
capable of making the enterprise worth while. In my judgment
Arthur Schopenhauer was one of them. His vision of reality
and of human life possesses a power of stimulus which is not
dependent on one's being a Schopenhauerian.

In regard to religion, Schopenhauer was not of course a
theist. And pantheism he considered even more absurd than
theism. But it by no means follows that he saw no value in
religion. On the contrary, he attached great value to certain
ideals of Christianity and of the great oriental religions. He
did not believe in God, but he certainly believed in a way of
salvation. And he saw exemplifications of it in the Christian
saints and the holy men of Hinduism and Buddhism. He
thought however that what the Christian saints discerned was
wrongly interpreted, in the light of pre-existing beliefs. And
his own interpretation of the way of salvation for human beings
comes much closer to Buddhism, with its doctrine of Nirvana,
than to Christianity, Judaism or Islam. As for Hinduism,
Schopenhauer's concept of the metaphenomenal Will differs
in important respects from the concept of Brahman. It is true
that he confines himself to representing the ultimate reality in
the light of its manifestation in the empirical world, while
admitting, whether consistently or not, that it might conceivably have aspects which are unknown to us. But the restless
tortured Will hardly corresponds to the concept of Brahman.
And emphasis is placed on negation, on the peace of Nirvana.
Those who are attracted by Buddhism might well feel an
interest in the philosophy of Schopenhauer.

The original preface to this reprinted book starts with a
quotation from Miguel de Unamuno in which the " inner biography " of philosophers is said to be the most significant factor
in explaining their ideas. This statement by the Spanish writer
gives rise to the question, to what extent, if any, is knowledge
about a philosopher relevant to an understanding of his
philosophy? On the one hand it may appear that Unamuno
is quite right, inasmuch as philosophical reflection is carried on
by human persons, each of whom exists in a given historical
and cultural situation, is subject to a variety of influences,
internal and external, and may very well be predisposed to see

the world in certain ways. When Unamuno goes on to say that it is usually not our ideas which make us optimists or pessimists, but rather our optimism or pessimism, whether physiological or pathological, which make our ideas, it may seem that this assertion is applicable to Schopenhauer. On the other hand it can obviously be argued that biography, even "inner biography ", is irrelevant from a philosophical point of view. For when a man has published his philosophical reflections, they take on, as it were, a life of their own. His assertions, if intelligible, are either true or false or, if complex, perhaps partly true and partly false. And such assertions can be evaluated without reference to their author. Similarly, the value of an argument can be assessed on logical grounds, and biographical details relating to the philosopher in question are irrelevant. Whether the philosopher was predisposed to see the world in a certain way or to focus his attention on certain aspects of it is a matter for psychologists to discuss From the philosophical point of view we are concerned with the ideas and arguments as expressed, not with the man and his psychological make-up.

It seems to me that no simple and universally valid and applicable answer can be given to the question whether or not knowledge of a philosopher's personality and life is relevant to an understanding of his philosophy. There are of course biographical anecdotes which please some readers, perhaps because they show that philosophers are human beings and not disembodied intellects, but which can hardly be said to be philosophically relevant. There is some material of this kind in the second chapter of this book, which treats of Schopenhauer's life. For example, the fact that the philosopher read the *Times* does not help us to understand his thought. But this sort of thing belongs to what Unamuno would presumably call ' outer ' biography. There are certainly ways in which our understanding of a man's philosophy can be helped by biographical knowledge. We may not be assisted in understanding Kant's *Critiques* by being told that he always took his afternoon walk at precisely the same time; but some knowledge of his intellectual development contributes to an understanding of what he was about. It is doubtless possible to confine one's attention entirely to the texts. And if we knew nothing about Kant himself but had his *Critiques*, this is what one would have to do. As things are however, we possess knowledge about the author which is clearly relevant to an understanding of his critical philosophy.

A good deal obviously depends on the sort of philosophy which we are considering. We do not really require a knowledge of Wittgenstein's life in order to evaluate the picture-theory of the proposition. But if a philosopher tends to universalize his own personal experience, as Kierkegaard did, some knowledge of his life and character may very well help us to see things in perspective. To be sure, if we had no knowledge of Kierkegaard's life but read a book which expounded his theory of the stages on life's way without mention of the author, our lack of biographical knowledge would not prevent us from understanding what we read. At the same time some knowledge of the man would help us to see why he concentrated on three particular stages, the aesthetic, the ethical and the religious, and why he described the transition from one stage to another in the way that he did. From one point of view such knowledge can be regarded as irrelevant to the truth or falsity of what he has written, which lies before us in print, detached, as it were, from the author. From another point of view it seems pretty obvious that in the case of a man such as Kierkegaard, under-standing of his thought as a whole is increased by a knowledge of what Unamuno describes as " inner biography ". The fact that Kierkegaard was much addicted to coffee-drinking may be irrelevant. But as his problems arise in the first instance out of his own life, in the form of alternatives presented for personal choice, it seems only sensible to admit that a knowledge of the background of these problems in the philosopher's life is help-ful, even if it is not strictly necessary. If a man's problems arise out of the contemporary historical situation, as in the case of the social thought of Hobbes, Locke and Marx, some knowledge of the situation in question is clearly helpful for understanding; and it would be thought rather odd if someone insisted on prescinding entirely from the historical background and on treating the relevant texts as though they were timeless realities, without historical roots. Why then should it be thought that " inner biography " is irrelevant, when it is precisely in this area that a man's problems have arisen?

It is reasonable to suppose that one main reason for declaring " inner biography " irrelevant is a certain idea of what philo-sophy should be. If we assume that worthwhile philosophy consists of logical studies, it is clearly arguable that biographical knowledge is without significance for the understanding of a man's philosophy. It may be the case, for example, that a given thinker has concentrated his attention on abstract logical themes as a means of transcending or escaping from acute personal problems. But this is a matter for the psychologists: it has no relevance when it is a question of evaluating logical theories or analyses. To be sure, " inner biography " may be helpful for an understanding of the thought of some people who are commonly described as philosophers, people such as Kierkegaard and Nietzsche. But the more an understanding of a man's philosophy demands a knowledge of the philosopher's personality, character and personal experience, so much the less can he be described as a real philosopher. He may be a great literary figure or religious thinker or prophet or what not; but he is not a ' scientific ' philosopher.

It is open to anyone to recommend this delimiting concept of philosophy. But I consider it too narrow. And while I have no wish to enter here upon a discussion of the range of meaning which it is desirable to give to the word ' philosophy ', I continue to regard persons such as Kierkegaard and Nietzsche, and Unamuno too for the matter of that, as philosophers. Hence I can only say that the question of the relevance of ' inner biography ' to the understanding of a man's philosophical thought is not one to which a simple and universally applicable answer can be given. This may be a banal conclusion. But it can be avoided only by talking about ' real ' philosophy and excluding from the class of real philosophers either those in whose case knowledge of the man is clearly helpful for understanding or those in whose case it is clearly irrelevant from a philosophical, as distinct from a psychological, point of view.

What about Schopenhauer? In his writings we come across a fair number of abusive references to other philosophers and some notoriously uncomplimentary remarks about women. The relevant remarks can obviously be understood without reference to Schopenhauer himself. At the same time some knowledge of the philosopher's life and character helps us to understand the relevant passages in the sense that it enables us to see them in perspective and not to take them with deadly seriousness. Schopenhauer's assertions about women however have little to do with philosophy. In regard to his general world-view, I think that this can perfectly well be considered on its own. Whether Schopenhauer was predisposed to focus his attention on the shadows in the world and in human existence and history seems to me a matter for psychological inquiry. The qualification which I should wish to make to the statement that his philosophy can be considered on its own, without reference to biographical material that is to say, is that a knowledge of Schopenhauer's attitude to Kant and to the development of philosophy after Kant is of considerable assistance in understanding his thought. Indeed, in certain respects it might be considered essential. For I have argued that a basic objection against his philosophy, in the actual form which he gives it, is precisely that he utilizes and develops Kantian themes and then goes on to claim access to and knowledge of the thing-in-itself.

In view of the frequent highly critical remarks about Schopenhauer's philosophy in the book which has been reprinted, it may seem odd that I should ever have written about him at all. One reason why I became interested in him was doubtless the influence which he had on Nietzsche, on whom I had already published a book (*Friedrich Nietzsche: Philosopher of Culture*, 2nd ed., 1975). It may also be the case that the notion, less common indeed in the second world war than in the first, that German philosophers bore a heavy share of responsibility for their country's behaviour helped to interest me in a German thinker for whom the Nazis would obviously have had no use at all. Schopenhauer's theory of a blind, striving and restless Will was not an exhortation to a policy based on the ideas of Blood and Race; and the ethics of the negation of life would hardly be congenial to Adolf Hitler and his associates. Even if however I came to Schopenhauer by way of Nietzsche, and even if I had a certain interest in him because his ethical ideals contrasted so sharply with the policies pursued by the Nazis, it is clear that I would not have written a book about his philosophy, unless it had impressed me. It is true that I criticized his philosophy severely, partly on the ground of internal inconsistencies and partly in the name of Christian optimism. The world however is ambiguous. To be sure, things are as they are. But if one looks for an overall view, there are different possible ways of interpreting them and of fitting them into a general picture. In its main lines Schopenhauer's philosophy represents one of these ways. At the same time I do not myself think it desirable that human beings should say No to life.

(London, 1974)   *F. C. Copleston*

PREFACE TO THE FIRST EDITION

'IN MOST OF THE histories of philosophy that I know, philosophic systems are presented to us as if growing out of one another spontaneously. . . . The inner biography of the philosophers, of the men who philosophized, occupies a secondary place. And yet it is precisely this inner biography that explains for us most things '.[1]

Histories of philosophy written from the Hegelian standpoint certainly tend to overlook the influence exercised on their thought by the personal character and temperament of the philosophers with whom they deal ; they tend to dwell exclusively on the abstract dialectic whereby one system develops out of another, showing how one system arises as the antithesis to a preceding system, owing to the one-sidedness of the latter, and how both systems, of which each is an exaggeration in a different direction, are brought together in a broader synthesis, which, in turn, manifests its insufficiency and so gives birth to a successor. Hegel himself is the supreme example (though not the only example) of this type of historian, for he regarded the whole course of philosophy before him as a propædeutic to his own system, as a dialectical ascent to Absolute Idealism. Yet in actual fact each system of philosophy was thought by a man, a concrete man, a man with a name of his own, a man of flesh and blood, a man who possessed a certain character and temperament, and is it to be supposed that the personal character and temperament of a philosopher was without any influence at all on his thought? Man is not a disembodied mind, nor is he infinite mind ; he is a finite, embodied spirit, who cannot comprehend the whole of truth, and the angle from which he contemplates reality will be partially determined by the sort of man he is, as will also his interpretation of reality. Although it is true that every positive philosopher worth the name has a guiding, leading, dominating idea, that informs the various parts of his system and welds them together, even if imperfectly, into a coherent whole, that leading idea is not an abstract idea which descended from the empyrean, but is an idea thought by a man, a real man, be it repeated, not man-in-himself, an abstraction. Is the difference in spirit

---

[1] Miguel de Unamuno in *The Tragic Sense of Life*, p. 2. Trans. J. E. Crawford Flitch (London, 1921).

between the philosophies of Plato and Aristotle without any relation to the respective characters of the two men ? Does it not at least manifest their respective interests ? We know comparatively little of these two men as men ; but, even if we had more extensive and reliable information about them than we actually possess, we could not write their biographies adequately without using their philosophies as a partial source. Does not the character of Leibniz reflect itself in his philosophy, and is not the same true of Locke, of Fichte, of Nietzsche, of many others ? Why did Berkeley reject Locke's concept of material substance ? Was it *only* because he felt himself compelled to do so for abstract, impersonal, theoretic reasons ? Not at all : Berkeley was a bishop, a believing Christian, and he tells us himself that he hoped, by that strange doctrine of his, to deprive the materialists of their *pied-à-terre*.

No, we cannot afford entirely to neglect the psychological factor in the history of philosophy and, if this is true concerning any philosopher, it is certainly true of the philosopher considered in this book, Arthur Schopenhauer. No systematic philosopher has given such an elaborate presentation of empirical and metaphysical pessimism as Schopenhauer (Eduard von Hartmann was an epigone), and this pessimism had its roots in the philosopher's personal character. If Schopenhauer had not been the man he was, his philosophy would scarcely have taken the exact form that it did, and it is important to know something of Schopenhauer's life and character, if we wish to understand how anyone could say the things that he said. To take two much less important examples than that of pessimism. Schopenhauer, as is well known, abused the celebrated German romantic metaphysicians with considerable verve and energy, Hegel being singled out as the special target for his abuse, and we should find it hard to understand Schopenhauer's ill-mannered abuse, if we knew nothing of the circumstances of his life. Again, his abuse of and cynical contempt for women in general, sprang, in part at least, from his own personal experiences and his somewhat coarse temperament (coarse in certain respects though not in all). The author has. therefore, devoted a chapter to a short biography of Schopenhauer, just as he prefaced his work on Nietzsche with a biography, for in the case of both thinkers biography is not without its importance for the understanding and interpretation of the philosophy.

But, while it is helpful to remember the personal factor when interpreting a given system, it is very necessary also to bear in mind that no system can be explained simply from the psychological standpoint : attempts have been made to do this, but such attempts are doomed to failure. To attempt to explain Leibniz' philosophy merely in terms of Leibniz' character, temperament and general interest would be ridiculous, just as it would be ridiculous in the case of Berkeley. That the personal factor influenced their respective philosophies and helped to determine the direction that each philosophy took is a fact that should not be forgotten ; but each man stood in a certain relation to his predecessors, and the genesis and development of his philosophy must be understood in relation to preceding thought.˙ We could scarcely appreciate adequately the philosophy of St. Thomas Aquinas, if we knew nothing of the re-discovery of Aristotle in the Middle Ages and the relation of the Angelic Doctor to the Augustinian tradition on the one hand and the philosophy of Aristotle, in itself and as presented by Arabian and Jewish commentators, on the other. Much of what Berkeley said stands in organic relation to the reflections of Locke and the philosophy of Leibniz did not follow on those of Descartes and Spinoza merely chronologically. In the case of Schopenhauer it would be a one-sided exaggeration to look on his voluntaristic system as *no more* than an experience of his character and temperament : it is partly that, it is true, but preceding and contemporary thought certainly contributed to determine the way in which that character expressed itself. The philosophy of Schopenhauer cannot really be understood, unless it is seen as following on the critical philosophy of Kant and the metaphysical systems of Fichte, Schelling and Hegel. (The author has devoted the introductory chapter to giving a brief sketch of modern philosophy up to the time of Schopenhauer ; but those who are well acquainted with that history or who are interested only in Schopenhauer may, of course, begin with chapter two.)

A further qualification. If no system of thought can be explained simply in terms of the thinker's temperament, it is also true that it cannot be explained entirely as a result of what has gone before. A philosopher can scarcely be wholly uninfluenced by preceding and contemporary thought (e.g., the questions he attempts to answer will, largely at least, be questions that arise out of the preceding philosophies or out of the general thought milieu) ; but he is a free man, free to choose his own premises and to draw his own conclusions. Moreover, the more he can rise above the limitations of his own temperament and the uncritical following of, or opposition to, his immediate predecessors, the more likely is he to approach objective truth. A philosophy will always be, to a certain extent, historically conditioned ; but, if philosophy be a science, then the more objective and ' impersonal ' it is, the better. A classic example is the philosophy of St. Thomas Aquinas. That that philosophy was, to a certain extent, historically conditioned cannot be denied : no one, for instance, would expect the Saint to deal with problems that could only arise in connection with modern physics, modern psychology or biology. To take a very trivial example. Some of the illustrations used by St. Thomas hardly carry much weight with us to-day because they were dependent on the scientific knowledge and speculations of the time. Nevertheless, St. Thomas' philosophy is objective and impersonal to a degree that is certainly not found in all other philosophies. He does not base his conclusions on ' intuitions ' or ' hunches ', but on arguments, and it would be very hard to discover the depth of the Saint's spiritual life from the pages of his theological and philosophical tomes : he kept himself in the background.

Every philosophical system, then, has an objective meaning of its own and can be considered according to the value or disvalue, the truth or falsity, of that meaning, quite apart from the character of the philosopher himself, though, as I have said, it is a help, in some cases indeed far more than in others, towards the understanding, appreciation and interpretation of the philosophy to know something of the personal character and history of the thinker. (For one thing, knowledge of the thinker as a man helps us to see what he is likely to have considered the important elements in his system.) In this book, therefore, the author has, after giving a biographical sketch of Schopenhauer, gone on to consider his thought as it appears in his writings, and he has not hesitated to criticize, and to criticize trenchantly, that thought. If a man gives his system to the world, he thereby lays it open to criticism on its own merits or demerits. Moreover, the author has endeavoured to present the philosophy of Schopenhauer as he presents it, and has resisted the temptation to attempt to read into that philosophy what its creator did not mean to put into it or to interpret it after an ' esoteric ' fashion. Presumably Schopenhauer knew better than anyone else what he meant to say. In other words, the book is an exposition of that system of philosophy which Schopenhauer propounded in *The World as Will and Idea* and, as far as space permits, a criticism thereof : it does not pretend to be an exposition of what Schopenhauer *might* have said, but of what he *did* say.

The author expresses his gratitude to Messrs. Kegan Paul, Trench Trübner & Co., Ltd., for their kind permission to quote from the English translation (R. B. Haldane and J. Kemp) of Schopenhauer's *The World as Will and Idea* and from the English translation of Eduard von Hartmann's *Philosophy of the Unconscious* (W. C. Coupland), both published by them. Thanks are also due to Messrs. Macmillan & Co., Ltd., for permission to quote the passage at the beginning of this preface from J. E. Crawford Flitch's translation of Miguel de Unamuno's *The Tragic Sense of Life in Men and Peoples* and to make two short quotations from Douglas Ainslie's translation of Benedetto Croce's *Aesthetic*. Quotations from Schopenhauer's *Parerga and Paralipomena* have been translated by the author himself from volumes five and six of Julius Frauenstädt's edition of the Works of Schopenhauer (Leipzig, 1877).

The English translation of Schopenhauer's *World* is published in three volumes, the first containing the first edition of the work, divided into four books, the other two containing the supplementary chapters, which were written subsequently. Footnote references to the *World* in my book are given according to the volume and page of the English translation, and when no book-title is either explicitly mentioned in a footnote or indicated by an *Ibid.*, the reference is always to Schopenhauer's *World*. References to *Parerga and Paralipomena* are given according to the volume and page of Frauenstädt's edition of the Works of Schopenhauer (in German) but I give the title of the essay concerned in English, in order to facilitate reference to the selections from *Parerga and Paralipomena* which have been published in English (e.g. *Selected Essays of Arthur Schopenhauer*, with introduction by E. Belfort Bax, George Bell, 1891).

(Heythrop, 1944) *F. C. Copleston*

Note: The translation of *Die Welt als Wille und Vorstellung* cited in this book is that made by R. B. Haldane and J. Kemp (3 volumes; 5th edition: London, Routledge, 1906). Another translation is available: *The World as Will and Representation*, trans., E. F. J. Payne (2 volumes; New York, 1958; New York & London, Dover, 1967). A new translation of *Parerga und Paralipomena* has also appeared, and was made by E. F. J. Payne (2 volumes; London, Oxford University Press, 1974).

CHAPTER I

THE PHILOSOPHIC SITUATION

IT IS A ROUGH truth (and one often repeated by historians of philosophy) that before the time of Kant there were two main tendencies in European philosophy of the post-mediæval period. The one tendency was represented by the line of Continental thinkers from Descartes to Leibniz, the other by the British empiricists from Francis Bacon to David Hume. To speak of a Continental School would scarcely be helpful, since the philosophies of Descartes, Malebranche, Spinoza, Leibniz can certainly not be united together as forming one system : that is sufficiently obvious. To the pluralism of Descartes is opposed the monism of Spinoza, and, however much one may play about with the logical similarity of the Cartesian and Spinozistic definitions of substance, or however much one may regard the deterministic monism of Spinoza as an extension to all Reality of the Cartesian view of the sub-spiritual, it remains true that Descartes was not, and that Spinoza was, a monist, and that this constitutes an essential and fundamental point of difference between the two philosophies. Similarly, the pluralism of Leibniz is radically opposed to the monism of Spinoza, while his dynamism and his doctrine of monads is not in harmony with the Cartesian physics. Again, Descartes and Leibniz were both theists, and in this important point (*pace quorundam*) their philosophies part company with the monism of Spinoza, for whom, *philosophically* (even if probably not *psychologically*) the term ' God ' is little more than a name or label. Yet, though the three most celebrated continental philosophers of the pre-Kantian modern period held different philosophies, they certainly all agree in Rationalism, in the sense that all three believed in the power of human reason to compass metaphysical truth and all three believed in the objective validity of a concept such as that of substance, even though each attached a different meaning and interpretation to the term. Kant was, therefore, justified in looking on the line of continental philosophy as a line of metaphysical Rationalism. In his view they were uncritical dogmatists, whose differing systems show clearly the powerlessness of metaphysics to reach abiding truth ; but, however little this conclusion may have been justified and whatever fairness or unfairness there may have been in the accusation of *a priori* reasoning levelled against these thinkers and in the importance attributed to e.g. Leibniz's conception of 'innate ideas', it is beyond dispute that the continental philosophers were not critical thinkers in the Kantian sense of the word. To this extent, then, they may be grouped together, even though their actual systems differed very much from one another.

If, therefore, we are justified in speaking of Continental Rationalism, we are also justified in speaking of British Empiricism, in the sense that the leading British philosophers of the period deny innate ideas and do not share the belief attributed to the continental metaphysicians (though it certainly cannot be justly attributed in the same extent to all) that the human reason is provided with a store of ideas of its own, 'innate' ideas of some type or other, enabling it to evolve philosophy from within. But though Locke, Berkeley and Hume all make use of the principle, that experience is the fount of real knowledge, they do so in very different ways. Locke, for instance, though he used this principle as a statement of origin and against innate ideas, did not question the distinction between sense and reason, and he admitted the power of the human reason to transcend sense. Locke did not reject metaphysics lock, stock and barrel, but insisted that reason employs the materials provided, by sense, arguing by the use of the causal principle to the existence of material substance, although this cannot be directly perceived by the senses. And if it cannot be said of Locke that he was an anti-metaphysician, still less can it be said of Berkeley, who, in spite of his attempt to be more consistently empiricist than Locke (an attempt which was partly responsible for his polemic against abstract general ideas, admitted by Locke), is one of the most outstanding speculative writers in the English language. However, although Berkeley criticized and denied Locke's doctrine of material substance in the interests of his spiritualist metaphysic, and although this spiritualist metaphysic is of the greatest importance if one is considering the philosophy of Berkeley in isolation, from the point of view of historical connection between succeeding thinkers this criticism marked a further step in the advance of empiricism in British philosophy, an advance that culminated in the writings of Hume. Arguing that all knowledge comes from experience and that any idea, if it is to vindicate a claim to objective validity, must have its direct origin in impressions, Hume criticized the conception, not only of material substance (admitted by Locke, though not by Berkeley), but also of spiritual substance (admitted by both Locke and Berkeley) and questioned the objective validity of the idea of causation. In this way certain knowledge of existent reality is undermined and metaphysics becomes a vain dream : we know (have experience of) only a succession of phenomena, in the internal world as in the extramental world, and, even if custom and association lead us to suppose spiritual and material substance and the objective validity of the idea of causation, and to act as if this supposition was grounded in reality, custom and association do not give us *knowledge*, though they make possible practical life. Hume *might*, of course, have gone on to ascribe to an *a priori* activity of the subject what he is content to ascribe to association, custom, etc., and so have anticipated Kant, but he did not follow out this train of thought : he endeavoured to be as consistently ' empiricist ' as possible, and it was in accordance with this attitude that he denied the power of reason to furnish the basis of ethics and made *feeling* the criterion of good and evil. Thus if for Locke there is a substantial spiritual world and a substantial material world, and for Berkeley a substantial spiritual world only, for Hume there is neither the one nor the other, but only a fleeting succession of phenomena or impressions. Hume alone of the three is radically sceptical, and he has to admit a dichotomy between theory and practice.

Kant (1724 1804) was, therefore, confronted with these two main philosophical tendencies or methods. Continental speculative philosophy had assumed the possibility of metaphysical knowledge, but its *a priori* character and its conflicting results (cf. Spinoza and Leibniz) cast doubt, in Kant's opinion, on the validity of the assumption. It was necessary, then, to institute an inquiry concerning the limits of human knowledge. (Locke had proposed an investigation concerning the objects with which the human mind is and is not not fitted to deal ; but he had not really carried out this investigation thoroughly or reached any satisfactory conclusion.) On the other hand, Hume had dissolved the world into discrete phenomena by pure empiricism, and, as the

principle of causality had been shown by him to be the subjective product of association, etc.; the general laws of science,
necessary laws, should go by the board. Yet Kant saw clearly
enough that we do make universal, necessary and instructive
judgments in science, and the very progress of science shows
that these judgments possess a real validity. The question,
therefore, arises : ' *How* are such judgments (synthetic *a
priori* judgments) possible ? ' Moreover, while the scientific
conception of the world regards all as determined and leaves
no place for freedom, we are certainly conscious of moral
obligation, which presupposes freedom. How are the two
conflicting positions to be reconciled ?

Unable to answer the criticism of Hume and believing
that Hume had shown that universality and necessity cannot
derive from sense-experience, Kant suggested that the notes
of universality and necessity, as found in synthetic *a priori*
judgments, derive from the *subject* and proposed his ' Coper-
nican revolution ', maintaining the hypothesis that, in order
to be known, objects must be conformed to mind rather than
the other way about. Into the details of the Kantian
Critique of the Pure Reason, e.g. the distinction between the
a priori forms of sensible intuition and the Categories of the
mind or the conditions of synthesis and into the details of
Kant's distinction between our freedom in the noumenal
world and our lack of it in the phenomenal world, it is unnecessary to enter in the present chapter, which is simply a
rough sketch of modern philosophy before Schopenhauer and
is designed to recall to mind the general philosophic situation.
(A reader who is entirely ignorant of the course of modern
philosophy has the simple recourse of skipping this chapter
altogether, if he does not wish to betake himself to a general
history of philosophy.) The point we wish to recall to mind
is this, that, while—on the Kantian hypothesis—the mind's
laws will govern all reality *as known*, only those objects will be
able to conform themselves to mind and become objects of
knowledge which are material and can conform themselves
to the mind's forms of sensible intuition, Space and Time,
since Kant accepts the position that all our knowledge begins
with sense-experience, even though he does not admit that all
the factors in knowledge arise from experience (there being
an *a priori* element, which governs knowledge, though it does
not of itself give knowledge). It follows that those objects

which, *ex hypothesi*, cannot conform themselves to the forms of sensible intuition (e.g. God) cannot be objects of knowledge, that metaphysical knowledge is impossible. It is true that the categories of the understanding, precisely because they are categories of the understanding, may seem to admit of an application beyond sense-objects (so that there arises what Kant calls the Transcendental Illusion) ; but their function lies in their application to sense-intuition, so that they cannot legitimately be applied to spiritual objects.

It might very well appear that the Kantian criticism, with its theoretical dissolution of speculative metaphysics, renders it impossible to attach any rational meaning or value to human life and that philosophy can be no more than an epistemology. But Kant, a resolute believer in moral obligation and the categorical imperative, tried to retain the ideas of personal immortality, of God (as Cause of the exact harmony of happiness with morality) and of freedom, as 'Postulates' of the moral law. Knowledge is *not* extended theoretically through the admission of these Postulates, but reason, if it cannot prove the validity of these ideas, is unable to disprove their validity, so that the Postulates are placed beyond criticism and reason makes way for 'Faith'. Kant, therefore, places before man the ideal of an unending approximation to moral perfection and also the final attainment of happiness as a concomitant of virtue. It is unnecessary to doubt Kant's personal good faith in his retention of the ideas of God, freedom and personal immortality as 'Postulates' of the moral law, even though we think that his criticism of speculative metaphysics on the one hand is invalid and that his mode of establishment of the moral law on the other hand is unsatisfactory ; but, though we have no wish to question Kant's personal sincerity, it can scarcely be denied that his criticism of metaphysics, if accepted, leads more naturally to agnosticism than to belief in his 'Postulates' and that agnosticism in regard to the objects of metaphysics leads logically to agnosticism in regard to any objectively given and objectively valid meaning and value in human existence.

Now, if the meeting of Continental Rationalism and British Empiricism took place in Kant (Kant was brought up in the tradition of the Leibni -Wolffian School and was awoken from his 'dogmatic' slumbers under the influence of Hume's criticism), how did it come about that immediately after the Kantian *Critique* German philosophy witnessed an exceptional flowering of speculative metaphysics? If we look at the dates of death of the celebrated German philosophers of the period (Kant died in 1804, Fichte in 1814, Hegel in 1831, Schelling in 1854, Schopenhauer in 1860), we see that they fall in more or less proximity to the dates of death of great German musicians (Mozart died in 1791, Beethoven in 1827, Schubert in 1828, Schumann in 1856), and of great German poets (Schiller died in 1805, Goethe in 1832, Hölderlin in 1843, Heine in 1856). Though it is extremely difficult—probably impossible—to define Romanticism in general, German Romanticism certainly meant in part the cult of subjectivism, of feeling and passion, the desire for a rich, wide and cultured life, an insistence on freedom and man's liberation from shackles. Among the characteristics attributed to German Romanticism by Gustav Pauli are 'the mystic welding together of subject and object, the tendency to intermingle the arts, the longing for the far-away and the strange, the feeling for the infinite and the continuity of historic development'. Now, the cult of subjectivism and immanentism, the tendency to bring together subject and object, the feeling for the infinite and the continuity of historic development, certainly find a place in the idealistic philosophical systems of the post-Kantian period, so that it is quite correct to see in post-Kantian idealism one of the manifestations of German Romanticism. The cult of subjectivism and immanentism, coupled with the feeling for the infinite, naturally expressed itself in the philosophical Absolutism of, e.g. Schelling and Hegel, while the very prominent position attributed to Aesthetic in the philosophies of Schelling, Hegel and Schopenhauer indicates the influence of the same Romantic Movement. There is really nothing to be wondered at in the Romantic Movement expressing itself in the philosophical sphere in an extravagant and sometimes bizarre metaphysic; rather would it be matter for wonder if German philosophers of the Romantic period had contented themselves with critical and epistemological questions, since the Romantics were concerned with the life of man in the broadest possible setting. (We may note in passing that, just as it is impossible to confine Goethe within the ranks of the Romantics, since Classicists as well as Romantics can find support in his words, so it is impossible to confine Hegel within the Romantic School. Hegel would never have said *Gefühl ist alles* and there is no cult of irrationality in Hegel, whatever we may think of the rational or irrational character of his system. But that is not to say that Hegel was not influenced by the Romantic Movement.)

Kant himself cannot be reckoned among the Romantic philosophers : nevertheless the idealist metaphysicians who followed him, and who are thought of as expressing the spirit of the Romantic Movement in philosophy, descend from Kant, as far as the purely philosophical *point de départ* is concerned. Kant had emphasized the part played by the subject in knowledge and had attempted to isolate the *a priori* element ; but at the same time he resolutely refused to allow that the object in its totality proceeds from the subject and left intact the *Ding-an-sich*, which is unknowable. Fichte pointed out that we are not justified in positing the existence of an unknowable entity, especially if the category of causality, declared subjective by Kant, is employed to demonstrate its existence. But, if there is no independent thing-in-itself, the extramental, phenomenal world must proceed from the subject, Fichte thought : he declared that Kant, with his dualism, was a 'three-quarters man'. Yet Fichte did not teach solipsism : he thought that the material world is formed for the finite ego (with a view to action, moral activity), through, and in a real sense by, the individual ego, but ultimately by the Pure or Transcendental Ego or Subject, from which proceed finite subjects and—*via* the finite subjects (idealism)—finite objects. He thus constructed a system of Subjective Transcendental Idealism. Fichte took over from Kant the conception of the Transcendental Ego, but in Kant the conception was *not* pantheistic : it denoted the principle of thought which is undivided subject and does not itself enter into consciousness. But as Fichte's ontological doctrine developed out of his original epistemological analysis, this Transcendental Ego took on the character of an Infinite Moral Will, which 'contracts itself', as it were, into individual egos. After a time it became in turn the manifestation of the Absolute or 'God', which is inexpressible in human language. If at first Fichte tended to identify God with a moral order which has to be created or which at least might seem to be little more than an abstract harmony of human moral wills, he later speaks of God as the Source of individual egos and as the One real Being, this conception of the Absolute becoming more marked as time went on. The fact of necessary principles in the theoretical and practical spheres points to a Real Existent Ground of both spheres, to an Absolute Being, which is the Reason of these principles, this Absolute being Pure Activity and Freedom, though it transcends human comprehension and human predicates such as 'personal' or self-conscious. The empirical or finite ego has as its goal the return to the Pure or Absolute Ego, a goal never completely reached in actual fact, though there is an unending approximation thereto by moral endeavour. The world of finite, material objects is simply the field of moral action, a world of stimuli and obstacles, as it were, set up by the subject that it may develop its moral character. Thus, while the thought of Fichte has as its point of departure the philosophy of Kant, Fichte developed his system in a meta-physical direction that is alien to the Kantian spirit and his conception of the Absolute and his insistence on freedom, self-development and dynamic activity link him up with the Romantic Movement. Fichte once observed that the kind of philosophy a man chooses, depends on the kind of man he is, and the central position given by him to the ideas of freedom and of activity, though having some relation to Kant's moral theory, certainly bear the imprint of Fichte's own character, of the man who delivered stirring ' *Addresses to the German People* ' at Berlin during the period of Napoleonic domination and wished to go as a sort of philosophic chaplain to the troops in the War of Liberation.

Schelling began with the position of Fichte, holding that the Ego is the supreme principle of philosophy, but he soon came to reject Fichte's view of external nature as being merely a means to man's moral action, a ninepin set up by the ego to be knocked down, having no real status of its own. This onesided subjectivism was rejected by Schelling in favour of the view that Nature, no less than Mind, is a manifestation of the Absolute. Both are real manifestations of the Absolute, though both—in some mysterious way—are identified in the Absolute. In his philosophy of Nature, Schelling depicted Nature as visible spirit, as the objective appearance of the ultimate Principle. Below man it is slumbering spirit ; in man Nature attains consciousness and becomes luminous to itself. Nature is thus a meaningful, if unconscious, Whole, possessing a World-Soul, which is really the principle of organization in the world, through which it strives upwards towards consciousness, so that, as with Leibniz (*mutatis mutandis*), there is no part of Nature that is essentially dead, mere stark materiality and passivity. Nature strives after the perfect representation of the Absolute, and the individuals of various species are attempts at different stages to represent the Absolute. Thus, while by Leibniz the emphasis is thrown on individuality, despite the world-harmony, Schelling is pantheistic, chiefly interested in the universalist conception of Nature. This philosophy he termed *Realidealismus*, so that we may say that Schelling came to oppose a system of Objective Transcendental Idealism to Fichte's system of Subjective Transcendental Idealism.

Driven to reflect more fully on the presuppositions of his Philosophy of Nature (and of his correlate System of Transcendental Idealism, into which we cannot enter) Schelling moved forward to his so-called System of Identity. The phrase ' Absolute Ego ' was abandoned, as savouring too much of Fichte's system, and in its place he postulated an Absolute, which is Subject and Object in identity. His *Realidealismus* would admit neither of an Absolute which was only Subject nor of an Absolute which was only Object (since it was *Idealism*, and not materialism), but rather an Absolute which is Subject and Object in one, so that in the long run Nature and Spirit are identical. The Absolute of Schelling is thus the all-embracing identity, the reconciliation-point of all differences, or—in Hegel's caustic phrase—the night in which all cows are black. God is, then, the Absolute Totality, the undivided Identity, and this panthcism is certainly in the spirit of the Romantic Movement. (Later on Schelling moved away from pantheism under the influence of the idea of freedom and developed a theism of a bizarre type ; but we cannot follow him into the theosophical flights of his old age, and in any case it was the Philosophy of Nature and the System of Identity that were of importance in the development of philosophy, i.e. of importance in the relation of Schelling to Hegel.)

If the pantheism of Schelling was in the spirit of the Romantic Movement, so also was the importance attributed by him to Aesthetic. For the first time in the history of philosophy a decisive position and function in the metaphysical synthesis of the universe was attributed to art as such. Kant indeed had written of Aesthetic in the *Critique of Judgment*, and had hoped to find therein an underlying unity between the sphere of freedom and the sphere of necessity ; but the very character of his thought and philosophy precluded him from adopting the ' absolute standpoint ' in regard to Art. Schelling, however, could, and did, adopt such a standpoint : indeed he was the pioneer in this direction. For him, every true work of art is a manifestation of the Absolute, freedom and design being perfectly united therein with necessity and law, and spirit attaining its highest concrete and objective expression. In this way Subject and Object, freedom and nature, are united and made one in the work of art, so that the Absolute, the infinite Identity of Subject and Object, is finitely represented in the artist's creation.

Schelling introduced notions from the Platonic theory of Ideas, maintaining (somewhat unexpectedly and inconsistently, it is true) that the Absolute expresses itself immediately in an eternal world of Ideas (God's intuitions of ' Himself ') which are the exemplars of all the differentiations in the empirical world and are the only true things-in-themselves. The artist's function is to represent these Ideas in the concrete, in a finite and spatial medium, so that true art, the work of creative genius, represents objectively and concretely what philosophy represents only abstractly. Beauty is thus the Infinite represented in finite form. (Schelling attempted a serial classification and systematic arrangement of the particular arts, but Bosanquet is doubtless right when he characterizes this arrangement as ' merely a piece of arbitrary formalism ',[1] and it is unnecessary to dwell upon it.)

Hegel was unable to rest content with the Absolute of Schelling, the indeterminate homogeneous unity or Identity or Indifference, in which all differences are merged ; for him the Absolute is not an abstract unity, in which the particulars disappear ; but a concrete unity, in which they are preserved. The Absolute is a single, self-dependent Principle, the ultimate explanation of the universe. Combining Plato's notion of the ' world of Ideas ', the noetic structure or hierarchy of Archetypal Principles, with the Aristotelian doctrine of the νόησις νοήσεως, Hegel depicted the world as

[1] *A History of Aesthetic,* by B. Bosanquet. George Allen and Unwin, Ltd., p. 332.

objective Thought—the manifold objects of this world embodying the Categories and yet forming together one great System or Thought-structure, which in its totality is the Objective Idea. Further, adopting from Christianity the notion of God, Hegel makes God the universal Reason, which is not simply the Archetypal Principle (' transcendent ' in religious terminology) but is also the immanent Principle and ultimate explanation and nature of the Universe, so that Plato's manifold Ideas, Aristotle's concrete ' universal ', Plato's unity of the world of Ideas in subordination to the Idea of the Good and Aristotle's νόησις νοήσεως are combined in the Hegelian Idea or God.

Now, for Plato particular things ' imitate ' the Idea, but are themselves fleeting and contingent, while Aristotle too admits the contingency of particulars (the species or essence abides, individuals pass). Hegel too admits contingency, and this is precisely the particularity or finiteness of individuals, though (following Aristotle) he insists that the individual has its universal or permanent aspect. This admission of contingency (most probably an admission inconsistent with the system as such) allows Hegel to protest that he is no pantheist, on the ground that he does not identify the particular object *in its particularity* with God, God (or the Idea) being transcendent in regard to the individual, if the latter be viewed under its aspect of particularity, but immanent in the individual, if the latter be viewed under the aspect of embodying the universal. God is thus, as it were, the *inside* of the world, its rational or ultimate Thought-structure. The world, as we know it in perception, consists of particulars, perishable objects, contingent beings ; this is the *outside* of the world, the Idea, or God, *in its otherness*, gone over into particularity. In its inner thought-structure the world is identical with God, but in its outward and contingent aspect it is not identical with God, so that, in religious language, God may be said to be both transcendent and immanent. (This attempt to combine Theism and Pantheism, or to avoid the consequenes of either pure Theism or pure Pantheism, was foredoomed to failure, and it is responsible for not a little of that extreme obscurity and ambiguity which is notoriously characteristic of the Hegelian system.)

Influenced by (*a*) Christianity, which looks upon the world as exhibiting God's action *ad extra* and (*b*) the sense of history

developed in the German Romantic School, Hegel regarded
the world as essentially a process, as history, for Reality is not
static, but dynamic. But, as God is thought, objective
Thought, and as thought, in Hegel's view, proceeds in the
dialectical manner (i.e. through thesis, antithesis and synthesis, or from an incomplete position, through the manifestation of the contradiction contained in its partiality, to a more
comprehensive position), the process is essentially logical,
though in part also temporal. God-in-Himself, or the Idea
looked at apart in its logical character, does not change
temporally and any advance that we may discern from less
adequate to more adequate concepts is exclusively *logical*,
but in so far as God goes out of Himself into otherness, i.e.
into nature, a temporal process follows. Thus, though the
transition from the Logical Absolute, God-in-Himself, to the
perceptible world of Nature was for Hegel most probably a
logical transition (the doctrine of creation in time being a
theological *Vorstellung* for the philosophical truth of the
logical transition), in Nature itself, God-in-His-otherness, the
process is temporal, the self-unfolding of the Absolute or
the *explicatio Dei*.

The three main stages of the Dialectic are :—

1. The Logical Absolute, God as He is in Himself—the
   Thesis. (This is the thought-structure, abstractly con-
   sidered, and one should not be misled by Hegel's frequent
   use of religious terminology into supposing that the
   Logical Absolute can be simply equated with the
   Personal God of Christianity.)

2. Nature, God in His otherness—the Antithesis. (As the
   Real is the Rational and the Rational the Real, and as
   the Rational is the Universal, the inner nature of the
   dialectical process will be less easy to grasp where there
   is more of contingency and particularity. Nature is thus
   harder to understand than e.g. the history of philosophy,
   i.e. harder to understand *philosophically* in its ultimate
   nature and dialectical development.)

3. God returning to Himself as concrete Spirit, i.e. the
   human spirit in its universal aspect. ' God ' comes to
   concrete self-consciousness in man ; but Hegel does not
   mean that *any* thinking on man's part can be considered God's thought : the identity is true of man's

thought only in so far as it is ' departicularized ', raised to the universal plane : it is true of it only in so far as it becomes truly conceptual, i.e. philosophic or universal thought. It is, therefore, not the thinking of Tom, Dick or Harry *as such* which is the self-thinking of the Absolute, but rather philosophic thinking, the succession of philosophic systems. (Hegel declared that he was, and would remain, a Lutheran, and he may have thought that his attempt to combine pantheism and theism was a successful attempt to give a truly philosophic interpretation of theism ; but to the simple mind his attempt will more probably appear to be singularly unsuccessful.)

These three main stages are divided and subdivided according to the triadic scheme of the dialectic. Thus the third stage has three main subdivisions, (*a*) subjective spirit (e.g. psychology), (*b*) objective spirit (the objective institutions of e.g. Morality and the State), and (*c*) Absolute Spirit (i.e. the Spirit's contemplation of itself), this final stage being subdivided into (i) Art, (ii) Religion, (iii) Philosophy. The Absolute manifests itself first in the form of immediacy, i.e. under the guise of external sense-objects, beauty being the ' sensuous semblance of the Idea '. The work of art, the beauty of which is superior to that of Nature, is an organic unity of parts and a concrete union of form and content, determining the division of art into its fundamental types. However, as Spirit finds that no sensuous embodiment is adequate for its expression, a new sphere is required for the self-revelation of the Spirit, and so we pass to Religion, in which the Absolute is not yet apprehended in pure thought (philosophy), though it is no longer revealed in a purely sensuous manner. Religion, then, stands between Art on the one hand and Philosophy on the other, having the same content as the other two spheres (i.e. the Absolute), but having an intermediate form of its own, namely figurative thought. For example, the dogma of the Incarnation is a pictorial thought or symbolization in reference to a particular historical Man of the universal and philosophic truth of the unity of God and man in concrete Spirit. (Hegel declared that Christianity is the absolute Religion, meaning, of course, that it is, in his opinion, the best possible presentation of the Hegelian philosophy under the guise of religious symbol or pictorial and figurative thought ; but it is clear that such a conception of Religion and of religious dogma is very far from being orthodox, since dogma is eviscerated and explained away and Philosophy is made essentially superior to Theology.)

Christianity, the absolute religion, possesses absolute truth as its content, but it presents that truth under the form of contingency. For example, the dogma of creation in Time represents creation as a free act of God, an act which might or might not have taken place. This form of contingency needs to be replaced by the form of necessity, the contingent historical events of dogma being shown in their inner form of universal and logical necessity, and thus we pass to the third sphere, that of Philosophy. However, just as Religion did not appear at once in its absolute form, but evolved through a dialectical process from the less adequate to the more adequate, so absolute philosophy (which, even if inconsistently, meant for Hegel pretty well his own system) did not appear all at once, but developed throughout the history of philosophy, until the Idea became perfectly self-luminous. In this final stage the Idea is both Subject and Object in unity, and ' God ' has become self-conscious.

Does this imply that, for Hegel, God in Himself is not self-conscious ? The Logical Absolute contains or *is* the category of personality or self-consciousness, and Hegel not infrequently speaks as though God in Himself were self-conscious and personal ; but his meaning is probably this, that, though God considered in Himself is the Category of self-consciousness, He is ' not yet ' *existentially* self-conscious : He becomes existentially self-conscious in the philosophic thought of man.

As Reason is operative in the world and as the world-process is rational, as it is the *explicatio Dei*, proceeding according to a logical and necessary dialectical advance, *optimism* results. Evil is admitted, since there is contingency and particularity, but, in the large, reason prevails and *must* prevail : what is evil for the particular object is good and for the best *sub specie dialecticæ*. This optimism is very apparent in Hegel's philosophy of history, in which he thought he could discern, in spite of all apparent aberrations, the rational process at work. The historical process is the dialectic of the National Spirits, and Reason and Right always prevail (' dialectically ', of course), so that the actual is justified as rational. It is in this sense that Hegel may be said to hold that Might is Right, and in this sense only. Hegel himself would never have said *tout court* ' Might is Right ' ; but, as he held that Right is Might, in the sense that the rational always prevails in the large, the *practical* conclusion is pretty well the same. In other words, Hegel did not go wrong through cynicism (he was not cynical), but through an unwarranted optimism. The Hegelian Philosophy of History may seem at first sight to be the same as the Christian doctrine of Divine Providence and Hegelian optimism may seem to resemble Christian optimisim ; but in reality, though there are certainly some resemblances, there is a deep-seated difference. Providence does indeed operate in history and God does bring good out of evil, using even immoral men and their actions to contribute to the final victory of Right ; but God does not override human liberty and Christianity does not teach that human history is necessarily and always an *ascent,* even a dialectical ascent. The Gospels tell us that the final ' Justification ' of God will be accomplished, not in any dialectical process of history but at the Last Judgment, whereas for Hegel *die Weltgeschichte ist das Weltgericht.* Moreover, the very character of the Hegelian philosophy of history precludes it from recognizing in any particular historical event the culminating point of human history on this planet. That is the reason why a thorough Hegelian must, from the philosophic viewpoint, interpret the Incarnation of the Son of God as a symbol for a universal thought. McTaggart was perfectly correct when he observed that, though Christian theologians might use the Hegelian philosophy as a weapon against e.g. materialism, they made a very big mistake if they regarded Heglianism as Christian or even as a loyal ally of Christianity: they would very soon find this supposed ally displaying itself as the most insidious foe of Christianity, all the more insidious in that it made such plentiful use of Christian terminology and professed to give the inward thought-essence of the Christian religion.

Against this exaggerated and doctrinaire optimism of Hegel, Schopenhauer revolted. If there was anything really clear about human life and existence, and indeed about life in general, he thought it was the fact of the prevalence of evil and suffering. To gloss over this fact with talk of the particular and the universal, the dialectic and the self-expression of the Absolute, was a foolish and cruel ignoring of a vital fact, only possible on the part of a professor of philosophy. (Schopenhauer, as we will see later, had a strong dislike of professors of philosophy—and a special grudge against Hegel in particular, partly for personal reasons.) Human life is a tragedy or, for most of us, a comic tragedy, so to speak, since in the case of most of us our lives and sufferings are not on the heroic and exalted scale required for Tragedy—though they are tragic none the less. In fact, if Hegel went to the extreme of unwarranted optimism, Schopenhauer went to the extreme of pessimism. *Virtus stat in medio.*

Hegel's optimism was not simply, of course, the expression of a tempermental optimism ; it was rather the logical conclusion of his metaphysical system. Similarly Schopenhauer's pessimism was not simply the expression of a pessimistic temperament or of a soured and embittered nature (which he was, in part at least), but stands in the closest relation to his philosophical system. If for Hegel the essence of the universe is Absolute Reason, for Schopenhauer the essence of the world, its inmost nature, is *Will*, and a blind, irrational, self-devouring Will at that ; for Schopenhauer there is no God and no Absolute Reason, no rational justification of life and existence. Schopenhauer thus reacted violently against the extreme rationalism of the Hegelian system and against the whole development of idealist, optimistic, rationalistic metaphysics that sprang ultimately from the *Critique of the Pure Reason* (though Kant himself would have been aghast, could he have foreseen his philosophical children and grandchildren !) In Schopenhauer and his system we find the swing-over from Reason to irrational ' Will ', from optimism to pessimism, from the exaltation of human history to the assertion of the valuelessness and meaninglessness of existence. After all, it was only to be expected that on one extreme another should follow by way of reaction—of antithesis, if you like. But though Schopenhauer reacted violently to the systems of Fichte, Schelling and Hegel, particularly to that of Hegel, he certainly belongs to the number of those German speculative philosophers who were influenced by the Romantic Movement. This will become apparent when we consider his system in succeeding chapters.

To conclude the present chapter I give a brief summary of the development from Kant to Schopenhauer.

1. *Kant* stresses the creative activity of mind, meaning the

individual human mind, and retains the 'Thing-in-itself.' (Critical Idealism or Critical Realism, according to the viewpoint, but certainly not either Idealism or Realism without qualification.)

2. *Fichte* suppresses the thing-in-itself and puts all the emphasis on the activity of the Subject, which appears as the Transcendental Ego and which (in opposition to Kant) is conceived monistically. Later it is 'pushed further back' and the conception of the Absolute gains in importance. (Subjective Transcendental Idealism.)

3. *Schelling* emphasizes the Object, Nature, which is an *immediate* manifestation (in opposition to Fichte) of the Absolute, the latter being conceived as the 'indifference point' of Subject and Object. (Objective Transcendental Idealism.)

4. *Hegel* rejects (*a*) the one-sided emphasis placed by Fichte on the Subject and by Schelling on the Object, and (*b*) the emptiness of the Absolute of Schelling. He then develops a metaphysic of 'God' or the Absolute as the *concrete unity* of Subject and Object, in which existence is not emptied out or the abstract stressed to the detriment of the concrete. (Absolute Idealism.)

5. *Schopenhauer*, rejecting the optimistic Rationalism of Hegel, accepts the Thing-in-itself from Kant but finds its reality and essence in Will, metaphysically and pessimistically conceived. (Voluntaristic Transcendental Idealism. In what sense the system of Schopenhauer is 'Idealism' will be shown later.)

It has been said that, whereas Fichte and Hegel develop, for the most part, the *Critique of the Pure Reason* and elaborate a rationalistic metaphysic, Schopenhauer starts rather from the *Critique of the Practical Reason* and develops a metaphysic of Will ; but, if this is said, it must always be remembered at the same time that Schopenhauer's 'Will" is something very different indeed from what Kant means by Will !

CHAPTER II

ARTHUR SCHOPENHAUER

THE PHILOSOPHER OF PESSIMISM was born on February 22nd, 1788, in the city of Danzig, which was at the time a free city, even if under the nominal suzerainty of Poland. His father, Heinrich Floris Schopenhauer, was a wealthy merchant, but came of an aristocratic family of Dutch origin. Though head of a leading business establishment he was a man of culture and refinement, as well as a man endowed with a strong and vigorous character, and he possessed strongly-marked cosmopolitan tastes. He read not only French, but also English literature, and it was even his wish that his son should be born in England, though the state of his wife's health before the birth of their first child, Arthur, prevented the fulfilment of this wish. In addition, moreover, to business capacity and cultured tastes, Heinrich Floris was possessed of a strong feeling for liberty, his personal inclination being in accord with the family motto, *Point de bonheur sans liberté* ; and when, in 1793, the free city of Danzig fell under the yoke of Prussia at the time of the second partition of Poland, he took his family to Hamburg and pursued his business in that city. This love of freedom, this dislike of state-absolutism and this cosmopolitan sympathy he bequeathed to his son, together with his force of character and his somewhat sombre and passionate temperament. There was a queer streak in some of the members of the Schopenhauer family (the elder brother of Heinrich Floris was mentally deficient), and though Heinrich Floris himself was certainly not mentally deficient—far from it— it is possible that his unexpected death in 1805 was self-inflicted.

The philosopher's mother, Johanna, sprang, like her husband, from an aristocratic family of Danzig, and, like her husband again, she was educated and cultured (as a widow she turned her hand to letters), but her temperament was not akin to that of Heinrich Floris, being what the French would call *spirituelle*. Arthur Schopenhauer believed that, while he owed his temperament and character to his father, he owed the quality of his intelligence to his mother.

However that may be, the difference between the temperaments of the two parents led to a certain unhappiness in the home and later on Arthur found that he could not get on with his mother, as she too found that she could not get on with him : the difference of temperament was too great to admit of real harmony, and both seem to have been egoistic in character. His relations with his mother were probably partly responsible for the philosopher's later professed contempt for women, though his own apparently irregular life at a certain period no doubt contributed to the formation of his exaggerated opinions on this subject.

Arthur Schopenhauer was thus brought up in a cultured and refined home, a circumstance that enabled him to develop his bent for study and thought, though his father destined him for a business career. In 1797 (the year in which Arthur's sister, Adele, was born) the latter took his nine-year-old son to France, where they visited Paris, and then left him for two years in the home of a business correspondent in Havre, in order that he might learn French (which indeed he did very well, becoming perfectly at home in that language). Afterwards Arthur was sent to a private school in Hamburg, where he remained for four years (a period broken by a tour of Germany with his parents), in order to prepare for a commercial career ; but his predilection for study made such a profession repugnant to the boy and he expressed his desire to continue his studies in a Gymnasium. His father opposed this plan, not apparently out of any insensitivity towards literature and learning, but partly because of his natural desire to see his son following in his own footsteps and partly because he associated a purely literary and studious life with poverty and loss of true independence. In the end Heinrich Floris hit on the following expedient. He offered his son a choice : he could either make a grand tour of Europe and afterwards fulfil his father's wishes as to career or do without the tour and continue his studies. Arthur, who shared to the full his parents' love of travel, chose the tour and spent two blissful years (1803–4) visiting England, the Low Countries, France, Switzerland, Austria and Germany. On his return to Hamburg he took up work in a business house, in accordance with his promise.

The opportunity for travel which Schopenhauer enjoyed in his youth intensified and developed his cosmopolitan spirit and by no means resulted in a loss of esteem for and interest in foreign peoples and ways of life. He always appreciated the culture of other lands, particularly that of France ; he came to read with ease the great European works of literature in their original languages and he was never a ' Fatherlander ' ; indeed, as a grown man, he was characterized by an almost complete lack of patriotic feeling. When, in later life, Schopenhauer had been holding forth one day on his regret at belonging to such a ' stupid ' nation, a Frenchman present remarked that if he entertained the same opinion about his own nation, he would at least have the grace to keep his opinions to himself. It is interesting to note that during his extended tour he spent several months at Wimbledon, at a school kept by a clergyman called Lancaster. He learnt English well, but complained in letters of the school-routine, of the lack of imagination in the instruction and of the Protestant bigotry of England, which he hated as much as the German variety. However, although disgusted with the pietism and bigotry he witnessed, he never ceased to admire the English character. In Paris, where he spent a winter, he became passionately fond of the theatre, a devotion that never left him. The tour also increased in him his pessimistic attitude towards human life which he shared with his father, though not with his mother, and in his travel journal appear the two contrasting impressions of the beauty of nature on the one hand and the misery of human life on the other.

I have said that, on his return to Hamburg, Schopenhauer entered dutifully on a business career, or rather on the immediate task of acquiring practical experience for such a career, but he was not happy, continued his studies ' on the sly ', and at length took the opportunity afforded by his father's death in 1805, to free himself from a life that he found very irksome. I say ' at length ', since he continued for two years at his post, out of respect for the wishes of his father and gratitude for all that his father had done for him, a gratitude later expressed in a dedication written for the second edition of *The World as Will and Idea*. Meanwhile his mother had moved to Weimar, together with his sister, and there established a *salon*, where she received Goethe, Schlegel, the brothers Grimm, and other noted literary figures. At length, then, Arthur Schopenhauer, unable to compensate himself for his hated occupation by the pleasures that Hamburg had to offer, wrote to his mother at Weimar, to obtain her consent to a change of life, and, after taking advice, Johanna agreed. Thereupon Arthur left Hamburg and entered the Gymnasium at Gotha (June, 1807), though he had to leave before long in consequence of a lampoon at the expense of one of the masters. He then went to Weimar and continued his classical studies (1808–9) under the guidance of the Hellenic scholar, Franz Passow, at the same time deepening his knowledge and appreciation of music in the town that liked to look upon itself as the German Athens.

It had been arranged that, while in Weimar, Schopenhauer should dine daily at his mother's house, but she found that her son's sombre temperament, his argumentativeness and dogmatism, disturbed her peace of mind and even the tranquillity of her sleep. Accordingly she wrote to tell him that, while it was necessary for her happiness to be assured that he was happy, it was not necessary that she should be an eye-witness of the fact. In point of fact both mother and son were 'egoistic' in character, bent on developing themselves, and the contrast between the gay and witty Johanna and the passionate, gloomy Arthur, who could not forbear from insulting his mother's friends and disliked her free and independent ways, made any truly sympathetic relations between them impossible. Moreover, as Arthur Schopenhauer attained his majority in 1809 and received his share of Heinrich Floris' fortune, he was in a position at last to lead his own life and so entered the University of Göttingen in 1809. He began by studying medicine, but changed to philosophy in his second year, countering the contrary advice of the poet, Wieland, with the observation that, as life was a great problem, he had decided to spend it in reflection on life. (At Göttingen he became an admirer of Plato.) However, drawn by the fame of Fichte, he left Göttingen and went for three semesters (September, 1811, to May, 1813) to the University of Berlin, though he was soon disgusted by Fichte's obscurity and rhetorical language and the *a priori* character of his philosophy. Schleiermacher too was an object of his sarcastic comments and, *apropos* of the lecturer's dictum that no man could be a philosopher without being religious, Schopenhauer observed that no one who is religious takes to philosophy, as he does not need it.

When the country rose against Napoleon, Schopenhauer hastened to leave Berlin (where Fichte gave himself to the care of the wounded) and betook himself to Rudolstadt, where he spent the summer of 1813, in the preparation of his doctoral dissertation, an essay *On the Fourfold Root of the Principle of Sufficient Reason*, which obtained for him the doctorate at Jena and was published in the same year, 1813. His precipitate retreat to Rudolstadt may not seem heroic, nor was it, but Schopenhauer had his reasons, of course, and he was quite frank in acknowledging them. Thus, in the *Curriculum Vitæ*, which he later sent to Berlin (when applying to the University for permission to lecture), he added quite gratuitously as a reason for his retreat (he might simply have mentioned his desire to prepare his thesis and have left it at that) that he detested military affairs and that in his isolated valley, hemmed in by mountains, he had had the good fortune never to see a soldier and never to hear a drum. However, in his Latin letter to the Dean of the philosophical faculty of Jena, written in application for his doctorate, he pointed out that he was not a Prussian citizen, and also that he felt himself called to serve humanity with his head and not with his arm : moreover, his fatherland was more extensive than Germany. Schopenhauer the cosmopolitan looked on himself as a citizen of the world and was a convinced anti-nationalist.[1] His retreat to Rudolstadt, therefore, though not heroic, was in accordance with his principles as well as with his inclinations : it was not due to admiration for the Emperor, whom he censured as using other men as instruments for the attainment of his own interests and as increasing the sufferings of humanity.

In his thesis Schopenhauer wrote under the strong influence of the Kantian *Critique*. The world of our experience is the phenomenal world, it is object, but object *for a subject*, and as known, as phenomenon, it is governed by the *a priori* in human cognition. All phenomena, all our representations, stand in a certain order and in certain relations to one another, this binding together of phenomena (in opposition to noumena or the noumenon) being governed by the general principle of human cognition, the principle of sufficient reason. But this principle is not simple and unitary : it

---

[1] A further indication of his cosmopolitanism was his fondness for *Fremdwörter*.

has four fundamental forms which govern the four fundamental types of human knowledge.

(1) By our intuitive, empirical and complete (complete,
as comprising both the form and matter of phenomena)
representations we have as object of cognition the world of
real objects ('real' only in opposition to the content of the
abstract concept) and the form of the principle of sufficient
reason characteristic of this class of representations is the
principle of causality in the strict sense, *principum rationis
sufficientis fiendi*, which is an *a priori* condition of experience
and governs phenomena as succeeding one another in time.
Thus representations of this kind are constituted by (*a*) the
matter of phenomena, elementary sensations, (*b*) the *a priori*
forms of sensibility, Space and Time, and (*c*) the pure form
of *Causality*, which (according to Schopenhauer, who here
simplifies the Kantian analysis) is the only category of the
mind. (These three together form indeed the principle of
individuation, according to Schopenhauer, which is the work of
Intellect in general ; but the principle of causality is the special
work of the understanding or *Verstand*, the mind creating a
world of objects, causally linked together.)

(2) In the second class of objects, the sphere of abstract
concepts, the governing principle is the *principium rationis
sufficientis cognoscendi*, which governs judgments, i.e. syntheses
of concepts, and is an *a priori* principle, governing logical
judgment and reasoning. It is to be noted that Schopenhauer's theory of concepts is *nominalistic* and that the faculty
of reasoning, according to him (as later for Bergson) has a
practical function and value : the reason does not transcend
phenomena and Schopenhauer has no use whatever for that
form of German idealism (Hegelianism, in particular) which
professes not merely to comprehend the essence of Reality
through abstract reasoning, but even to identify reasoning
with Absolute Knowledge and to make it the innermost
essence of Reality. (3) The third class of objects-for-the-
subject consist of the *formed* elements in our complete representations, i.e., they consist of the *a priori* perceptions under
the forms of external sensibility (space) and of internal
sensibility (time) and are, in brief, the objects of geometry
and arithmetic. Geometrical and arithmetical relations are
neither empirical nor logical in nature and have a special
justifying form of the principle of sufficient reason, which

Schopenhauer terms *principium rationis sufficientis essendi*. For example, if we say that the three sides of a triangle are equal, when the three angles are equal, this second judgment is not the physical cause of the first (there is no change, no effect), while on the other hand the relation is not a relation immediately between concepts or judgments, but between angles and sides. It is a case of pure intuition. (4) The fourth class of object is the subject itself as object of know-ledge, the operating and willing subject, attained directly through self-consciousness. This willing subject, which becomes the object of self-consciousness, does not act blindly, but according to motive, and so it is governed by the fourth form of the principle of sufficient reason, *principium rationis sufficientis agendi*. The principle of sufficient reason has thus four forms, (i) *essendi* (time and space), (ii) *fiendi* (cause), (iii) *agendi* (motive) and (iv) *cognoscendi* (abstract reason), and in all four forms necessity rules, so that we have (i) *mathematical* necessity, (ii) *physical* necessity, (iii) *moral* necessity and (iv) *logical* necessity. (Schopenhauer held that a man acts by necessity, reacting to motives according to his innate character. To this subject I return in a later chapter.)

This doctoral thesis (published in 1813, at Schopenhauer's own expense, and later on revised, in order to harmonize it with his general system) Schopenhauer regarded as an indispensable introduction to his thought. In any case it makes clear his dependence on Kant and shows his general acceptance of the Kantian theory of an *a priori* element in knowledge and of the distinction between phenomenon and noumenon. In his later metaphysic of the noumenon Schopenhauer, of course, pursued an original path ; but meanwhile we see that he regarded the world which we know as *phenomenon*, as owing its formal elements to the con-stitutive activity of the subject. It is in accordance with this doctrine, fundamentally taken over from Kant, that he is enabled to declare in his principal work that ' the world is my idea '. He is, therefore, to be termed an idealist ; but, as he found the essence of the world, its ' inside ', the nature of the noumenon, in *Will* (in opposition to the Hegelian Rationalism), he is to be called a voluntaristic idealist, a term which, if cumbersome and, it might perhaps seem, a *contradictio in se*, at least expresses his characteristic difference from the rationalist metaphysics of Hegel.

After the publication of his work (which made no stir and remained practically unsold) Schopenhauer went for a time to Weimar, where he lived with his mother for some six months, until incompatability of temperament led to their final estrangement from one another. Johanna, who had scant relish for serious studies of the type her son had just published, make a joke about the word *Wurzel* or ' root ' (in the title of the essay), saying that it reminded her of a chemist's recipe ; whereupon there ensued an acrimonious dispute, in the course of which Schopenhauer foretold the fate of oblivion that would overtake his mother's novels. Goethe, however, publicly congratulated the author in Johanna's salon on November 16th, 1813, and the result of this favour shown by the great man was Schopenhauer's essay *On Vision and Colours* (published at Dresden), in which he followed to a great extent the method of Goethe in his book on colours (1810). Both attacked Newton, but Schopenhauer introduced some more or less arbitrary speculations of his own. At Weimar he met, not only Goethe but also F. Mayer, an oriental scholar, who introduced Schopenhauer to Indian philosophical literature. His visit to Weimar was, therefore, not without permanent results for his thought, though, as far as his mother was concerned, it terminated in a letter from Johanna, in which she complained of his contemptuous, overbearing and critical attitude. (Schopenhauer used to complain of the light-hearted way in which Johanna spent her money, while his chief ground of praise for his father was that the latter had, by his industry, amassed sufficient fortune to enable his son to be independent.) The result was that the philosopher never saw his mother again, though she lived for another twenty-four years. Difference of temperament was largely responsible, as we have said, for this break between mother and son ; but Schopenhauer's character was not a pleasant one and the blame must probably be laid chiefly at his door.

From Weimar Schopenhauer went to Dresden in May, 1814, and remained in the art-centre of Saxony until September, 1818. It was from Dresden that he sent the manuscript of his essay *On Vision and Colours* to Goethe in 1815, saying that it was a development of Goethe's own theory and asking for his patronage. The Master apparently considered the essay to be over-subjective in its treatment of the matter and returned an evasive reply. Correspondence continued, but finally Schopenhauer had to have his manuscript returned to him, and published it in 1816, though relations between the two men remained on a friendly footing. But this work of Schopenhauer was really only a by-product : in the meantime he was constructing his philosophical system, taking notes of the ideas that occurred to him during his walks along the banks of the Elbe, while he also frequented the art-galleries and theatre and even had a few friends. His chief philosophical work, *The World as Will and Idea*, was finished in 1818 and committed to Brockhaus, the Leipzig publishers (whom Schopenhauer attacked in such a manner, during the passage of the book through the press, that the publisher felt compelled to sever all further correspondence with a man whose letters savoured ' more of the cabman than of the philosopher '). Schopenhauer was firmly convinced that he was giving to the public the solution of the world's enigma and that his work (which appeared at the beginning of 1819) would be the source of a hundred other books ; but, when it appeared, the serious reviewers were far from enthusiastic and, what was far worse, the book did not sell and soon passed, as we will see, into temporary oblivion. For the greater part of his life the philosopher met, not so much with hostility (which would have been at least a stimulus) as with indifference ; and this indifference of the learned world towards what he regarded as mankind's deepest thought was mainly responsible for his scurrilous attacks on his idealist predecessors and on professors of philosophy in general, whom he even accused of having entered upon a conspiracy of silence, in order to drown in oblivion a system that they were unable to refute.

In September of 1818, when the book had been sent to press, the philosopher, so devoted to travel, left Dresden for Italy, visiting Venice (though without meeting Byron, who was then in the city), Bologna, Florence, Rome and Naples, studying Italian, surveying the art-galleries and noting down his reflections in a diary. However, at Milan he learnt of the bankruptcy of the commercial house at Danzig, wherein his mother and sister had invested all their capital and he a part of his own. Schopenhauer had, therefore, to return to Germany and he again took up residence at Dresden, where he lived from September, 1819, to April,

1820. Writing to his sister, he offered to divide with her and Johanna what remained to them, an offer which was not accepted. In turn Schopenhauer refused to grant his sister's request that he would take part with her and their mother in the general arrangements of the creditors, with the result of a rupture of relations between himself and his relatives. Accordingly he went his own way, with such success that in two years he obtained possession of his whole capital plus interest, the other creditors being by no means so fortunate.

To return to the subject of his chief philosophical work, which consisted of one volume comprising four books or divisions. As we shall consider the system more in detail in succeeding chapters, it will be sufficient here to give a very brief sketch of his doctrine. The spatio-temporal world, consisting of individual objects, subject to the law of causality or bound together according to the cause-effect relation, is phenomenal, is ' idea '. This Schopenhauer stated in accordance with the theory of Kant. It will be remembered that he accepted from Kant the subjective, *a priori* character of space and time as conditions of experience and that he reduced the Categories to that of Causality, also an *a priori* form of experience, though pertaining to the mind. But whereas Kant, in declaring the world as experienced and known by us to be phenomenal, asserted the unknowability of the *Ding-an-sich*, Schopenhauer maintained that it is knowable and that it is a unitary Principle, which explains not only individual human nature, but the whole of Nature. This Principle he termed *Will*, meaning by this, not the rational will of Kant, but a force or energy that manifests itself in natural forces and energies, in unconscious instinct, in desire and feeling, etc. He called it ' Will ', and not ' Force ', since he considered that the former term is better known to us and understood than the latter. The *Ding-an-sich*, the noumenon, is therefore Will, which objectifies itself in the phenomenon or appears to perception in the phenomenon, the Will being the ' inside ' of the world, the multiplicity of phenomena being ' idea ', the ' outside ' of the world. Influenced by Indian thought (he read a Latin translation of a Persian version of the *Upanishads*) Schopenhauer declared that the multiplicity of phenomena is only appearance, Maya : they are the mere appearances of the one Will, which is in truth the sole Reality.

The Will is a blind will, a restless striving without intelligent aim, a blind impulse to self-objectification, to existence, never satisfied, never at one with oneself. This unsatisfied striving shows itself most poignantly in human life, in man's perpetual striving after happiness, a happiness which lies only in the future, the supposed attainment of which soon vanishes like a dream. Happiness and pleasure are merely negative in character ; suffering and pain are the prevalent and dominant notes of life. Schopenhauer's system was thus a system of *metaphysical* pessimism, for his pessimism does not consist simply in an empirical observation (whether true or false) that human life contains more pain than joy, more suffering than happiness, but is based on a metaphysical doctrine concerning the ultimate nature of Reality, a doctrine that is radically pessimistic in character. It is not simply that human life at present happens to contain more misery than happiness, but rather that human life *must* be dominated by suffering, since it is the expression, the objectification of a blind Will, essentially at variance with itself. The philosopher in this way presented the world with a system that stood in radical contrast to that of Hegel, the then dominant thinker of Germany. While for Hegel ultimate Reality was Reason, for Schopenhauer it was Will, and a blind Will at that : while for Hegel Reason was immanent in the world, in man and even in nature, the universe having a rational end, the manifestation and self-realization of the Absolute, of God, for Schopenhauer the world had no rational end and human existence was mere pain and suffering : while for Hegel history was the necessary process of Reason's manifestation, so that in the long run it is always progress, for Schopenhauer there was no progress, save a progress in increasing misery.

Schopenhauer offered, however, two ways of relief, one temporary, the other more complete. The Will, as we have seen, objectifies itself in particular objects, subject to space and time, but they are not the *immediate* objectification of Will. The Will objectifies itself immediately in the Archetypal Forms or Platonic Ideas, and it is the province of Art, the work of genius, to express these Ideas, that at which Nature is aiming, in its own medium. In the disinterested contemplation of these Ideas, expressed in the work of art, man's desires are temporarily stilled ; he becomes temporarily a ' will-less ' operator, and cognition, otherwise the servant of desire, becomes æsthetic contemplation. In listening to great music, which . is not the expression of an Idea but a revelation of the Will itself and is the highest of the arts, man can contemplate ' disinterestedly ' even the very Will that lies at the root of all things. Whether or not this theory of the Ideas or eternal patterns of things and the theory of art built upon this ideology are consistent with the doctrine of the Will, need not be discussed now : we would simply point out in passing the influence of Plato, whom Schopenhauer learned early to love and admire (even if he borrowed the Platonic theory of Ideas for use in a very un-Platonic system), and, in general, the welding-together of classicism with romanticism, that was not uncommon among prominent Germans of the time, for example, in the thought of Goethe himself.

If a temporary escape from desire, unsatisfied and unsatisfiable desire, is to be found in æsthetic contemplation, for a lasting escape we must turn to morality. There could, of course, be no real theory of moral obligation in a deterministic and ætheistic system, but Schopenhauer had his own peculiar theory of morality, closely linked with his metaphysical pessimism. The Will, the macrocosm, is objectified in each individual, the microcosm, and the inner nature of the individual is shown in his fundamental egoism : because he is the objectification of Will, indeed *is* the Will, he acts as if he alone mattered. This egoism shows itself most clearly in the lives of great tyrants and criminals and, wherever it appears, it is the unfailing source of misery and suffering. Now, when a man ' sees through ' the principle of individuation, realizes that all individuation is phenomenon, Maya, he realizes too that he suffers in all, that the suffering of all is *his* suffering, and he attains to love, the essential of which is *sympathy*. Knowing that the sufferings of others are, metaphysically, his own sufferings, he will do what he can to alleviate those sufferings. Sympathy, then, is an essential grade of morality, but it is not the highest stage : the complete penetration of the principle of individuation, the complete lifting of the veil of Maya which reveals the whole world as one and all suffering as one suffering, consequent on life itself, will lead a man, no longer to assert this life through the constant acts of the will and ever-renewed desire, but to deny the will to live, to turn away from life by voluntary renunciation, resignation, chastity and asceticism (*not*, as we might expect, by suicide). Beyond and above the ethic of sympathy there stands, therefore, the ideal of ' holiness ', exemplified in the lives of Christian, Hindu and Buddhist Saints. What the Saints really did, even those who would not recognize the fact owing to their dogmatic preconceptions, was, according to Schopenhauer, to deny the will to live and to attain that state in which the world was to them as nothing. This is the complete escape from the tyranny of desire and is entered upon by the transition from virtue or morality in the narrower sense (justice and, higher than justice, sympathy) to asceticism. In treating of this theme Schopenhauer utilized ideas from Christianity, but the general atmosphere is Oriental in character.

Such, in brief outline, was the solution to the world's enigma, that Schopenhauer gave to the world at the beginning of 1819. The leading ideas may seem bizarre and extravagant in the extreme, but in the work itself they are wonderfully expressed, in a manner that makes Schopenhauer an exception among the celebrated German philosophers of the period. One would scarcely go to Kant or Hegel in search of literary style, poetic imagery, sublime description (even if they do have their ' purple passages ') ; but when the system elaborated by the thirty-year-old Schopenhauer was published, a work of literature was added to the philosophical library of his country. Indeed, Schopenhauer and Nietzsche are really the only two stylists among the philosophers, i.e., more prominent philosophers, of Germany. Whatever contradictions or inconsistencies there may be in the system as such, the language in which it is expressed is easy to understand and is often beautiful, while the writer has a genius for poetic imagery which makes large portions of the work a real pleasure to read, whether one agrees with the thought or not.

The philosopher Herbart criticized the author of the *World as Will and Idea* for attempting to mingle the theories of Kant and Plato in such a way that the characteristic features and the real value of both systems evaporated in the process. On the other hand, Schopenhauer, said Herbart, was unjust in regard to his immediate predecessors, especially Fichte. None the less the work was learned and pleasant to read and might serve as an exercise in thinking and as a counter to the obscurity of Fichte and Schelling, even if the philosophy were false. Beneke, too, while praising Schopenhauer's acumen, his talent, literary clarity and frequent luminous observations, criticized the thought as full of errors. He did not, however, always give the exact quotations from Schopenhauer's work, and the latter took advantage of the fact to publish a denunciation of Beneke's behaviour. He was very pleased when Beneke had to retire from lecturing in 1822 in consequence of a publication on the relativity of morals and he later went so far, with his not uncharacteristic lack of good taste, as to joke about Beneke's death (apparently by suicide) in 1854. According to Jean Paul, on the other hand, Schopenhauer's book, original, acute and profound, was the work of a great philosophical genius, though owing to its pessimistic character he could not recommend it, even if he praised it. Schopenhauer had thus this consolation at least, that his book won some notice on its publication, even if the notice taken was not particularly favourable ; but this consolation did not last for long and when, in 1835, he made inquiries concerning the sale of the book he was informed that there was no sale—a somewhat exasperating thought to a man who believed that he had unveiled the mystery of the world.

After the publication of his work Schopenhauer set about obtaining an academic position, in order that he might expound the truth by word as well as by the pen and, after the necessary negotiations with the University authorities, he started lecturing at Berlin in 1820. *Arthur Schopenhauer privatim senis per hebdomadem horis universam tradet philosophiam, i.e., doctrinam de essentia mundi et mente humana.* In other words, Schopenhauer went to Berlin, in order to expound the truth in the very stronghold of Hegel himself, and he was so bold as to choose the very same hour for his lecture as that at which the great 'Sophist' was accustomed to lead an impressed if mystified audience through the subtle windings of the Dialectic. This determined offensive was a signal failure : Schopenhauer failed to entice away the pupils of Hegel to listen to a wiser than Oedipus and the lectures terminated at the end of the semester. The pessimist's philosophy was not only opposed to the spirit of the time, which found its embodiment in optimistic idealism, but also it did not lend itself to treatment in the dialectical manner which was then in fashion under the influence of Hegel, so that Schopenhauer was handicapped both by his matter and by the form in which he delivered it. Nor was he ever a man to remould his thought to suit prevailing fashions. He lived a retired life at Berlin and, though he was a faithful frequenter of the theatre and opera, he mixed little in society, and did not attempt to take part in university politics : in any case, as a *Privatdozent* he was hardly in a position to challenge effectually the supremacy of the *Professor ordinarius* : at least, in order to do so, he would have to have been a much more brilliant lecturer than he apparently was in actual fact. His failure can thus easily be explained, without having to suppose any deliberate conspiracy on the part of the professorial staff of ' Sophists '. However, in spite of his complete failure, Schopenhauer continued for several years to have his name printed in the University catalogue and to announce the subject of his course, though the lectures were never delivered. Later on he thought of renewing his academic career at Heidelberg, but the project came to nothing.

In May, 1822, Schopenhauer set off for Italy, to console himself beneath the southern sun, and visited Milan, Genoa and Florence, spending the winter in the latter city. In a letter to a friend he expressed his love for Italy, comparing her to a beloved with whom one quarrels one day, only to adore her the next, whereas Germany is like a house-wife, with whom one lives without anger and without love. Yet, in spite of his love for Italy, Schopenhauer found fault with the Italians, with their ' beautiful faces ', and ' vulgar souls ', largely because of the noise they made and their ' terrible voices ' in everyday life, which stood in such contrast with their singing in their theatre. Schopenhauer was extremely sensitive to noise and in his essay on the subject[1] he declaims against ' hammering, the barking of dogs, and the shouting of children ', the ' slamming of doors ' and the ' aimless drumming ' that goes on in Germany ; but his particular hatred was directed against the ' cursed cracking of whips ', which is ' the most unwarrantable and disgraceful of all noises '. ' I should like to know how many great and beautiful thoughts these whips have already cracked out of the world. If I had any authority, I should soon produce in the heads

[1] *Parerga and Paralipomena*, vi, pp. 678–682.

of these carters an inseparable *nexus idearum* between cracking a whip and receiving a whipping '. He quotes with approval Thomas Hood's dictum concerning the Germans : ' For a musical people they are the most noisy I ever met with '. One may smile at Schopenhauer's remarks on noise, but not a few thinkers and writers would sympathize strongly, even while smiling.

After spending the winter of 1824 at Dresden, Schopenhauer went to Berlin, because of a judicial process that had been dragging on for some years, and remained there till 1831. The judicial process in question, though somewhat comical, is revealing as to the philosopher's character. In 1821, Schopenhauer came one day upon three women who were chattering away on a landing outside his room. Irritated by their presence and the noise they were making Schopenhauer asked them to go away ; but one of them, a seamstress named Caroline Luise Marquet, refused to go. The end of it was that the philosopher, stick in hand, put the good woman out of the house by force, though he did not strike her, according to his own account. Be that as it may, the woman fell down in the process of being ejected and subsequently brought an action against Schopenhauer for assault and battery. The latter defended himself and the case was dismissed ; but the woman appealed and Schopenhauer, during his absence abroad, was fined. This did not satisfy the lady and she demanded a monthly allowance in compensation for permanent injuries received, with the result that Schopenhauer had to pay costs and to give her five thalers a month. When he returned to Berlin he tried to obtain the reversal of the judgment, but failed, and thus he was compelled to pay Caroline Marquet an allowance up to the time of her death in 1841. On her death certificate the philosopher commented, *Obit anus, abit onus*.

During his sojourn in Berlin thoughts of marriage occurred to Schopenhauer, but he could not bring himself to sacrifice his cherished independence : in any case he had before him the example of philosophers like Descartes, Spinoza, Leibniz, Kant, who had remained free from matrimonial shackles. Instead he turned his attention to translation. Already he had had the intention, during his last winter at Dresden, of translating into German *The Natural History of Religion* and the *Dialogues on Natural Religion* by David

Hume (of whom he thought highly) ; but the project proved abortive. Nor did his proposal in 1829 to translate the principal works of Kant into English, a proposal prompted by an article in the *Foreign Review* regretting the inaccessibility of Kant's works to English readers, prove any more successful —in spite of Schopenhauer's observation in a letter to Francis Haywood that a century might pass by before so much Kantian philosophy and so much English would meet together in one head. He also failed to find agreement with his proposal to collaborate in a French translation of the works of Goethe, and he was unable to find a publisher for his *Handorakel*, a German translation of a work by the Spanish Jesuit, Father Bathazar Gracian (1601–1658), which saw the light only after Schopenhauer's death. Altogether the period spent in Berlin was not a happy time for him, and in the summer of 1831 he left the city for ever, fleeing from the cholera, the disease that caused the death of his hated rival Hegel. (Characteristically Schopenhauer had paid attention to a dream he had had in Berlin which, he thought, foretold his death, if he remained in the city. Another dream, experienced after his arrival at Frankfurt, signified that he would survive his mother.)

From Berlin Schopenhauer went to Frankfurt-am-Main. After a short while spent in that city he went to Mannheim for a year, but returned to Frankfurt in June, 1833, and lived there until his death in 1860, with the exception of a few days' excursion in the Rhine valley in 1835. He had now apparently definitely renounced travel, matrimony and an academic career, and lived a retired life, preoccupied with the composition of his works and the desire of fame and popularity. His manner of life at Frankfurt is well known, though not so well known as that of Kant. The latter's habit of early rising was not to Schopenhauer's taste (he thought it a wasteful expenditure of valuable energy) and so he did not rise before eight o'clock. The forenoon he spent in study and writing, though he gave more time to thinking than to reading and writing, and then, after enjoying a little recreation with his flute, went to dine at an hotel. He ate well, we learn, and preferred wine to beer, the latter drink, together with duelling, being an object of destestation to him. Were not beer-drinking and duelling the delights of the German universities ? After a siesta he walked for a couple of hours in the country, with his dog as his companion. Schopenhauer had two dogs in succession (each of which was called Atman) and the second survived him : to these animals he was devoted, believing dogs to be much superior to men in point of sincerity. Apart from his walk the philosopher spent the afternoon in reading some classical author. (Schopenhauer left an annuity in his will to his surviving dog, payable, of course, to the dog's custodian.) Not only had he a great esteem for the Latin language, but he also read the literatures of France, Germany, England, Italy and Spain in their original tongue, besides trying to keep abreast of scientific development, alert to discover points that seemed to lend confirmation or support to his own philosophic system. The reading-room in the town always received a visit from the philosopher, who paid special attention to the English *Times*. Supper was taken at an hotel and, needless to say, he often visited the theatre or concert-hall, looking on the former as a mirror of life and comparing the man who does not go to the theatre to a man who makes his toilet without consulting his looking-glass. In music he preferred Rossini and Beethoven, but, in later years, his power of enjoyment was handicapped by increasing deafness. Schopenhauer was much subject to phobias, and he always slept with loaded weapons at hand, as a precaution against robbers, of whom he was singularly afraid.

Not a heroic life, it is true, and very far from attaining the ideal of ascetic renunciation that he set before the world in the last book of *The World as Will and Idea* ; but, as Schopenhauer himself aptly remarked, it is no more necessary that a philosopher should be a saint than that a saint should be a philosopher. However, though not a heroic life, nor even a life of constant study, it was an orderly existence, marked by prudence and care : at his death the philosopher had doubled his patrimony. His life was, however, marred by misanthropy. He had acquaintances indeed, but acquaintance did not ripen into real friendship : he was too intolerant and dogmatic for congenial relations to endure very long. Schopenhauer considered that his misanthropy was due to knowledge of mankind (though it was certainly also partly the result of his own difficult temperament) and he ceased to look for a real friend, believing that there are none. All men, he thought, are egoistic, the number of friends a man has depends on the number of compliments or other gifts he is prepared to present them with, and it is foolish to estimate the value of anyone according to the number of such friends. He made profession of a certain quiet irony and, believing himself to be a missionary of truth, declared that he ought not to compromise himself with the human beings to whom he stood in this relation, just as ' the missionaries in China do not think of fraternizing with the Chinese '. Such being Schopenhauer's attitude, it is scarcely a matter for wonder that he made no real friends, though he undoubtedly suffered from loneliness. His outstanding talent helped to isolate him, while his natural temperament made it difficult to be his friend. On the other hand isolation and loneliness increased his defensive attitude towards others. He was thus imprisoned in a kind of vicious circle.

In 1836, Schopenhauer published *On the Will in Nature*, containing what he believed to be corroborations contributed by empirical science to his philosophic doctrine, and in 1839, he won a prize from the Scientific Society of Drontheim (Norway) for the best essay on the question, ' whether free-will could be proved from the evidence of consciousness ', and was elected a member of the Society. The Royal Danish Academy of the Sciences at Copenhagen, however, which had instituted a prize-competition for essays on ' Whether the source and foundation of ethics is to be sought in an intuitive moral idea, and in the analysis of other derivative moral conceptions, or in some other principle of knowledge ', informed Schopenhauer that, though his essay was the only one sent in, it had failed to obtain the prize, one reason being that it failed to show proper respect towards the leading philosophers—an observation that naturally did nothing to increase Schopenhauer's affection for Fichte, Schelling and Hegel. This failure was a blow to the philosopher, since he had not only been confident of success, but had even made this confidence plain in his letter to the Academy. However, in 1841, he published both his essays together under the title of *The Two Fundamental Problems of Ethics*. As to freedom of the will, Schopenhauer denied *liberum arbitrium indifferentiæ* : a man can do what he wills and actualize his volitions, but he cannot will otherwise than he does. He maintained a form of character-determinism and considered that true ' liberty of indifference ' would contradict the principle of sufficient reason which everywhere rules the phenomenal world. As to the second essay, Schopenhauer criticized the Kantian ethic for maintaining a categorical imperative without at the same time asserting a transcendental Absolute and tried himself to found morality on ' pure piety' or sympathy (without sufficient justification in the opinion of the Danish Academy).

In 1844, appeared a second edition of *The World as Will and Idea*, in two volumes, since Schopenhauer added fifty supplementary chapters arranged in four divisions, to correspond with the four books of the original work. In the preface to this second edition, Schopenhauer expressed his opinion of German university philosophers in no uncertain terms. Whereas his sole star has been always that of truth, the university philosophers have had constantly before their eyes ' the fear of the Lord, the will of the ministry, the laws of the established church, the wishes of the publisher, the attendance of the students, the goodwill of colleagues, the course of current politics, the momentary tendency of the public, and Heaven knows what besides'. The young generation have wasted their time with the ' philosophemes of vulgar, uncalled men' and ' bombastic sophists', and minds have been drained of their freshness and ruined ' by the nonsense of Hegelism'. These outspoken words expressed Schopenhauer's disappointment and his disgust with the reigning philosophy, and his disappointment was not lessened when only one reviewer praised his originality, his sincerity and his style, and publicly recognized as cause of his failure the contrast between his philosophy and that of the period. But the time of disappointed waiting was soon to end and in the period of discouragement that followed the abortive political movement of 1848, Schopenhauer's philosophy had at last a chance to come into its own. (In 1859 Schopenhauer, then seventy-two years old, published a third, and augmented, edition of his chief work.)

The optimistic and democratic revolution of 1848 awakened no sympathy in Schopenhauer's heart ; he disliked and mistrusted it, not least because he feared it might result in the loss of his own property. All that he desired of a government was that it should preserve law and order : the State is a watchman to protect person and property and it has no moral function at all. If, therefore, Schopenhauer took the

conservative side, if in his will (1852) he left most of his estate
to be employed for the benefit of the royalist soldiers wounded
at Berlin in 1848 (Austrian soldiers used the windows of
Schopenhauer's room in Frankfurt to shoot at the demo-
crats below), this was certainly not because he had any
leanings towards a 'totalitarian' view of the State. On
the contrary, he regarded the 'ethical State' as a monstrosity, part of the Hegelian nonsense, and the revolutionary
movement, inspired to some extent at least by the School of
Hegel, was anathema to him. Let the State keep order :
then the servants of truth could continue their work in peace
—that was more or less his attitude. He was relieved and
glad, then, when the revolution failed, a failure that carried
with it the eclipse of optimistic Hegelianism, a failure that
made possible the rise of his own star.

In 1851 appeared a collection of essays, entitled *Parerga
and Paralipomena*. The essays, dealing with a wide variety
of topics, from religion to noise, are lively and witty, learned
yet thoroughly entertaining, garnished with quotations and
references furnished by the author's wide reading and written
in his beautiful prose style. It was refused by three publishers
and the fourth publisher approached, though he accepted,
gave no payment ; yet the book proved the most popular
of Schopenhauer's works and opened to him the gates of
success. The work was issued in two volumes, the first containing the *Parerga* or doctrinal developments, the second
the *Paralipomena* or isolated thoughts. One of the best known
sections of the *Parerga* is the celebrated *Aphorismen zur Lebens-
weisheit*, which contain advice and directions concerning
the leading of a life 'in the world' in such a manner as to
live with as little unhappiness as possible. These pages,
therefore, have not got in view the life of holiness (depicted
in the last part of *The World*), which consists in renunciation
of all desire and in asceticism ; they look rather to the lower
and more accessible levels of morality. The prudent man
will love solitude, and it is necessary for him to be possessed
of a sufficiency of property to enable him to lead an independent life, without the necessity of working to obtain a liveli-
hood. In this way he will be truly free and independent
and in a position to bring to maturity those fruits of wisdom
which, like lighthouses, illumine the darkness of the world
—a non-religious analogy to the Christian contemplative

who pays for his keep by the treasure of prayer. The direction of attention to the life of prudence rather than to that of heroism makes the *Aphorisms* somewhat akin to the *Hand-Orakel*, Schopenhauer's translation of Father Gracian's work. Gracian, like Schopenhauer, was pessimistic as to the majority of men, though his pessimism naturally found its place within the general framework of the Christian religion, whereas Schopenhauer's pessimism was metaphysical and fundamental.

In the *Parerga* occurs Schopenhauer's essay *On Women*, ' that undersized, narrow-shouldered, broad-hipped, and short-legged race ', the ' Number Two of the human race '. Neither for music, nor for poetry, nor for plastic arts, have they really and truly any sense or susceptibility ; it is a mere mockery if they make a pretence of it in order to assist their endeavour to please ; ' they are incapable of taking a *purely objective interest* in anything '. Woman indeed lives more in the present than man and so is more cheerful than man ; she is more ready to show sympathy for the unfortunate (owing to the weakness of her reasoning faculty) ; but she has no sense of justice, little sense of truth and is given to constant dissimulation. What was the reason for this very harsh judgment of women in general ? Apart from minor sources of annoyance (he was particularly annoyed by woman's habit of chattering in the theatre and suggested facetiously that St. Paul's maxim might be adapted and the words ' Let a woman keep silence in the theatre ' be put up in big letters on the curtain), Schopenhauer's relations with his mother undoubtedly contributed to the formation of his general attitude in regard to women. We have seen that the two were unable to live together and that all relations were broken off in consequence of the negotiations concerning the bankruptcy-affair ; and, though correspondence was renewed during the philosopher's Frankfurt period and though he had one interview with his sister, he never saw his mother again. Earlier in this chapter I said that, in my opinion, Schopenhauer himself was much to blame for this unfortunate episode ; but that should not be taken to imply that Johanna was a paragon among women. ' Madame Schopenhauer, a rich widow. Makes profession of erudition. Authoress. Prattles much and well, intelligently ; without heart and soul. Self-complacent, eager after approbation, and constantly smiling to herself. God preserve us from women whose mind has shot up into mere intellect '. Such is the independent testimony of Anselm Feuerbach in his *Memoirs*.

But, though his relations with his mother contributed towards his theoretical misogyny, we must not omit mention of the fact that Schopenhauer's experience of women in general was of a character hardly calculated to generate a real respect for and appreciation of the other sex. He had strong sensual desires and in his earlier years he apparently indulged these desires, while one of the joys of advanced age was that he was liberated from the slavery of passion. As he never married and his intercourse with women had been confined to more or less casual *amours*, he not unnaturally tended to take a cynical view of woman and to see in love little beyond the physical aspect, generalizing into judgments on womankind his individual experiences on the physical level. Moreover, his strong character, i.e., strong in will and tenacity of purpose, led him to over-emphasize the weakness of woman, in respect to character as well as physique, and in his essay *On Women* he commends the ancients for speaking of them as the *sexus sequior*. If Schopenhauer had ever known real love (for which his egoism and his difficult temperament unfitted him), he would hardly have taken up the attitude that he did in regard to the other sex.

Si quis tota die currens pervenit ad vesperam, satis est, says Schopenhauer in the preface to the third edition of *The World* (1859). With the publication of *Parerga and Paralipomena* in 1851, he had arrived at the evening of his life, and with the evening came fame, long hoped for yet so long delayed. Hostility was indeed not lacking, even at this stage, particularly on the part of German professors. After all, Schopenhauer had repeatedly castigated the *Herren Professoren* and they were not quick to forget the fact. Moreover, as functionaries of the State, they thoroughly disliked Schopenhauer's cosmopolitanism and his attitude towards Germany. The younger Fichte and the Hegelian Rosenkranz showed their hostility in their reviews ; but all this was powerless to reverse the tide which had now set in. In the *Westminster Review* for April, 1853, John Oxenford, in an article entitled *Iconoclasm in German Philosophy*, acted as Schopenhauer's herald in England, and the article was translated into German and published in the *Vossische Zeitung*. A similar service was accorded to the philosopher in France by Saint-René Taillandier in an article (*L'Allemagne littéraire*) in the *Revue des Deux Mondes* for August, 1856, while in December, 1858, Francesco De Sanctis published his *Schopenhauer e Leopardi* in the *Rivista Contemporanea* of Turin. Richard Wagner sent the philosopher a copy of the *Ring der Nibelungen* in 1854, 'in admiration and gratitude', while in 1853 E. Erdmann had given him an extended notice in his *Die Entwicklung der deutschen Spekulation seit Kant*, protesting against the oblivion into which he had unjustly fallen. Moreover, the fact that the philosophical faculty of Leipzig university offered a prize in 1856 for an exposition and criticism of Schopenhauer's system showed clearly (whatever motives may have led to the institution of the competition) that the philosopher could no longer be ignored, and by 1857 lectures were being delivered on his philosophy in the universities of Bonn, Breslau and Jena. Meanwhile disciples were declaring themselves, visiting the Master and corresponding with him—Frauenstädt, Becker, Lindner, etc. Richard Wagner was considerably influenced by Schopenhauer, as were also, later, Eduard von Hartmann, retired artillery officer and author of the *Philosophy of the Unconscious*, and Friedrich Nietzsche.[1] We may also mention the name of Paul Deussen, a friend of Nietzsche, who became professor at Kiel and who, though primarily an Oriental scholar, was a fervent admirer of the great pessimist.

Schopenhauer's hour was come. Visitors came from all sides, from Vienna, from London, from Russia, from America ; audiences of the great man were eagerly sought for and his more fervid admirers kissed his hand : students made pilgrimages to Frankfurt as they had formerly made pilgrimages to Weimar : the tables in the Hôtel d'Angleterre were filled by those who desired an opportunity to see him and he was the cynosure of all eyes : on his birthday flowers, gifts, compliments, verses, were showered upon him : his portrait was painted (thus the French painter Jules Lutenschütz painted at least three portraits in oils, in 1855, 1858 and 1859) : Elizabeth Ney, a descendant of Napoleon's Marshal, came from Berlin to make a marble bust of the

---

[1] For Nietzsche's relation to the philosophy of Schopenhauer, see Chap. VII in my *Friedrich Nietzsche, Philosopher of Culture* (2nd ed., London, 1975).

philosopher. All this devotion and even adulation was eagerly drunk in by Schopenhauer, who rejoiced that his philosophy had found its way to the world at last (he rejoiced also no doubt for more egoistic reasons) : no criticism was allowed, no praise of any other philosophy. Indeed, he was highly indignant that the University of Leipzig awarded the before-mentioned prize to a student who attributed greater import to him as a writer than as a philosopher. Yet there is certainly something to be said for the student's point of view, for, even if Schopenhauer did not merit the fame that came to him for the content of his work, he certainly merited it for his literary style, language and mode of presentation. He was quite right when he said in his essay *On Authorship and Style* that ' obscurity and vagueness of expression are at all times and everywhere a very bad sign ', since ' in ninety-nine cases out of a hundred they arise from vagueness of thought '.[1] Whether his judgment on Fichte, Schelling and Hegel, that ' they wish to appear to know what they do not know, to think what they do not think, and to say what they do not say ' is fully just or not, he hit the nail on the head when he spoke of ' the law of simplicity and naïveté ' and declared that ' the use of many words to express few thoughts is everywhere the infallible sign of mediocrity ; while to comprise much thought in a few words is the infallible sign of a distinguished mind '.[2] If he was correct in his opinion that ' the Germans are conspicuous above all other nations for neglect of style in writing ', it can hardly be denied that Schopenhauer himself set a good example.

Foucher de Careil (1826–1891) narrates how he was received by Schopenhauer in his library, where he saw about three thousand volumes, almost all of which had been read by the philosopher. Among them there were but few German books, many English and some Italian ones ; but the majority were French. (Schopenhauer had no high opinion of his fellow-countrymen and did not hesitate to give expression to those opinions.) The first time that Foucher de Careil saw the pessimist was in 1859, at table in the Hôtel d'Angleterre, and he has left us a vivid impression of the old man, with his blue, clear eyes, his thin lips about which played a somewhat sarcastic smile, his great brow framed by locks of white hair, his face stamped with an air of nobility and distinction,

---

[1] *Parerga and Paralipomena*, vi, p. 557.　　[2] *Ibid.*, vi, p. 558.

sparkling with wit and mischief. His clothes, his lace ruffle, his white cravat, recalled an old gentleman from the reign of Louis XV ; his manners were those of a man of good society. His movements were lively, with a liveliness that was accentuated in conversation ; he spoke French, English, German and Italian perfectly and Spanish passably and so enriched his talk with witticisms, quotations, precision and exactitude of detail that the hours sped by and sometimes the little circle of his friends went on listening to him until midnight without fatigue, while the brightness of his glance was never for an instant dimmed. He was like the last of the great conversationalists of a vanished century.

The last decade of Schopenhauer's life was, then, probably his happiest, certainly of his adult life : he had the popularity and fame for which he had so longed ; his wit and culture had at length an opportunity to show itself in intercourse with those who respected and admired him. But while we pay tribute to his ability, his learning, his powers of expression, we cannot help noticing his vanity and egoism. Schopenhauer was not a lovable man, nor was he a man who could really love others (and the second is often responsible for the first) : he was egoistic, passionate, suspicious, reserved, without patriotism or effective magnanimity of heart ; yet he was a man of strong character and will, steadfast in his purpose : he believed that he had the truth to give to the world and he was daunted by no opposition or hostility : he was sincere and spoke his mind openly. However much, therefore, we may feel that he was a man with whom we would not care to live and whom we could not really like, we need not withhold from him the tribute of admiration for those good qualities which he did possess. While we cannot feel for him that respect which a character like that of Bishop Berkeley must inspire, while we miss in him the practical idealism of a Leibniz or the public spirit of a John Stuart Mill, we acknowledge in Schopenhauer a certain rugged greatness, a strength of will, a breadth of culture, a theoretical sensitiveness to the suffering of humanity, that compensate in some degree for those qualities that repel.

In April, 1857, Schopenhauer was troubled with palpitations of the heart, which began again in April, 1860. He did not follow the doctor's advice to discontinue his cold baths and to breakfast in bed, and at the beginning of September inflammation of the lungs set in. He became somewhat better ; but on the morning of September 21st, when the doctor paid him a morning visit (Schopenhauer had taken his cold bath and his breakfast as usual), he found him peacefully seated on his sofa, dead. Some years previously, the philosopher obtained a statue of Buddha from Paris and had it gilded, and it was his custom, before retiring for the night, to meditate on the text of the Upanishads. Perhaps this had been his occupation on the last night of his life on earth, to meditate on the vanity of life and the fact of death. He was buried at Frankfurt and on the black tombstone were inscribed, according to his own wishes, simply the two words, *Arthur Schopenhauer*. On June 6, 1895, a monument to the philosopher was unveiled in the city that he had made his home for so many years.

CHAPTER III

LIFE'S A DREAM

' THE WORLD IS MY IDEA '—these are the first words of *The World as Will and Idea*, and they express, at first hearing at least, a very strange opinion. How can the world, the sun, the moon, the stars, and earth and all that it contains, be *my* idea ? These things are ' out there ' : I can see them, many of them I can touch and measure : I may perish but they remain. I am sitting at my table, with my books and my papers upon it : if I leave my room and cease to think of my table, my books and my papers, they do not cease to be. If I am run over in the street, the world still goes on : it is only I that cease to exist any longer in the world.

Now, Schopenhauer might say, we cannot speak of the world at all except in so far as it is an object of knowledge, an object of thought and consciousness. It would be absurd to assert the existence of an unknowable world, since by the very fact of asserting its existence we would at the same time assert that something is known about it : we cannot think an unthinkable world, since this would be a contradiction in terms. All that we know is object of knowledge and all that we think is object of thought. But there is no knowledge without a knower, no thought without a thinker : the world, then, which we know about and about which we think is object to the knower and thinker. But who is the knower and thinker? Each one of us can say, ' *I* am the knower, *I* am the thinker '. Each one of us, therefore, can say, ' The world is object to me, object to my knowledge, object of my thought : it is linked to me by an inseparable bond '. If I try to imagine the world existing without me, it may seem to me at first as though I could succeed in this—for cannot I imagine myself dead (as die I will) and the world continuing to exist? Let me reflect a moment. What is this act of imagination in its totality? Is it simply the world existing without me? Clearly not : it is *I* picturing the world to myself but leaving myself out of the picture : the imagination or the thought of the world existing without me is *my* imagination, *my* thought : I may try to leave myself out altogether, but I cannot : without me the imagination or thought is nothing. The world is thus the object of my knowledge, my thought : it stands in an essential relation to me. But the objective as such, the object of knowledge, exists in the consciousness of the subject ; it is the subject's idea. The world, then, is my idea.

(What this really amounts to is that one cannot think of the world without thinking of it or imagine it without imagining it. Similarly, my idea of the world is my idea of the world. The world is known by me, the individual subject of knowledge, only imperfectly and partially, and this partial and imperfect knowledge, which may be called my idea of the world, perishes with me, cannot exist without me, precisely because it is my idea and no one else's. If we wish to call my idea of the world, which, as a subjective act, is peculiar to me ' the world ', then, of course, the world is ' my idea '. But is this anything more than saying that my idea is my idea? I know the world directly, even if only partially and imperfectly, and the reflection of this knowledge in my consciousness cannot exist without me ; but it does not follow that the world, of which I have knowledge, is ' my idea '. Cæsar's knowledge of the world perished with him ; but the world of which Cæsar had knowledge did not perish with him and can very well exist without him. The world, *precisely as* finitely known, has no existence apart from the finite knower ; but the world, *of which* the finite knower has finite knowledge, certainly has existence apart from the finite subject.)

But I am self-conscious, I can make myself an object of my

knowledge : am I, then, my own idea ? In so far as I really
can turn myself into an object of self-reflection, know myself,
I exist for my consciousness and am my own idea : but that
is only one side of the matter, since to the self as known, as
object of consciousness, there must correspond a self as knower,
as subject. I reflect on myself : the ' myself ' is object, the
' I ' is subject. I then reflect on the ' I ' : very well, the ' I '
becomes object and ' another I ', an I further back, as it were,
becomes subject. In other words, there is always presupposed
an I that is subject and subject only, that can never be object.
It can never be apprehended or grasped in the sense of becoming object : but it is necessarily presupposed : it transcends
the I as appearing to consciousness, as phenomenon. Consciousness, therefore, means the subject-object relation, and
neither can the object be resolved into subject (Fichte) or the
subject into object (Schelling). The whole world (including
e.g. my body) is object of my consciousness, is my idea ; but
the I does not exist without the object. The two belong
together, and both, the individual subject and the object of
his consciousness, are governed by the principle of sufficient
reason which, as has been shown (cf. *The Fourfold Root*) is the
principle of subjectivity, governing the phenomenal world.
The whole world, individual subjects and individual objects, is
phenomenon, appearance, Maya.

But what does Schopenhauer mean by ' idea ', when he
says that the world is my idea ? He means that the world,
as essentially object in the subject-object relation, is essentially
for the subject, is an appearing-to or a perceived-by the subject.
He entirely agreed with Berkeley's criticism of Locke's theory
of material substance : there is no matter-in-itself : there is
only what we perceive, so that *esse est percipi*. For Schopenhauer,
then, the material objects of the world, including the human
body, have no other existence than in their being perceived :
they are *ideas of perception*. Distinguishing ideas of perception
from abstract ideas (concepts) he remarks of the former that
they ' comprehend the whole visible world, or the sum total of
experience, with the conditions of its possibility '.[1] They are
not, therefore, ideas in the ordinary sense of the word, but are
presentations, existing *for* the subject and having no independent reality of their own in the empirical world. While,
then, he would not agree with Berkeley's speculative meta-

[1] I, p. 7.

physic as a whole, he agreed with Berkeley's doctrine that the essence of the material world of individual objects lies in their being perceived, in their being presentations of a percipient subject. *Esse est percipi*. Abstract ideas are peculiar to man alone and are not shared in by the irrational animals ; but ideas of perception are common to men and animals alike. To each there is a world of nature, an object.

At first sight at least this theory would seem to rob the world of all reality whatsoever, to place it on precisely the same level as the dreams that come to us by night or the fanciful images that flit through our minds by day. It is because of this impression of the conclusion to be drawn from idealism, says Schopenhauer, that appeals have been made, now to ' irresistible conviction ' (in the independent reality of the external world), as by the Scotch School, now to ' faith ', as by Jacobi. In fact, however, true idealism does not rob the external world of any of its reality *on the level of experience*. I, the individual subject precisely as individual, am also appearance ; according to the full doctrine of Schopenhauer, I as an individual am also to be reckoned among phenomena : as far, then, as mere phenomenality is concerned, the external world and I am on the same level : the whole subject-object relation belongs to the realm of phenomena. To say that the world (i.e. the external world) is my idea robs neither me nor the world of empirical reality, but asserts the transcendental ideality of both the phenomenal self and the world of individual objects without. ' The true idealism is not the empirical but the transcendental '.[1] Thus just as Berkeley could claim that his theory left untouched the empirical reality of the external world, since it asserted that the external world is just what it is perceived to be and nothing else (without any matter-in-itself or unknowable material substance in the Lockean sense), so could Schopenhauer protest in turn that his own theory did not affect the empirical reality of the world when it asserted that the world consisted of ideas of perception or presentations, without the thing-in-itself (as understood by Kant). ' With all *transcendental* ideality the objective world retains *empirical* reality ; the object is indeed not the thing in itself, but as an empirical object it is real '.[2]

But, though the world is empirically real, the empirically real in general is conditioned by the subject in a twofold

[1] II, p. 170.　　　　　　[2] *Ibid*, p. 184.

manner, first, as we have already seen, *materially* or precisely as *object*, as opposed to a subject, as idea or presentation of the subject, and secondly *formally*, i.e. according to the mode of its existence or according to the mode of its being perceived. As I have already mentioned in the biographical sketch, when treating briefly of *The Fourfold Root*, Schopenhauer accepted the Kantian analysis of experience and his doctrine of the *a priori*, though he reduced the *a priori* elements to time, space and causality. It is these formal factors that determine the mode of experience and so the mode of empirical existence of the object. It is to these conditions of experience that Schopenhauer refers, when he remarks in the already cited words that ideas of perception ' comprehend the whole visible world, or the sum total of experience, with the conditions of its possibility '.[1] In accordance with this doctrine Schopenhauer observes that ' with the simple or Berkeleian idealism, which concerns the object in general, there stands in immediate connection the Kantian idealism, which concerns the specially given *mode or manner* of objective existence '.[2] In this way Schopenhauer combined Berkeley's *esse est percipi* with the Kantian *a priori* in order to explain the matter and form of the phenomenal world, thus doing away with the unknowable thing-in-itself of Kant, that ' *ignis fatuus* in philosophy ",[3] which was supposed to be neither idea nor will (the true thing-in-itself, according to Schopenhauer). The world of empirical reality and the world of dreams are ' different as regards their matter ', yet are moulded in the same form and ' this form is the intellect, the function of the brain '.[4] Kant, says Schopenhauer, did not speak of the brain but of ' the faculty of knowledge ' : he himself, however, declares that time, space and causality are ' nothing more than functions of the brain '.[5] This may not seem to be an improvement upon Kant ; but, if irrational animals perceive objects, not only in time and space but also in causal connection (as Schopenhauer thought they did), it is difficult to see what else he could say.

Ideas of perception, therefore, are common to men and to irrational animals ; so the faculty by which these ideas are perceived must also be common to them both. What is this faculty ? It is the faculty of *understanding*. It might appear that Schopenhauer, by attributing understanding to the

[1] I, p. 7. [2] II, p. 170. [3] I, p. 5.
[4] II, p. 164. [5] *Ibid.*, p. 170.

animals, is denying their irrational character ; so it is very
necessary to bear in mind the fact that he does not mean
precisely what we would naturally be inclined to think he
meant. We say, ' I understand this problem,' referring to the
rational apprehension of e.g. an abstract mathematical problem, an apprehension which is beyond the power of a dog or
a cat : we have no reason to suppose that a dog can understand the theorem of Pythagoras or solve abstract mathematical problems. But Schopenhauer is not referring to
understanding in this sense ; by ' understanding ' (*Verstand*)
he means ' knowledge of causality, transition from effect to
cause, and from cause to effect, nothing more '[1] Of course,
the use of the word ' knowledge ' is unhappy, since animals
have no knowledge of causality as such (nor does Schopenhauer
really mean to imply that they have) ; but the underlying
meaning of the statement can be seen from an example. A
dog, when it has been beaten, does not associate the beating
with the dog-biscuits regularly provided for it, but e.g. with a
stick held by the man, and when on future occasions it perceives a man standing over it with a raised stick (especially if
it has again performed the action for which it received the
former beating) it shrinks away or cowers down. This may
very well be no more than the effect of association of images ;
but, leaving the explanation out of account, it is clear that
there is some transition, by whatever mechanism, from effect
to cause and from cause to effect, *in the concrete*. The simple
forms of this transition Schopenhauer choose to call ' understanding ' and found it in men and animals alike, though ' the
degree of its acuteness, and the extension of the sphere of its
knowledge, varies enormously with innumerable gradations
from the lowest form, which is only conscious of the causal
connection between the immediate object and objects affecting
it . . . to the higher grades of knowledge of the causal
connection among objects known indirectly, which extends to
the understanding of the most complicated systems of cause
and effect '.[2] That a process analogous to that in the animal
takes place in man is only to be expected, since he is animal as
well as rational and will have reactions on the purely sensitive
level similar to those in irrational animals ; but it is unfortunate that Schopenhauer should have called this process
' knowledge of causality ', for this phrase immediately suggests

[1] I, p. 26.   [2] *Ibid.*,

an intellectual knowledge of causality such as is possessed by man alone. Moreover, knowledge of causal connections between objects known indirectly, as possessed e.g. by scientists, is specifically different, and not merely different in degree, from an animal's concrete perception of a given causal relation, even if Schopenhauer would say that the form is essentially the same, while the abstract and reflective character of man's knowledge is peculiar to him.

' Understanding ' is, therefore, according to Schopenhauer, common to both men and animals ; but reasoning and the formation of abstract concepts is found only in man. Reason (*Vernunft*), the intellectual power which is distinctive of man, is the faculty of conceptual, abstract, reflective thought. Concepts are a distinct class of ideas, says Schopenhauer (i.e. distinct from ' ideas ' of perception) and exist only in man's mind : they cannot be perceived but can only be thought, yet they have a necessary relation to ideas of perception, since the abstract world of concepts is the repetition in reflection and abstraction of the originally presented world of perception. An abstract idea, a concept, may, it is true, stand in immediate relation to another abstract idea, as its ground of knowledge ; but, however long the chain of abstract grounds of knowledge may be, it must end in a concept which is grounded in perceptive knowledge, ' for the whole world of reflection rests on the world of perception as its ground of knowledge '. The abstract concepts ' man ' or ' horse ', for example, are immediately grounded in the world of perception (i.e. on empirically real men and horses), whereas the abstract concepts ' relation ' or ' virtue ' are not immediately grounded in the world of perception. We perceive men, and we form the abstract, general concept of man immediately ; but we do not perceive directly a relation as such : we form abstract conceptions of particular relations concretely perceived and then, by a second act of reflection, as it were, we form the abstract concept of relation in general from the abstract concepts of particular kinds of relation. The concept is thus the ' idea of an idea ', i.e. its whole nature consists in its relation to another idea '.[1] Schopenhauer's idealism naturally leads to a certain confusion, since, though it is quite true that concepts are founded on perception, some directly and others indirectly, the phrase ' idea of an idea ' is used, and must be

[1] I, p. 54.

used if his idealism is accepted, ambiguously. A concept
formed by further abstraction from other concepts is an ' idea
of an idea or ideas ' in one sense, while a concept formed
directly from perception is, on Schopenhauer's theory, also an
' idea of an idea ', but in another sense. But I will return later
to a criticism of Schopenhauer's idealism.

Reasoning or conceptual thinking, is, says Schopenhauer,
' feminine in nature ; it can only give after it has received '.[1]
It is only the four principles of identity, contradiction, excluded
middle and sufficient reason, to which Schopenhauer attributes
' metalogical truth ', that constitute absolutely pure rational
knowledge : the rest of logic presupposes the relations and
combinations of concepts, and concepts presuppose experience,
so that even the science of logic as a whole cannot justly be
termed absolutely pure rational knowledge or *a priori*. However, it is true that no particular content is presupposed for
these concepts, ' but merely the existence of a content generally ' (e.g. if we speak of ' species ' in logic, we do not presuppose a special and definite species, such as horse), so that,
in comparison with other sciences, logic may pass for a pure
rational science. In the case of all other sciences, on the
other hand, reason definitely receives its content from ideas of
perception (to use Schopenhauer's terminology), as is clear in
the case of natural science. As to mathematics, the relations
of space (geometry) or of time (arithmetic) are presented prior
to experience (notice the Kantian influence) ; but they are
presented in intuition or perception and are received by
reason. Rational knowledge (*Wissen*) in general, therefore,
means to have in the mind or in the memory, in such a way
that they can be produced at will, ' such judgments as have
their sufficient ground of knowledge in something outside
themselves, i.e. are true '.[2] ' Rational knowledge (*Wissen*) is
therefore abstract consciousness, the permanent possession in
concepts of the reason, of what has become known in another
way '.[3]

This rational knowledge is, as we have said, peculiar to
man and is not possessed by the animals, which are irrational.
In dealing with this point Schopenhauer does something to
dispel the unfortunate impression he gave when he attributed
understanding to the animals. (In the Supplement he explains
that by understanding he means what Kant called *pure sensi-*

bility). In the first book of the *World*[1] he observes that animals apprehend what is presented in perception and remember it and possess imagination, as is proved by the fact that they dream, while in the Supplement[2] he says that they lack a ' proper memory ' and that it is which constitutes the principal difference between their consciousness and that of man. Animals have no distinct consciousness of past and future *as such* ; they cannot recall the past at will in an orderly and connected fashion ; they lack general conceptions, which are necessary for a ' proper memory ', i.e. an intellectual memory. The memory of brutes is always dependent on on what is actually present : it is the present perception that excites the mood produced by an earlier sensation. Something analogous occurs in the case of human beings too : for example, the sight of someone may induce in us the impression that we have seen the person before, although we are quite unable to recall when or where we saw him. The perceptive or sensitive memory is at work, we are dependent on the present perception : the brute's memory is always of this kind, they are entirely dependent on the present and cannot recall the past as past. ' The consciousness of the brutes is accordingly a mere succession of presents, none of which, however, exists as future before they appear, nor as past after they have vanished ; which is the specific difference of human consciousness '.[3] Nor is any brute capable of possessing a purpose, properly so-called : to conceive a distinct purpose, to hold it before the mind, to follow it out deliberately, is a prerogative of man : we should not confuse purpose, distinctly conceived and deliberately followed, with the instinct of a migrating bird or a bee. Schopenhauer, therefore, did not mean to minimise the difference between man and animals or to hold that the latter are rational. Nevertheless, in accordance with his theory of understanding, he remarks that ' the brutes have only a *single* intellect, we a *double* intellect, both perceptive and thinking ', thus using the word ' intellect ', just as he uses the word ' idea ', ambiguously.[4] Moreover, he tones down what he has said on the subject of the difference between men and brutes by declaring that, though in producing the human intelligence nature took the greatest step she has ever taken, there is discernible in some of the higher brutes a faint trace

[1] pp. 65–66. [2] II, pp. 228 ff.
[3] *Ibid.*, p. 230. [4] *Ibid.*, p. 232.

of reasoning, of purpose, deliberation, foresight. He quotes a report from an English paper of 1830, concerning the killing of a keeper by an elephant, which he had injured two years previously by pricking it with a needle. The animal had never forgotten the injury and, when a favourable opportunity presented itself, killed its keeper.[1] Elsewhere Schopenhauer mentions the sagacity of an elephant who crossed many bridges in Europe, but once refused to go on a certain bridge, fearing it would not stand his weight, although he saw the rest of the party, men and horses, doing so, though he admits that orang-outangs, who warm themselves at a fire they have found, do not throw wood upon the fire to keep it alight, thus shewing themselves to lack the power of deliberation for which abstract concepts are necessary.[2] We must, however, beware of interpreting the behaviour of animals anthropomorphically and thinking that, because a certain type of behaviour in man is the product of intelligence, an analogous type of behaviour in a brute is necessarily the product of even an inchoate intelligence, whatever that may be. If conceptual reasoning is the prerogative of man and if conceptual reasoning is necessary for deliberation properly speaking, then brutes are incapable of such deliberation and any behaviour on their part that seems to presuppose it must be explained on the sensitive, and not on the intellectual level. In the incident of the elephant that killed its keeper, one naturally tends to think anthropomorphically and to suppose that the elephant went about for two years deliberating how best to accomplish its conscious intention of revenging itself ; but we ought at least to inquire first of all what were the immediate circumstances that led up to the attack on the keeper, for it might have been that some circumstance excited in the elephant the mood attendant on the former injury. In any case the whole affair could be explained on the perceptive level (and Schopenhauer probably meant little more than this, though he spoke of ' perceptive *thinking* '), so that, on the principle *entia non sunt multiplicanda præter necessitatem,* we are not justified in ascribing intelligence to brutes. (As a matter of fact the words ' intelligent ' and ' intelligence ' are frequently used ambiguously. We may say, ' What an intelligent dog ! ' without at the same time meaning to ascribe to the animal the intellectual activity enjoyed by a human being.)

[1] II, pp. 232-3.　　　　　　　　[2] I, p. 29.

As we might expect, Schopenhauer takes the occasion of his denial of the knowledge of past and future as such to animals and its restriction to man to point out the bearing of this on the question of suffering. The mere animal, by the fact that it lives in the present alone and neither cherishes nor is haunted by memories of the past and hopes and fears for the future, is relieved of a great deal of that suffering which falls to the lot of man. An animal may shrink away instinctively from an action that would be fatal to it, that would actually result in its death ; but it has no abstract idea of death, it cannot reason from the sight of dead animals to the conclusion that it must itself inevitably die. An animal cannot have conceptual knowledge of the fact that it must die ; but man has this knowledge, he can reason concerning the vanity of human life, the apparent waste of so much that was good and noble, the frustration of so much that was promising, the flourishing of the wicked like the green bay tree. Though an animal may, through association of images, have an expectation of e.g. punishment, it does not conjure up to itself all manner of possible pains and disasters and render itself miserable thereby ; but a man can anticipate consciously what will happen to him, what might happen to him, can render the passing hours a torture by brooding on the past, on what has been, on what might have been, while his reflective consciousness makes his present ills all the more painful and intense. Moreover, as error lies in the judgment, the brute cannot, properly speaking, err ; it cannot lie, it cannot proclaim false systems (like Hegel, that ' repulsive, mindless charlatan ', that ' unparalleled scribbler of nonsense ') ; it cannot err from the path of nature. Man, on the other hand, can practise every sort of insincerity and trickery and fraud, can proclaim and accept error, can indulge in monstrous actions, such as the sacrifice of children to Moloch, can use his reason to think out exquisite tortures to inflict on his fellow-men. The possession of reason, then, that sets man above the brutes, may be used by him to sink himself below them, though, on the other hand, he may use it to promote truth and benevolence, to create speech and literature and science.

How is science principally formed and advanced, according to Schopenhauer ? By the faculty of judgment, which consists in translating rightly into the abstract sphere that which is known in perception, so that judgment is ' the mediator between understanding and reason '.[1] Primary judgments are those which are founded directly on perception and such judgments ' are to science what the sun is to the world '.[2] Advance in science requires an outstanding power of judgment, a power to conceptualize, to lay down in a permanent storehouse, as it were, what is known directly to perception, and to do this properly (so that what is common to many empirically real objects may be known as one through the concept, while at the same time differences are not confused but are carefully distinguished, and all in accordance with the special end or aim of the scientist), requires more than a mere mediocre power of judgment, since it is easy to miss the partial difference of concepts which in one aspect are the same or the identity under one aspect of concepts which under another aspect are relatively different. If we take the example of astronomy, it is clear that the science has a foundation in perception, since the existence of planets, for instance, is known empirically, as is also their apparent motion. The science of astronomy, however, does not advance purely empirically : the astronomer makes use of mathematics, which rest upon *a priori* intuition, and reasons to hypotheses, which are confirmed or otherwise, by induction, i.e. empirically. The construction of the hypotheses was the work of judgment comprehending the empirically known facts and rightly expressing them. But the reasoning of the astronomer, the long process of calculation that he makes, could be supplanted by direct empirical observation, were it physically possible to make such observation. For example, if I want to know the width of my table, I measure it directly, though it *could* be calculated in other ways, as by observing the time taken by an object travelling with uniform velocity from one side of the table to the other. The astronomer, however, cannot measure the distance from the earth to the sun with a measuring-rod, and must accordingly have recourse to reasoning, calculation, the process of calculation or reasoning thus taking the place of direct observation, which is impossible. Again, if the astronomer who discovered the existence of Neptune by calculation had been able to see it directly, the process of calculation would not have been necessary. The employment of calculation, of reasoning, of syllogizing, which is peculiar to man, is thus ' only a makeshift '.[3] Natural science in

[1] I, p. 84. [2] *Ibid.* [3] *Ibid.*, p. 88.

general, therefore, is empirical or *a posteriori* (as are also ethics
and history, founded on ' the doctrine of motives '), even if it
uses mathematics, which Schopenhauer classes as ' *pure a priori
science* ' together with logic.   (The latter subject to the quali-
fications already given.[1])   His efforts to belittle the syllogism
or to restrict its scope are due to his insistence on perception
and on intuition.

Schopenhauer's view of the function of concepts anticipates
in this respect the theory of Bergson, that he emphasizes the
practical function of human reason.   Conceptual reasoning,
dialectical processes *as such*, provide us with no new positive
knowledge : to help us to attain knowledge they must draw
their content from perception or from self-consciousness.   Why
then do we form concepts ?   For practical ends.   We abstract,
we leave out the unessential, in order that we may more easily
handle the original material of knowledge.   ' The great value
of conceptions lies in the fact that by means of them the
original material of knowledge is more easily handled, surveyed, and arranged.'[2]   In the concept the differences of
particulars are omitted (e.g. in the concept ' man ' the differences that exist in the concrete between individual men are
omitted), so that the concept represents things to the mind in
a very imperfect manner ; but, although ' the most perfect
and satisfactory knowledge is that of perception '[3], it is limited
to the particular, and for practical purposes we require something more comprehensive and something *communicable*.   ' The
greatest value of rational or abstract knowledge is that it can
be communicated and permanently retained '.[4]   Perceptive
knowledge through the ' understanding ' is sufficient for
practice, if it is a question of a man putting his knowledge
into practice himself, but it is not sufficient for the communication of that knowledge to others.   A first class batsman
(Schopenhauer takes the example of a practised billiard-
player) may have great skill but little theoretical knowledge ;
he possesses, Schopenhauer would say, knowledge of various
laws concerning the impact of bodies, velocity, direction and
so on, but he possesses this knowledge ' merely in the understanding, merely for direct perception '[5] : he has little theoretical knowledge and cannot explain to others ' how it is done '.

---

[1] For Schopenhauer's classification of *a priori* and *a posteriori* sciences
according to their dependence on the several forms of the principle of sufficient
reason, see II, p. 317.

[2] II, p. 258.   [3] *Ibid.*, p. 335.   [4] I, p. 72.   [5] *Ibid.*

He can say ' watch me ', he can correct somebody else's
stance, for example, by eye ; but he has not worked up his
implicit knowledge into explicit theoretical knowledge, he has
not conceptualized and rationalized his skill, he cannot impart
theoretical knowledge to others.   Thus it may be that he is a
very fine player, but a very poor coach.   Or take the example
of the building of a palace, on which many men are to be
employed.   It is essential that the architect should have
thought out the plan, it is essential that he who is to organize
and direct the whole operation should possess a theoretical
knowledge of the work to be performed and of the different
parts that individual workmen are called upon to play.   Co-
operative activity may be pursued very well by ants or bees
without the assistance of reason ; but in the case of men the
assistance of reason is necessary.   A modern army cannot be
supplied in the field through a series of ' hunches ' on the part
of the commander.   Again, for the adequate formation and
development of speech or language, which is the means of
communication among human beings, concepts are necessary.
Social intercourse would be impossible otherwise.

Schopenhauer also insists on the practical function of reasoning in the sphere of ethical conduct.   Through conceptual
knowledge a man is liberated from the domination of immediate and present stimulus and can guide his conduct.   In so
far as a man does guide his conduct by conceptions his conduct
is rational, proper to man, a type of conduct of which the
brutes are not capable.   We do not think that a man acts in
a way fitting his nature if he surrenders to every passing
incitement of lust or pleasure or anger, but rather if he guides
his conduct according to principle.   But how can he possess
principles without concepts ?   If he had no concepts, he could
not form judgments, could not form principles of conduct.
Now, leaving out of account Schopenhauer's doctrine of
motives and his own peculiar ethic, we do not see how anyone
could deny the fundamental truth of his observation.   Even
an intuitionist in ethics, who held that we recognize immediately our duties and that no one could prove to a man by
reason that any particular action was his duty, could hardly
deny that moral generalizations, maxims and principles have
a real practical utility and function.   I may recognize that
this particular action is a duty here and now, that I ought to
do it ; but I may feel strongly disinclined to do it, I may even

feel strongly attracted towards doing something which I know to be wrong. I may then fortify myself by considering some general principle such as ' I ought to do actions of the type *x* and it would be quite unworthy of me to surrender to laziness or to passion or to selfishness ' (as the case may be) or even only such as ' I ought to do my duty '. Even if a principle does not show me what my duty is in the concrete, even if I recognize this immediately and intuitively, I may help myself to *do* my duty, may *have* to help myself to do my duty, by attending to some principle, by re-enforcing my will by some general consideration. But I could not formulate such a principle without abstract concepts, could not understand it without conceptual knowledge.

Schopenhauer, however, does not content himself with pointing out practical applications of concepts and conceptual knowledge : he asserts that cognition is essentially the servant of the ' will '. In animals perception serves a practical purpose, serves for the satisfaction of desire and bodily needs. (Did not Aristotle observe that an animal which possesses the power of locomotion and has to go in search of its food needs the senses, in order to enable it to find its food and recognize it ?) Nature has provided the brutes with the organs necessary for their sustenance, and the weapons necessary for attack or defence, and her provisions suffice for them ; but with progressive development of the animal organism and its cerebral system (Schopenhauer speaks of intellect as a function of this system) there likewise occurs a progressive multiplication of needs and wants, so that a higher type and wider range of knowledge is required in order to obtain their satisfaction. In man, then, more highly developed physiologically than any other animal, reason appears : he can deliberate, invent new ways and means of supplying his wants, fashion tools, and so on.

Nature, therefore (or the Will that objectifies itself therein), produces the human reason, that man's wants and needs may be satisfied ; his reason is thus the handmaid of his body, cognition is the servant of Will (of which the body is a phenomenon, an objectification). It is true that in man alone ' does a *pure separation of knowing and willing* take place '[1], so that he is enabled to use his reasoning power for purposes not immediately connected with his bodily wants and is thus differen-

[1] III, p. 15.

tiated from the brutes ; but nature takes the step of perfecting
the brain, and so of increasing the powers of knowledge, only
in view of the increased needs of the organism and the species.
What nature ' aims at and attains in man is indeed essentially
the same, and not more than what is also its goal in the
brutes—nourishment and propagation '.[1]

This being so, it follows that the reason is not designed for
comprehending the inner nature of things, but rather to know
them in their phenomenal character, apprehending them only
in their relation to each other and not according to their
inner essence. ' For our intellect, originally only intended to
present to an individual will its paltry aims, comprehends
accordingly mere *relations* of things, and does not penetrate
to their inner being, to their real nature.'[2] The world of
phenomena, which are object for the subject, are as motives
to the will or to that objectification of it which is the body, so
that the intellect, which—genetically considered—exists simply
for practical ends, is ' merely the *medium of motives*, and therefore fulfils its end by an accurate presentation of these ' [3]: it
does not penetrate to the thing-in-itself. ' It results from this
whole objective consideration of the intellect and its origin,
that it is designed for the comprehension of those ends upon
the attainment of which depends the individual life and its
propagation, but by no means for deciphering the inner
nature of things and of the world, which exists independently
of the knower '.[4] We are reminded of Bergson's dictum, that
' the intellect is characterized by a natural inability to comprehend life '.[5] However, if the human reason, because of its
essentially practical orientation and its relation to will, is
unable to penetrate to the inner side of the world, to the thing-
in-itself, if it is limited to the phenomenal, it follows that
the truths it establishes are not unconditional truths. For
example, if we are forced to recognize matter as the permanent
being, the *mater rerum*, the naturalistic or materialistic conclusion, though based on empirical reality, is limited to that
reality, to the phenomenal world, in its application : it cannot be an unconditional truth, applying to ultimate reality,
to the thing-in-itself. Schopenhauer thought this doctrine,
which disposes of the unconditional truth of naturalism, ' very

[1] III, p. 15.   [2] *Ibid.*, p. 25.   [3] *Ibid.*, p. 24.   [4] *Ibid.*, p. 21.
[5] *Creative Evolution*, p. 174.   Trans. Arthur Mitchell (London, 1911).

consoling '[1] ; but it may well be questioned if his own theory of ultimate reality is any more consoling than the sheerest materialism. If it is consolation that we seek, we shall hardly go to the metaphysical pessimist in order to find it.

I have mentioned Schopenhauer's theory that in man the intellect is more loosened from the will than in animals below man. The will is the basis of intelligence, but intelligence in man develops to such an extent that a surplus of intelligence, as it were, comes into being, and it is this surplus, this measure of intelligence greater than that which is required for the service of the will, which renders possible the æsthetic consciousness, treated by the philosopher in the third book of the *World*. When the intellect acquires great energy and becomes truly separate from the will, when the will retreats into the background, then is the intellect enabled to comprehend the external world in an objective manner, i.e. apart from the interests of the will. The highest grade of objectivity of the intellect is found in the *genius* (of whom more in a later chapter), who apprehends in the individual thing, not merely the individual thing itself but also the nature of its species, its archetypal pattern, the Platonic Idea. The true artist, the genius, apprehends the Platonic Idea in the individual thing and expresses it in a concrete work of art, and this he is enabled to do because in him the intellect has become, at least temporarily (i.e. during æsthetic contemplation), separate from the will, free from the service of desire, a pure and disinterested spectator.

But contemplation of the Platonic Idea is not comprehension of the thing-in-itself, and the following question will naturally occur to the reader. If the intellect is unable to penetrate to ultimate reality, if it is confined to the phenomenal, to the physical, with what justification can Schopenhauer pretend to present us with a true and valid metaphysic, with a doctrine of ultimate reality, of the thing-in-itself? We might suppose that the philosopher would have recourse to ' intuition ', as a sure refuge against attack ; but, for reasons which will become apparent shortly, it is not possible for him to say *tout court* that his philosophy is based on intuition and to leave it at that. Schopenhauer does indeed sing the praises of intuition at the expense of abstract knowledge, especially in regard to practical life, as when he remarks that a man

[1] III, p. 26.

might know by heart all the three hundred maxims of Gracian and yet make the most stupid mistakes in life if he lacks the intuitive knowledge of men or observes that in ' real life ' the scholar, whose pre-eminence lies in the sphere of abstract knowledge, is inferior to the man of the world, whose pre-eminence lies in the sphere of intuitive knowledge.[1] ' All truth and all wisdom ', he says, ' really lie ultimately in perception '.[2] But, as he goes on immediately to state that the intuitive knowledge of perception ' can neither be retained or communicated ', it is quite obvious that this intuitive knowledge cannot, by itself at least, constitute philosophical knowledge, for, if the latter can neither be retained nor communicated, there would be no point in writing a lengthy philosophical tome or attempting to reveal the enigma of the world in a course of lectures at the university of Berlin. The only kind of knowledge that is properly speaking and without qualification communicable is the ' worst knowledge, abstract, secondary knowledge, the conception, the mere shadow of true knowledge '.[3] This being so, philosophy, to be communicable, must on the one hand be expressed in abstract and conceptual form, while, on the other hand, if it is to be worth anything, it must be based on intuition. ' To enrich the conception from perception is the unceasing endeavour of poetry and philosophy '.[4] Philosophy, therefore, must be intuitive knowledge raised from the condition of immediate knowledge to that of mediate or abstract knowledge. We are reminded of the doctrine of Bergson on philosophical method, which, according to him, consists in the proportionate interplay and combination of sensible experience and reasoning founded thereon, of intuition (in the *Bergsonian* sense, of course) and conceptualization thereof.

But the matter is not so simple as that for Schopenhauer. Metaphysical knowledge is supposed to attain to the ultimate, to the thing-in-itself (which is not a particular and individual object), whereas he has roundly declared that intuitive knowledge ' always apprehends only the particular ' and ' stands in immediate relation to the present case '.[5] Intuition is thus asserted to be limited to the particular and so the phenomenal world : how, then, can it be a means for attaining the noumenon, which is impervious to perceptive intuition ?

[1] II, pp. 250–1.   [2] *Ibid*., p. 248.   [3] *Ibid*.
[4] *Ibid*.   [5] *Ibid*., p. 250.

Schopenhauer has not left room for an intellectual intuition which is *above* intelligence and which is capable of attaining ultimate reality directly : the mental activity of the genius may attain the Platonic Idea, but the Platonic Idea is not the thing-in-itself, which is Will. Intuition or perception is directed to the individual and particular on the one hand, while on the other hand it is ' not only the *source* of all knowledge, but is itself knowledge κατ' εξοχην is the only unconditionally true, genuine knowledge completely worthy of the name ".[1] Somehow or other, then, perceptive knowledge of the individual must be made the basis of philosophy, and Schopenhauer finds this fundamental intuition in the perception or immediate consciousness of the identity of body and will or of my body as the objectivity of my will. ' My body considered apart from the fact that it is my idea is still my will '.[2] This identity of will and body, says Schopenhauer, can be proved only in this sense that it is ' raised from the immediate consciousness, from knowledge in the concrete to abstract knowledge of the reason '[3] : it can never properly speaking be demonstrated or derived from a more immediate knowledge, just because it is itself the most direct knowledge. He then argues by analogy to a general philosophical position, subserving the less known (e.g. force in nature) under what he considered the better known, i.e. the will. Philosophy is thus founded on an immediate consciousness of a special kind, and Schopenhauer is quite prepared to admit that such knowledge is of a special kind, being ' the relation of a judgment to the connection which an idea of perception, the body, has to that which is not an idea at all, but something *toto genere* different, will. I should like, therefore, to distinguish this from all other truth, and call it κατ' εξοχην *philosophical truth* '.[4]

Yet, if philosophy rests on an immediate consciousness, an intuition, of a special kind, how can Schopenhauer avoid his own condemnation of systems which ' start from an intellectual intuition, i.e. a kind of ecstasy or clairvoyance ', which is subjective and, even if it actually existed ', would not be communicable ' ?[5] The philosopher, when he penned his condemnation of such systems, was, of course, writing polemically and he considered such claimed intuitions to be fanciful; but his real point of attack is that such claimed intuitions, even

---

[1] II, p. 252.   [2] I, p. 133.   [3] *Ibid.*
[4] *Ibid.*   [5] II, p. 393.

if existent, would be *abnormal*, and as such incommunicable, and so useless for philosophy. ' Only the normal knowledge of the brain is communicable ; if it is abstract, through conceptions and words ; if purely perceptible or concrete, through works of art '.[1] It is true that those philosophers who attempt to found systems on such intuitions would claim that these intuitions, even if not normal, are empirical data and that their system is a conceptualization of the intuition ; but Schopenhauer claimed for his fundamental immediate consciousness that it is *normal*, that everyone, if he reflected, would recognize the fact. (He certainly thought too that the main truth of his system was supported by independent truths, born of contemplation of empirical reality.) Kant, according to Schopenhauer, proved irrefutably that experience contains two elements, an *a priori* element and an *a posteriori* element, and it is possible to say what belongs to the form of the phenomenon, what is conditioned by the intellect, and what remains over. One may not be able to discern the thing-in-itself through the veils of perception directly ; yet everyone carries the thing-in-itself within himself and everyone can penetrate thereto through self-consciousness, attaining the noumenon within himself. ' Thus the bridge by which metaphysics passes beyond experience is nothing else than that analysis of experience into phenomenon and thing-in-itself in which I have placed Kant's greatest merit. For it contains the proof of a kernel of the phenomenon different from the phenomenon itself '.[2]

I shall deal later with the metaphysic of the Will ; but it is relevant to the present subject to mention a pertinent objection which was raised by Herbart. In the chapter of the Supplement entitled *On the Possibility of Knowing the Thing-in-itself*[3] Schopenhauer declares that ' all knowing is essentially a perceiving of ideas ', from which it follows that we cannot attain the inner nature of things in this way. Our knowledge consists in framing ideas by means of subjective forms and so ' affords us always mere *phenomena*, not the true being of things '. However, we are not merely the knowing subject, for we also belong ourselves to that inner nature which we desire to know, we are ourselves the thing-in-itself. Thus, though we cannot penetrate to the latter from without (' everything objective is idea, therefore appearance, mere

[1] II, p. 393.   [2] *Ibid.*, p. 389.   [3] *Ibid.*, pp. 399 ff.

phenomenon of the brain ') we can penetrate to it from within : the thing-in-itself is itself conscious of itself. This consciousness is not perception (which is subject to the form of space) nor is it *a priori* and merely formal : it is immediate consciousness within ourselves and is ' the single narrow door to the truth '.[1] But, even if inner knowledge is free from the form of space and the form of causality, which are the forms of outer knowledge, is it not, asked Herbart, still subject to the form of *time* ; do we not know our will only in its successive acts ? Schopenhauer concedes the difficulty, but maintains nevertheless that in the affections and acts of our own will ' the thing in itself most directly enters the phenomenon '[2] and that the act of the will is ' only the closest and most distinct *manifestation* of the thing in itself '. Yet, even if this is accepted, will not the act of the will, volition, be subject to the principle of sufficient reason, just as are all phenomena, and how then are we ever going to attain to the thing-in-itself as it is in itself ? Schopenhauer allows the force of the difficulty to this extent that he concedes that the question, what the will ultimately and absolutely is in itself, can never be answered, since ' becoming known is itself the contradictory of being in itself, and everything that is known is as such only phenomenal '.[3] The will in itself, apart from all phenomenal appearance, may have ways of existing which to us are entirely unknown and incomprehensible. It is really very difficult to see how, after laying down his theory of knowledge and his doctrine of the phenomenon, Schopenhauer can give any satisfactory formal justification for a metaphysic. Either all knowledge is knowledge of the phenomenal, in which case there can be no knowledge, at the very least no communicable knowledge, of the noumenal, or there can be knowledge of the noumenal, in which case knowledge is not essentially knowledge of the phenomenal.

According to Schopenhauer's theory my body is the objectification of will and a phenomenon ; indeed the whole ' I ' is phenomenal, precisely as an individual. On the other hand, according to my inner nature, I am identical with the noumenon, with Will. But by the very fact that I turn my attention to myself I turn myself into an object and in so far as I turn my attention to Will, with which I am said to be identical according to my inner nature, I turn Will into an

<hr />

[1] II, p. 406.   [2] *Ibid.*, p. 407.   [3] *Ibid.*, p. 408.

object. But if it becomes object, does it not become object for a subject and so phenomenal ' idea '? And, if this is so, then am I not still shut up in the phenomenal world, in the world of presentations ? It may be said that Will knows itself in immediate self-consciousness. To this three objections at least may be made. (i) Whatever may have been the case with Schopenhauer most of us are probably unprepared to lay claim to a complete and perfectly luminous self-consciousness, in which there is no distinction of subject and object. And there is distinction of subject and object precisely because we know ourselves in our acts, which are ' phenomenal '. An act of self-intuition, in which there is no distinction of self as knowing and self as known, is beyond our power, and if this distinction remains, then we are, on the Schopenhauerian theory, still within the phenomenal world. (ii) How can the noumenon know itself through the phenomenon ? If it know itself through the phenomenon in actuality, then the knowledge itself will be phenomenal. In any case how can the noumenon, which is *Will*, know at all, especially as the metaphysical Will of Schopenhauer is blind ? To speak of it as providing itself with a body or an intellect is to use mere metaphor—and quite unjustifiable metaphor, if the Will is blind. If the Will is blind, it cannot know itself either directly or through the phenomenon, while, if it is the phenomenon, it must recognize itself as phenomenon, setting itself in distinction, under its phenomenal aspect, from the noumenon and so turning the latter into object, into idea, into phenomenon. (iii) Schopenhauer may say that philosophical truth lies in a judgment as to the connection of the body, an idea of perception, to the will, which is not an idea at all ; but what is the justification, on Schopenhauer's premises, for affirming that the will is not an idea ? Will is an abstract term and a concept : it must be either mere phantasy or based on an idea of perception, in neither of which cases can it be an adequate expression of the noumenon. In short, the proper conclusion from Schopenhauer's epistemology, as from that of Kant, is agnosticism : a metaphysic is quite out of place. It is true that sometimes Schopenhauer admits a certain agnosticism in regard to the Will ; but the question is, ' how, on his premises, can there be *any* knowledge of the Will at all, whether real or partial ? ' The assertion that consciousness of the identification of body with Will is in a privileged position needs a strict proof, for it is by no means self-evident to all ; yet Schopenhauer admits that it cannot be proved. But *quod gratis asseritur, gratis negatur*, as the Scholastic adage has it.

Again, Schopenhauer's contention that cognition is the servant of will or desire is open to criticism. That the human intellect fulfils a practical function is obvious, and it is clear enough that, when the conditions of life are primitive, the practical function of the intellect will be the function most in evidence : in a nomadic tribe, living by hunting and fishing, or in a primitive pastoral people we would scarcely expect to find academic metaphysicians, though we should no doubt find ' sages ', men distinguished for their ripe, if limited, experience. Apart from all other (some of them very important) considerations, the necessary preoccupation with the means of subsistence would preclude prolonged reflection of the type required for philosophic thought : there would be no leisured class. But it is one thing to say that the intellect exercises a practical function (which in certain circumstances may be its most obviously predominant function) and quite another to say that nature provided the human body with an intellect, in order to satisfy more completely the needs and wants of the body, so that service of desire is *the* essential function of intellect. Let us suppose for a moment that man developed through specific evolution (without entering upon the question, whether or not this is a true supposition). If man's body developed from the body of lower animals of one kind or another, then his intellect either was given him directly by an external Cause or ' appeared ' as an epiphenomenon, consequent on cerebral organization and refinement, or ' evolved ' out of a preceding state in some mysterious manner. Now, the first mode would certainly necessitate the existence of an external intellectual Cause, and such a Cause is ruled out by the philosophy of Schopenhauer, while the third mode, to be intelligible at all, presupposes a panpsychism, which is quite alien to Schopenhauer's characterization of the Will. But if intellect simply developed as an epiphenomenon of the cerebral organism (and does not Schopenhauer speak of it as a function of the brain ?) then, apart from the difficulty of seeing how a new factor could evolve without the agency of an external Cause, intellect will have those functions which we find it to exercise in actuality, and no particular function can legitimately be chosen out and termed its *essential* function. If we find it used for theoretic contemplation as well as for practical purposes, we might just as well say that its essential function lies in theoretic contemplation as in practical service. If historical investigation showed that the use of the intellect for purely theoretical purposes occurred later in time than its use for purely practical purposes and that a great deal of the theoretic activity, when it did come, was devoted to practical ends, that would not necessarily prove that the intellect was essentially the servant of desire or the will, save in the sense that its most rudimentary function was to satisfy physical needs. Moreover, we could not legitimately speak of the body providing itself with an intellect or nature or will providing the human body with an intellect for practical purposes, unless the will were capable of rational purpose, which could be known by us. But how could Schopenhauer's Will, which, though the will to live, is blind, have any purpose at all? And to read a purpose into its activity, or to speak as though it had a purpose, would be the sheerest anthropomorphism. Why, in any case, did the Will provide the human body, which has to be sustained by intellect? To objectify itself? Now, either the Will consciously willed to objectify itself in human intellect or it did not. If it did, then it is a *rational* Will, which is inadmissible according to Schopenhauer's system : if it did not, then it just happened that the Will objectified itself in this and we are not entitled to say that the intellect has any essential purpose at all : it just is, and there is an end of the matter.

Schopenhauer's thory of knowledge obviously depends to a great extent on the Kantian Critique. The world is object for a subject : as known, it is phenomenon, governed by the *a priori* conditions of knowledge, the Categories being reduced by Schopenhauer to causality. In regard to the last point it is difficult to see how the philosopher did not ultimately lay himself open to the same objection which critics have so often brought against Kant. The latter made causality a subjective category of the mind, while at the same time he affirmed the existence of the *Ding-an-sich*—and continued to affirm it, in spite of Fichte's appeals to him to renounce it. Yet what justification could Kant have for affirming the existence of the thing-in-itself other than that its existence is required as objective cause or ground of the material element in the phenomenon ? This, however, is hardly consistent with the subjective character of the principle of causality. Now, although Schopenhauer rejected the Kantian thing-in-itself in the precise form in which Kant asserted it, he certainly maintained the existence of the thing-in-itself and identified it with Will, which objectifies itself in the phenomena. But if such self-objectification is not an instance of objective causality and not subject to the principle of sufficient reason, what is it ? The world may be appearance or illusion, but it is an appearance with a ground or cause : the world may be a manifestation or phenomenon of the noumenon, but, if so, it is an effect of the noumenon.

Again, Schopenhauer's doctrine on the pure forms of sensibility or ' understanding ' is also open to the same objections that can be brought against the position of Kant. It seems to be true that space and time are *a priori* conditions of sensible cognition in this sense, that a finite subject or form will, as finite, accomplish its cognitive operations in time or succession, while a finite subject that is embodied, a finite form which is intrinsically the form of a material compositum, will accomplish the cognitive acts of the compositum in dependence on the concrete mode of extension. If the soul has no innate ideas but depends for the formation of ideas on sense-perception, space or extension will be a condition of experience, and the synthesis of the discrete data of sense will be accomplished according to time. For example, when we listen to a piece of music being played on the piano, parts of the organ of hearing are affected by the extended medium of sound, both simultaneously and successively. But in order that the tune should be grasped as an intelligible whole, the subject must unify the discrete data of sense, and this it does by taking them up, as it were, in a definite temporal sequence, accomplishing the synthesis of space according to time. But, even if space and time are conditions of the experience of a finite and embodied subject, it certainly does not follow that space and time are merely subjective : indeed, the very *opposite* is demanded, for spatial and temporal conditions on the part of the subject demand spatial and temporal conditions on the part of the object. An inextended and timeless object could by no means be received and placed under the *a priori* forms of space and time. Moreover, Kant himself seems to have felt the difficulty, for in the *Metaphysical Foundations of Natural*

Science, he remarks that ' to every given spatial determination there must be a ground which is in itself unknown ' ; and in his observations on the first Antimony he declares that ' things, as appearances, determine space, that is, of all its possible predicates of magnitude and relation they determine this or that particular one to belong to the real '. What is this ground ? It can only be spatial conditions on the part of the object.

Now, the world, according to Schopenhauer, is phenomenon, is ' my idea ', consists of my ideas of perception. On the other hand my intellect is a function of my brain, and my brain is a part of my body, the whole of which is objectified will. But objectified or manifested will is phenomenon : therefore I also am phenomenon. The world is accordingly both phenomenon of the will and also object for me, who am a phenomenon, and I am phenomenon of the will and also subject for the world. The total complex of subject-object is, then, phenomenal, the Will manifesting itself or objectifying itself in both subject and object, the plurality of subject and object being the ' outside ' of the world, the noumenal unity of Will being the ' inside ' of the world. If this be so, *all* my ideas, *all* my thoughts, are phenomenal : they are objects for ' me ', i.e. the pure knower, just as much as the objects of the external world are objects for me. In this case not merely is the subject-object distinction phenomenal, but my assertion, my knowledge, my thought of the subject-object distinction is also phenomenal, it is my idea. More than that, the distinction I make between phenomenon and noumenon, between the subject-object distinction on the one hand and the metaphysical unity of Will, the ' inside ' of the world, on the other hand is also phenomenal. (In fact, the whole philosophy of Schopenhauer is phenomenal !) But if phenomenal means illusionary, as it clearly does in Schopenhauer's doctrine concerning the external world as contained in the last book of the *World*, then any distinctions I draw, any thoughts I think, any philosophy I formulate, are also illusionary. In brief, *La vida es sueño*. In this way, the philosophy of Schopenhauer, in the opinion of the present writer, negates itself.

The foregoing criticisms may seem to be over-academic in tone, perhaps even carping : so it may be as well to close this chapter with a few words of appreciation. Apart from

Schopenhauer's epistomological theories and the relation of the external world as idea of perception to the subject, one might say that a central point of the theory of the phenomenal character of the world is that the world, which is the object of our knowledge, is not ultimate reality and that it is not truly known unless it is known in its relation to that reality. That the world is phenomenal in this sense, that it is the manifestation of the ultimate reality, is perfectly true. While certainly not prepared to agree with Schopenhauer that the world *is* the ultimate reality in its phenomenal objectification, that it is the ' outside ', as it were, of ultimate reality, and while equally disagreeing with the philosopher's characterization of the ultimate reality, we are at once with him in affirming that the world of nature, though real, is a manifestation, i.e. an external manifestation, of ultimate reality and that it is known very imperfectly if it is not known in its relation to ultimate reality, since it has an essential relation thereto, a relation which is identical with its being. If we mean by ' real ' existing extramentally and apart from the finite subject, then the world is real ; but if we wished to restrict the term ' real ' to that which is self-dependent or utterly independent, then the external world could not, in that sense, be termed real. On the contrary, born of nothing, it hovers over the abyss of sheer unreality, nothingness, kept from falling into that abyss by the continued action of the ultimate reality that lies behind it and is not itself dependent on the world. ' Behind ' and ' within ' the world that appears to us in sense-perception and which we apprehend in our ideas, there remains Subsistent Being, Eternal, Immutable, Infinite, the ultimate reality that appears or is manifested to the finite intellect in that constantly changing, fleeting object, that we call the world. From this point of view the philosophy of Schopenhauer is far preferable to any system that would make of the material, spatio-temporal cosmos the true and only *Ding-an-sich*, the one ultimate reality.

That the appearance of the world, i.e. the manner in which it appears to us, depends to some extent on the subject as well as on external conditions, can scarcely be denied even by the most fervent realist. Centuries ago in ancient Greece it was pointed out that the same wind may appear warm to one man, cold to another, according to their bodily condition, just as water flowing from the cold tap may feel

warmish to a man who has just come from the cold and rain
outdoors, but quite the reverse to one who comes from a warm
room or a cosy bed. *Quidquid recipitur, secundum modum reci-
pientis recipitur.* The grass in the meadow may not seem very
tall to the man walking in it ; but to the insect crawling along
one of the blades it presumably appears as a great forest would
appear to a man. Again, anyone who held the fundamenta-
list view of colour would have to admit that the world does
not appear exactly as it, in his opinion, is in itself, for it is
coloured objects that we see and not atoms or electrons. But
we explain all these things on the assumption of the extramental
reality of the world. For instance, if colours are formally
subjective (a view to which the present writer does not
necessarily commit himself), they are nevertheless fundamentally objective, and it is on this basis that the funda-
mentalist would explain colour-perception. Thus we may
admit that the world is phenomenal in a certain sense, without at the same time being compelled to admit that the world
is simply ' my idea ' or that we cannot attain real knowledge
of the world by means of rational activity (unless, of course,
we were to adopt the theory of the idea as the *medium quod
cognitionis*, in which case we should be logically pushed into
an agnostic position concerning the external world, or would
be compelled to have recourse to some such device as that of
Descartes, in order to prove that our ideas correspond to
objective reality. For, if it is ideas that we know directly and
not things, how are we ever to get outside the circle of our
ideas, to compare them with extramental objects ?).

A final remark. To the unreflective man, for whom ' seeing
is believing ', nothing is more substantial, more objective,
more real, than the external world of nature. We come up
against it, so to speak, we have to respect its laws, we depend
on it for our life, our bodies come from it and dissolve again
into it : it is brute, crass ' matter ', mountains and rocks and
earth, abiding and comparatively changeless realities. But
the more we penetrate the nature of the external world, the
more elusive, the more unsubstantial (in a popular sense) it
becomes. The modern scientific conceptions of matter's
constitution dissolve the sure and solid world of the old-
fashioned materialists into something very intangible, into
electric charges, into waves, into symbolic conceptions or
mathematical formulæ, which, while expressing the inner

nature of empirical reality, almost deprive of reality the world as it appears and resolve it into something very unlike the world as it appears in sense-perception. In actual fact, of course, modern scientific conceptions do not deprive the ' phenomenal ' world of its reality (the world remains for us precisely what it always was), but they do suggest that the material cosmos is not, in its ultimate constitution, quite that crude, hard thing-in-itself, which some have thought it to be. The philosophizing of some recent scientists may be some-what crude ; but it does perhaps help us to see that, though the world can exist apart from the finite subject, it cannot exist apart from the infinite Subject, Whose (external) manifestation it is. If we think of matter-in-itself as existing in its own right, apart from any Thinker whatsoever, then we are indeed living in a dream-world. ' The dreamer ', says Santayana in *Dialogues in Limbo*—' the dreamer can know no truth, not even about his dream, except by awaking out of it '; but we can awake out of our dream, if we recognize the world of nature, with all its suns and milky ways, as—not nothing— but as an external phenomenon, veiling, yet manifesting, the ultimate Reality, the one transcendental Subject, Who is His own Infinite Object in undivided substantial unity.

CHAPTER IV

THE TRAGEDY OF LIFE

OPTIMISM AND PESSIMISM, as the words are often used in daily intercourse, denote two attitudes to life which do not necessarily suppose two different metaphysical conceptions. For example, in a period of great national danger and distress, when the very existence of a State as an independently sovereign and autonomous entity is threatened by a powerful foe, one man may continue to believe and hope, even in the darkest hour, that the danger will somehow be averted, that his country will rally sufficient forces and possess sufficient material to repel the invader or that the latter will make some fatal mistake which will snatch the prize of victory from his outstretched hand, while another man, abandoning hope, resigns himself to what he considers the inevitable calamity. The first man we would, in common parlance, call an optimist, the second a pessimist ; yet both men may be at one in their belief in the existence of a Divine Providence that watches over all things and that eventually brings good out of evil. Both may believe that in the end Right will certainly triumph, though the first thinks that the immediate disaster to his country will be averted, while the other thinks it most unlikely that the temporary calamity can be avoided. There is no difference in metaphysical outlook between the two men, any more than there is necessarily any difference of metaphysical outlook between two individuals of whom one, in the less sensational and trivial affairs of daily life, is inclined to fasten his attention on the black side of things, whereas the other, in similar circumstances, habitually sees the ' silver lining '. The pessimism of the one and the optimism of the other may be largely a matter of temperament, of health, of low vitality or high vitality, and both might agree that in the long run all will be well and that little sufferings may have their value and contribute towards a greater good. Again, one man may be inclined to a pessimistic view of human nature, always ready to suspect low motives, deceitful cunning, mean and egoistic aims, while another man will be more ready to attribute unselfish and noble aims to others, to see the good points in a human character, to be perhaps over-trustful : yet both may believe firmly in the value of human personality, in man's vocation, in his great possibilities. Such optimism and such pessimism might be termed practical (often simply temperamental) optimism or pessimism. If two men are believing Christians, their belief, though affirming for both of them a fundamental optimism, since both will believe that God has the last word and that the sufferings of life are subordinated to Divine Providence, does not of itself tell them that this or that particular historical calamity will or will not take place, that their earthly lives will be afflicted with many or with few misfortunes, that their fellows will act on high principles or on low and unworthy maxims.

But, if there are, as we all know there are, predominantly optimistic and predominantly pessimistic attitudes to life, which may not derive at all from metaphysical tenets but rather from temperament, upbringing, particular experiences, happy or the reverse, psychological factors of one sort or

another, there are also an optimism and a pessimism which
derive logically from different metaphysical systems. We say
' *logically* ', since, from the *psychological* viewpoint, it may be
temperament, experience, or some other purely personal factor
that determines a man's choice of an optimistic or a pessimistic
metaphysic : there are at least some cases in which Fichte's
dictum is verified, that the sort of philosophy a man chooses
depends on the sort of man he is. But once a man has chosen
his philosophy, then a certain attitude towards life should
logically follow therefrom. If, for instance, a man is a convinced Hegelian, he should logically view the process of
history as a rational, self-justified process, and if he adheres to
the nineteenth century doctrine of Progress, based, whether
justifiably or not, on the scientific theory of evolution among
other factors, he should logically expect the human race to
pursue a continuous upward path from darkness into light.
Similarly, if he believes that finite existence is a metaphysical
evil, something that ought not to be, he is logically debarred
from adopting an optimistic attitude towards human life in
the concrete.

Now, the philosophy of Schopenhauer is a philosophy of
metaphysical pessimism. That Schopenhauer's personal
character and temperament, together with his own experiences
and his observations of human suffering and the apparent
futility of life, contributed to the formation and elaboration
of that philosophy, is no doubt correct ; but he was convinced
of the truth of his metaphysical system and, if that metaphysic
were actually true or if it were only held to be true, then from
the logical standpoint, the one possible attitude towards life
would be a pessimistic attitude. A man might hold the dogma
of Progress and later, under the pressure of fact, economic
crises, world wars, widespread sufferings, relapses into sava-
gery and barbarism, find himself compelled to modify his
former naïve outlook ; but he might still believe that these
very crises and relapses would lead men to examine and
renounce their causes and so pave the way to an advance in
civilization and a happier and more rational human life ; he
might consider these periodical relapses to be no more than
the antithesis which has to be experienced before the higher
synthesis can be attained. But if a man held the philosophy
of Schopenhauer, he would be debarred from any such optimistic outlook : for him the passing years, the succeeding

phases of history, could mean only a progressive increase in
suffering and misery ; true happiness would be an illusion,
life a mockery, a tragico-comedy. ' I think ', says Pirandello,
' that life is a very sad piece of buffoonery ', and these words
might be uttered by a disciple of Schopenhauer, not simply
because his own observation had taught him to consider them
true, but on *a priori* and metaphysical grounds. The philosophy of Arthur Schopenhauer thus raises what we might call
empirical or practical pessimism on to the theoretical level,
giving it a metaphysical foundation and justification.

On what is the metaphysical pessimism of Schopenhauer
logically based ? On his conception of the *Ding-an-sich*, which
he views as Will, an irrational, blind, self-conflicting impulse
to existence. ' Thing-in-itself signifies that which exists
independently of our perception, in short, that which properly
is. This was, for Demokritos, formed matter. It was the
same at bottom for Locke ; for Kant it was $= x$; for me it
is Will '.[1] We have seen how, according to Schopenhauer, the
whole world of nature, of individual objects of perception, is
but phenomenon, ' my idea ' ; but this is only the ' outside '
of the world, and there is also an ' inside ', the metaphysical
and ultimate reality, the true thing-in-itself. Whereas for
Kant the thing-in-itself was unknowable, impenetrable to the
speculative reason, for Schopenhauer it is knowable, it is Will,
the principle which explains not only individual human
nature, but the whole of the world. But Will for Schopenhauer
is very far from being the free and rational will of the Kantian
Ethic : on the contrary it includes unconscious instinct,
desire, feeling, also all force and energy manifested in nature,
comprising ' the force which germinates and vegetates in the
plant, and indeed the force through which the crystal is
formed, that by which the magnet turns to the north pole, the
force whose shock he experiences from the contact of two
different kinds of metal, the force which appears in the elective
affinities of matter as repulsion and attraction, decomposition
and combination, and, lastly, even gravitation, which acts so
powerfully throughout matter, draws the stone to the earth
and the earth to the sun '.[2] All these forces and impulses are
different only in their phenomenal nature : in their inner

---

[1] Some Reflections on the Antithesis of Thing-in-itself and Phenomenon
from *Parerga and Paralipomena*, vi, p. 96.

[2] I, p. 142.

nature, they are all identical, the manifestation of the meta-phenomenal Will.

In the last chapter I mentioned that, in Schopenhauer's view, we penetrate to the thing-in-itself through inner consciousness. Subject and object are correlative, and it is impossible to arrive at the one principle through a consideration of the world as idea : we cannot reduce the object to the subject with Fichte or the subject to the object with Schelling. However much we investigate nature as perceived, ' we can never reach anything but images and names. We are like a man who goes round a castle seeking in vain for an entrance, and sometimes sketching the façades. And yet this is the method that has been followed by all philosophers before me '[1] Ultimate reality must be beyond the cognitive relation of subject and object, and it is in ourselves that we find the key to reality. (Schopenhauer commended Descartes for taking self-consciousness as his *point de départ*.) In reflection on ourselves we recognize that our bodily actions are nothing but the acts of our will objectified, that the act of the will and the movement of the body are not two separate things, of which the latter stands to the former in the relation of effect to cause (though they are so related in perception for the understanding), but rather are one and the same, the bodily action being nothing but the act of the will objectified, i.e. passed over into perception : in fact the whole body is nothing but objectified will or will which has become idea. When a man has realized this, that his body is simply his will become ' idea ', that the inner nature of his phenomenal being is will, he has found the key to the knowledge of the world in general, and he is enabled to unlock the door of nature, penetrate its phenomenal character as ' idea ' and attain to its noumenal character as will.

In the last chapter I pointed out that, in view of what Schopenhauer has to say on the subject-object relation and cognition in general, the acts of our will and our will itself ought logically to be considered as belonging to the phenomenal order in such a way that reflection on self is really of no more help to attaining the thing-in-itself than sense-perception, and agnosticism in regard to ultimate reality should be his position. But it is unnecessary to press this criticism any further, as Schopenhauer's metaphysic of Will is the product of a comprehensive ' intuition ' of reality, suggested by tempera-

[1] I, p. 128.

ment and observation of life and other factors, rather than the conclusion of a coldly rational argument. That was probably one of the reasons contributing to the failure of his lectures of Berlin, inasmuch as his philosophy did not lend itself to the dialectical treatment then in vogue. It is also no doubt one of the reasons why his system, in spite of inconsistencies and illogicalities, gives an impression of grandeur and simplicity, for it centres round one idea which, though false, represents a definite *Weltanschauung* and corresponds to an undeniable aspect of finite existence in general. The whole system, though its creator certainly believed that it embodied the truth, might perhaps be profitably viewed as an æsthetic whole, a work of the creative imagination, in spite of all the attempts made by Schopenhauer to confirm his metaphysic by appeals to empirical reality. Seen in this light, prescinding from its truth or falsity, it is a great achievement, and it is not difficult to understand how it may arouse interest and even a certain sympathy in some natures. To the superficial and unreflective optimist, it can scarcely be anything else but repellent in the extreme ; but in one for whom the dark side of life is a grim reality, a reality that he does not fear to face, it may awaken a certain regard, even though he considers it one-sided and extravagant.

Having found the ' key to reality ' in inner consciousness, Schopenhauer proceeds to extend his discovery of the noumenon to the world at large through an analogical treatment. The identity of the noumenon with will, first known directly *in concreto*, ' i.e. as feeling ',[1] and then lifted by Schopenhauer on to the plane of abstract knowledge, is recognized to express the inner nature, ' the kernel, of every particular thing, and also of the whole '.[2] ' If we observe the strong and unceasing impulse with which the magnet turns ever to the north pole, the readiness with which iron flies to the magnet, the eagerness with which the electric poles seek to be re-united, and which just like human desire, is increased by obstacles—if we observe the choice with which bodies repel and attract each other, combine and separate, when they are set free in a fluid state, and emancipated from the bonds of rigidness ; lastly, if we feel directly how a burden which hampers our body by its gravitation towards the earth, unceasingly presses and strains upon it in pursuit of its one tendency ; if we observe all this,

I, p. 141.   [2] *Ibid.*, p. 143.

I say, it will require no great effort of the imagination to recognize, even at so great a distance, our own nature'.[1] In us indeed the will pursues its ends by the light of knowledge, while in nature apart from man it pursues its ends in blind activity (as when, says Schopenhauer, the larva of the stag-beetle makes the hole in the wood of double size, if it is going to be a male beetle, in order that there may be room for the horns), but it is the same Will that is operative in both cases.

Why, then did the philosopher choose to call the noumenon *Will*, rather than *Force* or *Energy*? His reason was this. If we subsume the concept of will under that of force, we have subsumed the better known under the less well known, where-as, if we refer the concept of force to that of will, we thereby refer the less known to the better known. In our inner con-sciousness of will we find the only immediate knowledge that we possess of the inner nature of the world, and it would be absurd to resolve the concept of will into another notion, that of force, abstracted from the phenomenal sphere.[2] This obviously presupposes that the concept of will is the expression of a direct consciousness of the noumenal : in any case its extension to the world in general by absorption of all that which we would normally term manifestations of force or energy or life involves attaching a very wide connotation to the word ' will ' and a dilution of its common meaning. Thus Schopenhauer finds will in the irrational animals and declares that in every animal consciousness there is always present. as its foundation, ' an immediate sense of *longing*, and of the alternate satisfaction and non-satisfaction of it '.[3] The animal wills existence, well-being, life and propagation, we are told ; but it is obvious enough that willing in this case does not refer to a tendency towards an end presented by reason, since the brutes have no reason, but to an instinctive impulse, an infra-rational desire. Much less in the case of inorganic things does the manifestation of will approach the rational level : it is not accompanied by consciousness of any sort. It is necessary to bear this in mind when considering Schopenhauer's meta-physic of the will : if the latter is thought of as rational, purposeful volition, the whole tone of the system will be mis-understood. The philosopher's doctrine is summed up in words that he quotes from Vanini, *Voluntas potentia cœca est.*[4]

[1] I, p. 153.   [2] Cf. I, pp. 143-4.   [3] II, p. 414.   [4] III, p. 32.

The thing-in-itself is, therefore, Will, which objectifies itself in the phenomenon or rather in phenomena, in the world as ' idea '. This Will, which is the inner nature of the world, is *one* Will, the multiplicity of things being appearances, phenomena thereof. Multiplicity, individuality, particularity, is thus phenomenal, being conditioned by space and time, the *principium individuationis*, and being only empirically real, i.e. existing only as ' idea ', in relation to the knowing subject. The Will, considered in itself, apart from all its manifestations, lies outside space and time and consequently beyond all multiplicity. It is, therefore, one and undivided, and it should not be viewed as being partially present in a stone, partially present in a man, for the relation of part and whole is a spatial relation and is entirely foreign to the thing-in-itself. Yet this one and undivided Will objectifies itself, renders itself visible, in a multiplicity of phenomena, according to different grades of objectification. Universal forces of nature, such as gravity and impenetrability, represent the lowest grades of the Will's objectification, while organic objects, plants, brutes, men, represent progressively higher grades of the will's objectification : yet the individuality which belongs to the phenomenal world, an individuality which increases in proportion to the elevation in grade and reaches its culminating point in men (whose bodies and characters are seen to be so markedly different and individual, when viewed in relation to e.g. the brutes) does not affect the Will-in-itself. Schopenhauer declares that if, *per impossibile*, a single existent thing were entirely annihilated, the whole world would perish with it, and he quotes two lines of Angelus Silesius :—

" I know God cannot live an instant without me,
He must give up the ghost if I should cease to be."[1]

Not, of course, that Schopenhauer means that the Will is God (his system is atheistic) : his words are meant to convey simply the unicity and indivisible character of the metaphysical Will, which constitutes the inner nature of all phenomena. (Strictly speaking, the *immediate* grades of the Will's objectification are the ' Platonic Ideas ', which are related to individual things as their eternal prototypes and are severally indivisible ; but it is more convenient to discuss them in the next chapters, because of their intimate connection with Schopenhauer's aesthetic theory.)

Considered in itself, Will is 'merely a blind incessant impulse ',[1] ' an endless striving '[2] ; ' eternal becoming, endless flux, characterizes the revelation of the inner nature of will '.[3] It is to be called free, inasmuch as it is not subordinate to the principle of sufficient reason, not determined as a consequent ; but this freedom is simply groundlessness, the Will is free merely negatively, in that it is subject to no necessity, knows no cause whatsoever. Yet Schopenhauer characterizes the Will as will to life, will to existence. The will as phenomenon, the particular will, has its end, the Will in itself has no end,[4] and it may well appear strange that Schopenhauer should go on to characterize it as will to life ; but life, by which is meant the visible world, the phenomenon, is no conscious end and, according to Schopenhauer, ' it is all one and a mere pleonasm if, instead of saying simply ' the will ', we say ' the will to live." '[5] Life, or the visible world, is said to be the mirror of the Will and to accompany it as inseparably as the shadow accompanies the body, so that, if Will exists, life on the world will also exist. It might perhaps be considered a childish criticism to point out that though shadow cannot exist apart from the body the shadow of which it is, and on which it depends, it cannot be said to *be* the body, and that it does not follow from the dependence of the visible world on the noumenon that it *is* the noumenon ; but even if it would be unjust to press the metaphors and the comparisons employed by Schopenhauer, the fact remains that the world, even if it is phenomenal and exists only for perception, is a phenomenon, an appearance, a manifestation, an objectification of the Will. But how can we conceive an ' endless striving ', an irrational impulse to live, to objectivity itself, that is not at the same time the striving of some subject ? The philosopher may say that we must liberate ourselves from the shackles of a reason that thinks in terms of individuality, of subject and object, and so on ; but to demand this is to demand that we free ourselves from the forms of human cognition and, since no other form of cognition is attainable by us, this means that we should pass into mere not-knowing. We can, of course, write down or utter the words, ' the noumenon is a blind impulse to live, to exist,

[1] I, p. 354. [2] *Ibid.*, p. 213. [3] *Ibid.*, p. 214.
[4] *Ibid.*, p. 215. [5] *Ibid.*, p. 354.

which is not the impulse of any subject whatsoever and is not substantial but eternal becoming, endless striving ' ; but it does not follow that we can conceive the reality which is supposedly expressed in these words. Moreover, how could this mysterious Will objectify itself in intellect, in the world as idea, if it is of itself irrational and blind ? Schopenhauer, thinking that life as we know it is senseless, declared that the ultimate Principle, which manifests itself in life, is also senseless, and, if he had contented himself with a materialistic position, with saying that matter of some form or other is the *ens a se*, we would, while disagreeing, understand what was meant ; but, as he endeavours to transcend experience and postulates an ultimate principle, the being of which transcends the forms of human cognition, we are introduced into the ' night in which all cows are black '. And let it not be said that, just as God transcends human cognition and yet can be partially apprehended by way of analogy, so Schopenhauer was justified in proceeding by way of analogy to his noumenon, for analogy demands that the ultimate principle be not *less* than that of which it is the principle, whereas Schopenhauer's Will is obviously incommensurable with its effect, not because it is infinitely higher than the effect but because it is immeasurably lower. The philosopher would remark perhaps that for him the world is *not* the effect of the Will, any more than Will is the cause of the world : the world is the inseparable mirror of the Will ; but if the world is not the effect of Will, it is the Will itself in its phenomenal aspect, and, if it is the Will itself in any sense, then the Will itself must be rational, which *ex hypothesi* it is not. But you cannot have it both ways. Either the world is a true mirror (or the ' outside ' aspect, if you like) of the ultimate principle, and then the latter cannot be simply irrational, for there is reason in the world, or the world is no true mirror of the ultimate principle, the latter being in itself irrational. In the first case you will be driven to admit in the end that the world is the mirror of Absolute Reason, is the *explicatio Dei* : in the second case you will have to explain how phenomenal reason can possibly issue from what is itself irrational. It is no good saying that reason simply ' appears ', whether as phenomenon or epiphenomenon, for to state that reason ' appears ' is no more than saying that it ' is there ' or exists (whether it ' appears ' early or late in the world's history is simply irrelevant), and that is the very point that needs explanation. A scientist may, if he chooses, say that at a certain stage of development reason ' appears ' and leave it at that, since he is not concerned, precisely as a natural scientist, with metaphysical themes ; but the philosopher cannot stop there and will be compelled either to adopt an impossible materialistic position (making reason *no more* than mere matter) or to accept a panpsychistic doctrine (which will soon land him in insoluble difficulties) or to admit frankly that reason cannot be explained in terms of the irrational and that the ultimate principle is Reason in itself.

Schopenhauer insists that will to live is not ' an arbitrary hypostasis or an empty word '[1] and that the characterization of ultimate reality as will to live is confirmed by observation of the world. In surveying organized life we see the one ' intention ', the maintenance of the species, the individual having value only in so far as it contributes to this end. ' Apart from this its existence is to nature a matter of indifference ; indeed nature even leads it to destruction as soon as it has ceased to be useful for this end '.[2] This explains the existence of the individual ; but what of the species itself? If we observe the untiring diligence and ceaseless labour of bees or ants, the regular migrations or nestings of the birds, we ask ourselves what is attained by all this labour, all this preparation, and ' there is nothing to point to but the satisfaction of hunger and the sexual instinct '[3] or a little transitory comfort that now and again falls to the lot of the individual animal. The disproportion between the trouble taken and the reward attained is to be seen also in human life, with its industry and trade, its inventions and technical developments, its intriguing politics and its wars, all of which serves but to sustain ephemeral, transitory, suffering individuals through a short span of life, and, more ultimately, to contribute to the maintenance of the species, to its constant striving. In all this is seen a motiveless and groundless tendency, the impulse to live, to exist, even if life spells suffering.

The unity of the Will, as also its character as will to live, is manifested in teleology, both inner and outer.[4] Inner teleology, the ordering of all the parts of an organism in such a way that they contribute to the preservation of the whole, shows the unity of the Idea (i.e. Platonic Idea) that is the

<hr />

[1] III, p. 107.　　　　　　　　　[2] *Ibid.*, p. 108.
[3] *Ibid.*, p. 111.　　　　　　　　　[4] Cf. I, pp. 201 ff.

archetype of the species in question and is the immediate objectification of the one Will. The unity of the Idea, therefore, which reveals the unity and indivisibility of Will, is itself revealed in the relations of the parts of the organism to one another and of all the parts of the organism as a whole, which stands to its parts as end to means. For example, the lungs in a dog have a definite function to fulfil in regard to the blood, but both lungs and blood subserve the dog as a total entity. The empirical character or form of the dog is worked out or developed through time, but it is the manifestation of the intelligible character and this intelligible character is one, manifesting the one Will. ' Outer ' teleology shows itself, not in the relations within the organism itself, but in the support and assistance an organism receives from inorganic nature and from other organisms, e.g. in the adaptation of this animal to the air, of that to the water, of the camel to life in the desert, of the eye to light, and so on. The way in which, for example, birds build nests for the young that they do not as yet know or insects deposit their eggs where the larva may find future nourishment, shows us external teleology in a marvellous form, and all this external teleology is simply a revelation of the unity of the indivisible Will, which objectifies itself in inter-related phenomena. Moreover, inasmuch as teleology in general subserves the life and preservation of the individual, and still more, of the species, it reveals not only the unity of Will, but also its character as will to live, to exist.

Now, that Schopenhauer admitted design, teleology, in nature is admirable ; but is this admission compatible with his characterization of the ultimate principle as irrational, as a mere striving ? Schopenhauer gives a varied number of examples and illustrations, in order to show that there is subordination of means to end, accommodation of phenomena to one another, in short finality and design ; but if there is design in nature, then either the Will must itself be capable of designing or some other organizing principle must be introduced. If Schopenhauer had denied design in nature and had declared that the apparent finality and design in the world is read into nature by man under the influence of a tendency to view all things anthropomorphically, we would have disagreed with his denial of finality, but his denial would have been consistent with his characterization of the metaphysical Will. In fact, however, he admitted design in nature, and had to, for, if the world of nature is simply ' my idea ', it would be quite redundant to say that I read design into nature and quite unjustifiable to conclude that the fact that I read design into nature means that it is not really there : if it is there for perception, then it is there according to all the reality that Schopenhauer allows to nature. As a matter of fact there appears to be a double standpoint involved. The world, according to the one standpoint, is my idea ; and in this case the design in nature belongs to my idea and nothing can be argued from design in nature as to the character of the noumenon. The world, according to the other standpoint, is the self-revelation of the noumenon, in which case, once given teleology and design in any real sense, the Will cannot be irrational and blind. To prove design may not be so easy as it appears to be in the eyes of some (we cannot be expected in an exposition of Schopenhauer's philosophy to enter upon such a proof here) ; but, once design has been proved, it is scarcely legitimate to declare that the world is the mani-festation of an irrational impulse. It may be said that Schopen-hauer is merely stating a *de facto* adaptation of parts to the whole, of an organism to its conditions, etc., and that by ' design ' he does not mean to indicate the work of a designer, so that there is no real inconsistency in admitting, for example, adaptation to environment, which even the mechanistic materialist must admit, and at the same denying the existence of any designer. In reply I would point out that Schopenhauer is constantly speaking of nature as providing for this or that and that the whole tenor of his language presupposes the existence of at least a World-Soul, the existence of which he denies. Since he termed the noumenon *Will*, it appears less strange that he admitted teleology, as the word ' will ' uncon-sciously suggests rational purpose : if, however, we substitute ' blind impulse ' for ' will ' (and that is what he thought the noumenon to be), we shall see more easily the strangeness of a theory, according to which blind impulse, an ' unattached ' blind impulse as it were, reveals itself in an organized cosmos, in which there is adaptation of means to end and in which the peak-phenomenon is a rational being, capable of deliberately subordinating particular means to particular ends.

It is, however, quite true that in the *Supplement* Schopen-hauer explains or modifies his position, with the purpose of excluding the theistic conclusion from teleology. He asserts that final causes are the clue to the understanding of organized nature, as efficient causes are the clue to the understanding of unorganized nature,[1] and adds that in regard to the latter ' the final cause is always ambiguous, and especially when the *efficient* cause is found, leaves us in doubt whether it is not a merely subjective view, an aspect conditioned by our point of view '[2]. Schopenhauer commends Aristotle for admitting teleology without trying to find an external Cause for nature (and it is true that the God of the *Metaphysics* at least is only a Final Cause, though the absence of a transcendent efficient Cause is precisely one of the defects of Aristotle's philosophy and a point where it is inferior to Platonism). Leibniz he condemns for saying, ' *Les causes finales, ou ce qui est la même chose, la considération de la sagesse divine dans l'ordre des choses* '.[3] Teleology, according to Schopenhauer, in no way leads to theology ; but what proof does he offer for this assertion ? It is that of Kant, to whom it was reserved ' really to refute ' the physico-theological proof, Kant, the ignorance of whose philosophy ' is principally responsible for this whole outcast position of the English '.[4] (Schopenhauer thought of the English as greatly given to adopting the position of Leibniz in regard to teleology.) Ignorance of the Kantian philosophy is largely responsible for ' the nefarious influence of the detestable English clergy, with whom stultification of every kind is a thing after their own hearts, so that only they may be able still to hold the English nation, otherwise so intelligent, involved in the most degrading bigotry '. (Schopenhauer is perhaps thinking partly of the months he spent in England as a boy.) Kant, as is well known, had a great respect for the ' physico-theological ' proof (' it is the oldest, the clearest, and most in conformity with human reason '), but the conclusions he came to in regard to the speculative reason forbad his accepting as demonstrative any speculative proof for God's existence. This is really the main objection of Kant, since his assertion that, in order to proceed from the idea of an Architect of the universe to that of the Supreme and Necessary Being, recourse must be had to the so-called ontological argument, is simply false. As, then, Kant's only real objection to the teleological proof rests on his theory of the limitations of pure reason, we must suppose that Schopenhauer who appeals

[1] III, p. 80.   [2] *Ibid.*, p. 88.
[3] *Ibid.*, p. 91.   [4] *Ibid.*, p. 92.

to Kant's supposed refutation of the proof, accepts the compelling nature of his objection. It would be clearly impossible,
and also out of place, to attempt an answer here to the *Kritik
der reinen Vernunft* ; but we might observe that, if Schopenhauer
accepted Kant's objection, he would have done well (i.e.
from the *logical* viewpoint) to acquiesce in the agnostic position
which follows from that objection and to refrain from dog-
matizing about the noumenon and postulating an ultimate
principle which is quite incompatible with the presence of
design in nature.

The Will, which objectifies itself in the world, is not only
one, not only will to life, but also at variance with itself, in
conflict. Will, that ' striving without aim or end ',[1] shows in
all its manifestations ' that variance with itself which is essential
to the will '.[2] Just because it is a striving without end, Will
never attains final satisfaction : a partial and transitory satisfaction, as experienced by an individual man, for instance,
soon turns to ennui. Will-in-itself is, therefore, always unsatisfied, always desiring, never at rest, constantly reaching
out as if it could be satisfied and yet never finding satisfaction
in anything. This conflict, which is involved in the desire to
find satisfaction on the one hand and the inability to find it on
the other hand, belongs to the Will itself (for it is at once an
endless striving-after and an endless inability-to-find), and is
reflected in nature through all its grades. ' Every grade of the
objectification of will fights for the matter, the space, and the
time of the others '[3] Schopenhauer finds illustrations of this
conflict in the inorganic sphere, but it is seen more clearly in
the organic sphere, particularly in the animal kingdom.
Animals not only use the vegetable kingdom, but also (i.e.
some of them) prey upon one another. In this we see the
matter in which one Idea expresses itself destroyed or ' con-
quered ' by the matter which expresses another Idea, as when
the hawk destroys the small bird or the cow feeds upon the
grass ; and, since both Ideas are objectifications of the *one*
Will, the conflict is ultimately the conflict of the Will with
itself. The insect that lays its eggs in the body of the larva of
another insect, the parasitic growth that chokes the mighty
tree, the magnet which ' forces its magnetism upon iron, in
order to express its Idea in it ',[4] all this shows the conflict

---

[1] I, p. 414.   [2] *Ibid.*, p. 191.
[3] *Ibid.*   [4] *Ibid.*, p. 193.

that exists in both inorganic and organic nature. ' Thus the will to live everywhere preys upon itself, and in different forms is its own nourishment, till finally the human race, because it subdues all the others, regards nature as a manufactory for its use '.[1]

But if this conflict shows itself throughout all the grades of the Will's objectification, it shows itself most clearly and most poignantly in man—*homo homini lupus*. The individual is identical, in his inner nature, with Will and the Will's striving reflects itself in him as *egoism*, so that he regards himself as the centre of the world and has respect only for his own existence and well-being, not caring for the existence and welfare of others. Man (unless indeed he has advanced to the state in which he can penetrate the veils of appearance and realize the underlying unity of all things and the futility of egoism), is imprisoned in the phenomenal world, the world of perception, and looks upon all other beings as means to his own satisfaction —in philosophic language, looks upon them, not as manifestations of the one Will equally with himself but as his ' idea ', dependent in some way upon himself. He is ready, therefore, to annihilate the whole world, if that were necessary, in order to preserve himself in existence a little longer : his own being and its maintenance are of more importance to him than the being and maintenance of all others together. This natural egoism is seen, as regards its terrible side, ' in the lives of great tyrants and miscreants, and in world-desolating wars ', as regards its absurd side, in petty self-conceit and vanity.[2] ' The chief source of the serious evils which affect men is man himself : *homo homini lupus*. Whoever keeps this last fact clearly in view beholds the world as a hell, which surpasses that of Dante in this respect, that one man must be the devil of another '.[3] Apart from the arch-fiends, who appear in the guise of conquerors and set thousands of men to shoot each other, this fact appears in the general injustice, unfairness, hardness and even cruelty displayed in the conduct of men, one towards the other. ' How man deals with man is shown, for example, by negro slavery, the final end of which is sugar and coffee '.[4] The mechanical and monotonous labour in factories, which is the lot of millions, is another example. It is shown most distinctly when a mob of men is set free from

[1] I., p. 192.
[2] *Ibid.*, p. 429.
[3] III, p. 388.
[4] *Ibid.*

all law and order, upon which follows the *bellum omnium contra omnes*, ' which Hobbes has so admirably described '. (Schopenhauer, it will be remembered, hated and feared the revolutionary movement of 1848.) ' Upon this depends the necessity of the State and legislation, and upon none of your false pretences '.[1] In other words, the State exists simply to keep human egoism, man's predatory instincts, within reasonable bounds : it has no ethical or educative end. It is directed against the unbridled egoism of one man or a few men ; but it is *not* directed against egoism as such ; on the contrary, ' it has sprung from egoism and exists only in its service ', it is instituted on the supposition that pure morality is not to be expected.[2]

When a man is driven on by an intense pressure of will and, though he takes every means to slake the thirst of his egoism, finds that all satisfaction is merely apparent, the intense pressure of his volition does not allow him to acquiesce in the consequent melancholy, but impels him to seek the mitigation of his own suffering in witnessing the sufferings of others, ' which at the same time he recognizes as an expression of his power. The suffering of others now becomes for him an end in itself, and is a spectacle in which he delights ; and thus arises the phenomenon of pure cruelty, blood-thirstiness, which history exhibits so often in the Neros and Domitians, in the African Deys, in Robespierre and the like '.[3] Schopenhauer thus finds a metaphysical explanation of cruelty, which may appear far-fetched, but his suggestion that cruelty is loved as an expression of personal power (and so as an expression of egoism) is undoubtedly true in many cases. It has become the fashion for writers in magazines and papers to speak of all love of cruelty as ' sadistic ' ; but there is really no reason to suppose that all love of cruelty is an expression of the sexual libido. That sadism is a real phenomenon, it would be folly to deny ; but the fact that some people are sadists does not show that *all* cruel people are sadists, for the deliberate infliction of pain on others may be loved, not only as a stimulus to or expression of libido, but also as an expression of the will to power, of perverted egoism of a type not directly connected with sex. Sadistic impulses and impulses to the unbridled expression of the will to power may run together to constitute an individual's impulse to deliberate cruelty ;

[1] III, p. 388. [2] I, p. 445. [3] *Ibid.*, p. 470.

but it will not do to fall a victim to pan-sexual theory and to view all cruelty as essentially connected with the sexual libido. Sex-perversions there certainly are ; but not all perversions of human nature are sex-perversions.

Though conflict between individuals, both on the great and petty scale, is a fruitful source of suffering in human life, it is not the only source, for life itself, according to Schopenhauer, necessarily involves suffering. Will is an endless striving, a striving after satisfaction, and when it is hindered from obtaining its goal, there is suffering. The goal, satisfaction, is unattainable, just because the Will is essentially an endless striving, and all temporary satisfaction that comes to the Will in this or that phenomenal manifestation, soon turns to ennui and forms the starting-point for fresh discontent, renewed striving. Happiness is, therefore, merely negative, a temporary quietening of desire, and real, lasting happiness is impossible : the reality of life is suffering. ' The striving we see everywhere hindered in many ways, everywhere in conflict, and therefore always under the form of suffering. Thus, if there is no final end of striving, there is no measure and end of suffering '.[1] Just because the individual is one with Will, his desire is limitless, his claim to happiness inexhaustible; the satisfaction of any desire gives rise to a new desire and no possible satisfaction could still the infinite craving of the will. Suffering is present indeed in the animal kingdom, but it increases in proportion to the increase in consciousness and reaches its highest degree in man, the more intelligent the man, the greater being his suffering and pain; since he realises that his phenomenal existence is a ' constant transition into death, a constant dying ', that ' the present is always passing through his hands into the past ', that ' the future is quite uncertain and always short ', that, though man pursues life with solicitude as long as possible, death will inevitably conquer in the end, death which plays with its prey for a little while before swallowing it up.[2] The reflective man, the true philosopher, realizes that willing and striving constitute man's nature, that this striving is like to an unquenchable thirst, and that ' consequently the nature of brutes and man is subject to pain originally and through its very being '.[3]

Human existence, therefore, is but vanity and suffering. ' The wish is, in its nature, pain ; the attainment soon begets

---

[1] I, p. 399.   [2] Ibid., pp. 401–2.   [3] Ibid., p. 402.

satiety : the end was only apparent, possession takes away the charm ; the wish, the need, presents itself under a new form ; when it does not, there follows desolateness, emptiness, ennui, against which the conflict is just as painful as against want.[1] The life of most men is no more than a constant struggle for existence, a struggle amid the rocks and whirlpools ; but, although they may succeed in avoiding many of these, they approach nearer and nearer every moment to the inevitable, complete, irremediable shipwreck of death. All living things are indeed occupied with the striving after existence ; but if for a few moments it seems to be assured, then they do not know what to do with it and have to ' kill time ', in order to escape from ennui. It is ennui that ' makes beings who love each other so little as men do, seek each other eagerly ' ; and it is ennui that is the scourge of the fashionable world, as want is the scourge of the people. ' In middle-class life ', Schopenhauer caustically remarks ', ennui is represented by the Sunday, and want by the six week-days '.[2] Purely intellectual pleasures are not accessible to the great majority of men and, in any case, great intellectual power involves an extended capacity for suffering and a greater isolation.

Taken all in all, therefore, life is nought but a tragedy and optimism is unwarranted self-delusion. It is true that the trivial irritations and mishaps of our day by day existence may take on the character of comic scenes ; but this is one of the most poignant facts about the tragedy of life, that fate adds derision to the misery of our existence and that, while life contains all the woes of tragedy, ' we cannot even assert the dignity of tragic characters, but in the broad detail of life must inevitably be the foolish characters of a comedy '.[3] If the confirmed optimist were to be shown the blackest scenes of earth's misery, if he were to be conducted through the hospitals, infirmaries and operating-theatres, through the prisons and torture-chambers, through the battle-fields and places of execution, he would realise the true nature of this ' best of all possible worlds '. In fine, ' whence did Dante take the materials for his hell, but from this our actual world?'[4] The optimism of Leibniz and his followers is a mockery : ' *Optimism*, when it is not merely the thoughtless talk of such as harbour nothing but words under their low foreheads,

---

[1] I, pp. 404–5.
[2] *Ibid.*,
[3] *Ibid.*, p. 416.
[4] *Ibid.*, p. 419.

appears not merely as an absurd, but also as a really *wicked* way of thinking, as a bitter mockery of the unspeakable suffering of humanity. Let no one think that Christianity is favourable to optimism ; for, on the contrary, in the Gospels world and evil are used as almost synonymous '.[1] Schopenhauer commends Hume for exposing the untenable character of optimism in his *Dialogues on Natural Religion* and *Natural History of Religion*, works far superior to those of the German ' home-bred boastful mediocrities, who are proclaimed great men '. ' From every page of David Hume there is more to be learned than from the collected works of Hegel, Herbart, and Schleiermacher together '.[2] Leibniz may talk of the best possible world and bring ' palpably sophistical ' proofs to show that our world is such, but in actual fact it is the worst of all possible worlds and a worse world than this could not possibly continue in existence.

> ' Count o'er the joys thine hours have seen,
>   Count o'er thy days from anguish free,
> And know, whatever thou hast been,
>   'Tis something better not to be '.[3]

It might be thought that in view of this grim picture of human life, Schopenhauer would recommend suicide ; but, though he refused to recognise any valid moral reason for condemning suicide, he considered that it is no real solution to life's tragedy. A man may be so overcome by suffering that he takes his own life, but he will not find annihilation in this way, for annihilation is impossible. ' Really the most solid ground for our immortality is the old principle : " *Ex nihilo nihil fit, et in nihilum nihil potest reverti* ".[4] (The quotation is, *ad sensum*, from Lucretius.) Individual consciousnesss is indeed destroyed, i.e. phenomenal existence, but man's inner nature, identical with Will, persists and can never be destroyed. Annihilation on the one hand is thus unattainable, while on the other hand, if the man who commits suicide is putting a question to nature, an experiment, to find out what life is like after death, ' it is a clumsy experiment to make ; for it does away with the identity of the very consciousness that is to hear the answer '.[5] (As a matter of fact,

---

[1] I, p. 420.   [2] III, p. 394.
[3] Byron, quoted by S. in III, p. 400.   [4] *Ibid*. p. 280.
[5] From the essay on suicide in *Parerga and Paralipomena*, vi, p. 333.

of course, it is in his phenomenal nature that man suffers consciously, and if his sufferings impel him to commit suicide, the destruction of that individual consciousness, which makes possible the awareness of his sufferings, might be the very thing that he desired, irrespective of whether or not he would persist in an unconscious and impersonal fashion. But we will return to this point in a later chapter, when dealing with what Schopenhauer considered the true solution to the tragedy of existence.)

Such being Schopenhauer's conception of the world, it is not surprising that he entirely rejected pantheism. According to pantheists, he says, the inner nature of the world is to be called God, so that the world is a theophany. But only look at the world ! See the suffering and misery, see men and animals killing and devouring one another :—" a God who could think of changing Himself into such a world as this must certainly have been tormented by the devil '.[1] But the pantheists, instead of looking at the world as it is, start with God, Who is not their *quæsitum*, but their *datum*. ' If they were boys, I would then explain to them that this is a *petitio principii*, but they know this as well as I do '.[2] In his short essay on pantheism in *Parerga and Paralipomena* Schopenhauer delivers some telling blows at the pantheists.[3] ' Against Pantheism I have principally only this objection, that it says nothing '. As he very rightly observes, to call the world God is not to explain it, it is merely to give it a superfluous label, and whether we say ' the world is God ' or ' the world is the world ' comes to the same thing. (Though Schopenhauer is undoubtedly right in saying that the mere identification of the universe with God, is merely to give a superfluous label to the former, one ought to remember that the *psychological* attitude of the pantheist may be at variance with his professed philosophy and the attitude which that philosophy would logically demand. As Prof. A. E. Taylor remarks in the *Faith of a Moralist*, the source of Spinoza's actual piety is not to be sought in the *Ethics*, but in the deep impressions of his early life in a Jewish family and community.) Thus, if we start from the world as given and go on to call it God, we have really said nothing at all. If, however, we start with the idea

---

[1] II, p. 106.   [2] *Ibid.*

[3] VI, pp. 104-7. Schopenhauer remarked (edit. Cotta, xii, p. 275) that pantheism is in general no more than a polite form of atheism.

of God as theism presents Him and then identify Him with the world, we commit the absurdity of transforming God into a very imperfect world, and identify Him with e.g. ' six million Negro slaves, who daily on the average receive sixty million blows of the whip on their bare bodies ' or with ' three million European weavers who, amid hunger and misery, feebly vegetate in musty rooms or wretched workshops '. Schopenhauer rejected theism, because he did not admit the validity of the proofs for God's existence and because he considered the character of the world to be incompatible with the existence of a Being at once omnipotent, omniscient and good ; but he considered pantheism to be considerably less acceptable than theism, and declared that the supposed progress from theism to pantheism, ' if one takes it seriously and not merely as a masked negation ', is a progress from the ' unproven and hardly thinkable to the actually absurd '. In the opinion of the present writer Schopenhauer's attack on pantheism is extremely apt : from the philosophic viewpoint (to be distinguished from the viewpoint of romantic natures who do not really understand what they are saying) pantheism is absurd, an example of a contradiction in terms.

The system of Schopenhauer is thus a system of atheistic voluntaristic idealism, if such a strange combination of terms may be admitted—but then the system is itself a strange combination. It is indeed inconceivable that the *Ens a se* should be an endless striving, and it is inconceivable that this endless striving should objectify itself in the phenomenal world of multiplicity and individuality, a world in which teleology exists and intellectual beings are found : the *Ens a se* must contain within itself *modo eminentiori* the perfections of creatures, and, if intellect is found in the world, then the *Ens a se* must be intelligent. If we see a conjuror producing rabbits out of a hat, we may not know *how* it is done, but we presume that the conjuror knows and it would not occur to us to suppose that the conjuror was an unconscious robot, producing rabbits out of thin air. It may be said that Schopenhauer clothes an essentially scientific view of the world, or a hint of that view, in the garments of fantastic metaphysic, and that, when the trappings have been removed, the truth within lies revealed. But the inconceivable is no wit more respectable in pseudo-scientific trappings than in the colourful trappings supplied by Schopenhauer, and the appearance of intellect is no better explained by the pseudo-scientific jargon of the Marxists than by the bizarre metaphysics of the German pessimists. A real scientist will, quite justifiably, omit metaphysics in his strictly scientific work, but a philosopher who supposes that the empirical scientist says all that there is to be said about the world, bar the addition of some grandiose phrases, understands neither science nor philosophy. Schopenhauer himself, of course, never supposed that empirical science can explain all things—far from it ; but anyone who wishes to make out that the essential of Schopenhauer's philosophy, when the latter is stripped of the meretricious ornaments of metaphysics and idealism, is at once truly philosophic, truly scientific and true, shows that he is aware neither of the possibilities of metaphysics nor of the limitations of empirical science.

From the practical viewpoint it is perhaps better to look on the philosophy of Schopenhauer as an extreme statement of the problem of evil and suffering and to criticize it from that angle than to consider it purely academically : at least it is probable that the general reader is more interested in the problem of life's tragedy than in minute discussion of e.g. the question whether or not Schopenhauer's idealism, as presented in the first book of the *World*, is compatible with the voluntaristic realism presented in the second book. The problem of evil and suffering is a real problem and it perplexes many who are not the least bit concerned with the internal consistency of Schopenhauer's system, but who might feel that the latter's description of life, even if exaggerated and too highly coloured or rather too thickly blackened, is the statement of a real objection to theism. Schopenhauer had a clear perception of the evil and suffering in the world and he declined to take refuge in resounding phrases and airy explanations, such as *sub specie æternitatis*, thesis, antithesis and synthesis, and so on. No one could possibly accuse him of superficial and careless optimism, that ignores the dark side of life, and in *this* respect he certainly comes nearer, as he himself claimed, to Christianity than those who speak as if Progress were the one obvious fact of human history and who suppose that ' education ', increase of knowledge, necessarily augments happiness. According to the Bible one of man's first acts was to fall from a higher to a lower state, and the Scriptures give no reason to suppose that man is always progressing towards the light or that development of technical civilization always brings with it true happiness, while it is notorious that Christian writers have often spoken of this world (though they do not, of course, regard finite existence as inherently evil) as a ' vale of tears '. Schopenhauer is thus quite justified when he asserts that neither he himself nor the orthodox Christian are deceived by an unwarranted and blind optimism. It is perfectly true that Christianity is fundamentally optimistic, while the philosophy of Schopenhauer is fundamentally pessimistic ; but they are, despite this fundamental difference, at one in refusing to disregard the shadows in life's picture.

It would be as well first of all to criticize one of Schopenhauer's leading ideas, the idea that happiness is simply negative in character. Suffering is essentially ' deficiency, want, care for the maintenance of life '[1] : happiness is ' always really and essentially only *negative*, and never positive ', being ' always the satisfaction of a wish ', a want or need, which latter is pain. Happiness is, therefore, no more than the temporary cessation of pain, ' the deliverance from a pain, from a want '.[2] ' Only pain and want can be felt positively, and therefore announce themselves ; well-being, on the other hand, is merely negative '.[3] Now, that want, need, wish, desire is sometimes painful hardly needs elaboration : the craving of a starving man for food (before lassitude sets in, at least) is painful to him, the drug-addict's craving for his drug is extremely unpleasant to him, the longing of a really lonely and abandoned man or woman for the sympathy that is denied could scarcely be termed a joy. But is it true that *every* want or need its *ipso facto* painful ? A good appetite is the expression of a want, but if a man knows that dinner will be forthcoming as usual, it is at least no unmixed pain. It might be replied, of course, that the deficiency as such is painful and that it is only the anticipation of the stilling of the want which is pleasurable ; but a healthy appetite follows the normal functioning of bodily processes and it may well be that, though a want, it is not unaccompanied by pleasure. Some people would scarcely admit that being in love, though it involves want and deficiency, is altogether unpleasant, even if it is bitter-sweet. Lessing declared that, if God offered him the pursuit of truth with one hand and the final attainment of truth with the other, he would choose the former, and a

[1] I, p. 406.   [2] *Ibid.*, pp. 411–12.   [3] III, p. 385.

scientist who spent his life investigating some problem without, however, attaining its complete solution, would probably not reckon his life one of mere suffering : the mere search for truth may be a pleasure. It is true that it is the employment of the rational faculties that is pleasurable, and not the mere ignorance of truth or the failure to attain it ; but this simply goes to show that pleasure attends the proper functioning of a faculty, so that, even if we admitted that all want or desire is painful, it certainly does not follow that pleasure and happiness are essentially negative in character. As Aristotle said centuries ago, pleasure accompanies the normal and un-impeded functioning of a faculty and man's true happiness is to be sought in the highest, completest and most elevating and all-embracing activity open to him. Now, activity is something positive and not negative, and the accompanying pleasure is also something positive. Schopenhauer declares that health, for example, is a negation, on the ground that we only become conscious of it when we have lost it.[1] It may indeed be true in practice that we learn to attach great value to health only through experience of ill-health ; but that does not show that health as such is not pleasurable, even if the healthy man has never been ill in his life, or that the pleasure accompanying health is merely something negative. If Schopenhauer's contention that pleasure, happiness and well-being are no more than the cessation of pain were correct, it would follow that, to the man who has never been ill, health is not pleasur-able, since it is preceded by no pain—a conclusion which is patently false. One may meet someone who has never been really ill, but who is yet filled with *joie de vivre*. Again, it would require some subtle reasoning to show that the pleasure the mathematician takes in his calculations is *no more* than the cessation of pain or that the mystic who experiences experi-mental union with God enjoys no positive happiness. A happy and loving family may spend a fine day in the country and they would hardly allow that the pleasure they took in their excursion was no more than a temporary relief from suffering. In fine, Schopenhauer's contention that pleasure, happiness and well-being are essentially negative, the tem-porary relief of suffering or cessation of pain, will pass the test of neither theory nor practice. It may perhaps seem that we have laboured an obvious fact unnecessarily, but it is an

[1] III, p. 385.

important point in the present discussion, since the philosopher's picture of human life depends in some measure, though by no manner of means entirely, on his contention that suffering and pain are the positive factors in human life, whereas happiness is only negative. As a matter of fact, if life were essentially suffering and happiness only negative, happiness could really only be obtained in oblivion. There may be some people who are so overwhelmed by suffering, mental or physical, that they would welcome oblivion as the lesser of two evils ; but there are certainly many who find positive pleasure and positive happiness, and their existence is sufficient to prove that pleasure and happiness are not merely negative and so to reduce, to that extent at least, the justifiability of Schopenhauer's pessimistic picture of human life.

But, though happiness and pleasure are positive, it does not thereby follow of necessity that there is a great deal of happiness in human life. It would indeed be futile to attempt to assess the amount of happiness and the amount of unhappiness experienced by mankind : we have not the means to carry out any such assessment and we should in any case have to decide first of all whether under ' happiness ' we were going to include anything that anyone ever thought of as happiness or only what *we* would recognize as happiness. However, leaving aside all question of the impossible and impracticable, it must, I think, be admitted that Schopenhauer greatly exaggerates the suffering in the world. The lives of the ' European weavers ' of whom Schopenhauer speaks, were most probably not lives of unmitigated suffering at all : hard lives certainly, monotonous and laborious lives, a form of life which would no doubt have been extremely painful to Schopenhauer himself, but not a form of life which allowed no enjoyment at all to those who were brought up to it. Suffering there is in the world, more than enough, but, generally speaking, men and women cling to life, as Schopenhauer himself admits, e.g. when he remarks later that those who commit suicide are actuated by the desire, not to escape from life as such, but to escape from some particular suffering or sufferings, so that, if they had the option of living a life of happiness or of committing suicide, they would certainly not choose suicide. Normally the life of a human being is a mixture of joy and sorrow : he tends to remember the joy and to forget the sorrow : he does not, normally again, look forward to death as such. People may, of course, look forward to death for various reasons, as a relief from great suffering, for example, or as the gateway to a fuller and more secure joy than is attainable on earth ; but normally they do not look forward to a supposed extinction of all consciousness merely to be rid of life as such. In other words, they recognize implicitly that life is not unmixed sorrow, and very many would admit on reflection that happiness has on the whole counterbalanced, and even outweighed, the sorrow they have experienced.

I have made the foregoing rather obvious remarks simply in order to indicate a necessary correction to Schopenhauer's one-sided view of the world and not at all in order to belittle the very real suffering in the world or to gloss over the wounds and tears of humanity. If we think of the hatred and envy and violence, the oppression and injustice, the crimes and sins, the wars and pestilences, the tortures and barbarities, that have stained human life and brought misery to so many in all ages ; if we think of the social evils of the industrial era and of the slavery of the ancient world ; if we think of the world-wars of our own time, and hear the groans of the wounded and the dying, the sobs of the bereaved ; if we see the hospitals filled with the diseased and maimed—how can we be indifferent to the sufferings of men or women or pretend that all is joy in the best of all possible worlds ? No, suffering and sorrow, pain and anguish are terrible realities, and all honour to Schopenhauer that he recognized the fact, even if he recognized it only from the seclusion of a comparatively sheltered life. The fact that the philosopher was in comfortable circumstances, that he never had to struggle for the means of existence, never took part in any war, may tend to make us regard his pessimism with a cynical eye ; but we must not forget that the very circumstances of his life would have permitted him, had he so chosen, to gloss over the sufferings of others with high-sounding terms and specious phrases, as he accused his arch-enemy Hegel of doing.

The suffering of men and women is real, and Schopenhauer considered that this fact constitutes an insuperable objection to theism. That he exaggerated the dark side of life is no real answer to his objection ; something more is required. We cannot embark on a complete Theodicy here ; but it seems desirable to say something on the point, and first of all we will make the following remark. When people bring up the problem of evil and suffering as an objection to the existence of a good God, they mean by ' God ' God as He is presented by Christianity. Now, the God of Christianity, the Father-God, is revealed to us in the Gospels ; He is not presented to us in the philosophy of e.g. Aristotle. If, therefore, an objection is brought against the existence of a God, Whose character is revealed in the Christian Religion, it is only just that reference should be permitted to other Christian doctrines, when one attempts to meet the objection. If no reference to such doctrines is to be permitted, on the ground that they are theological and not philosophical, then the objection should be brought, not against God as revealed in Christianity but against God as He is presented by philosophy, apart from Christianity altogether and apart from even the guiding influence of Christian dogma. One might, then, not unjustifiably claim that the objicient who refuses to allow a reference to Christian dogma in the answer should bring his objection against e.g. the God of Aristotle. If he knows anything at all about the Aristotelian theology, he will hardly wish to do this, and will press his objection against the Christian conception of God as Love. Very well, then, let him not complain, if we refer to Christian doctrine in an attempted answer. If a similar objection were raised against the Hegelian God, no one would be indignant if Hegel pointed to other aspects of his system when attempting an answer : similarly, if an objection is raised against the Christian conception of God, the respondent must be allowed to refer to other Christian doctrines in his answer.

In considering physical suffering we should not lose sight of the fact that the capacity for bodily suffering attends an animal organism in the natural course of events, and that this capacity is by no means an unqualified evil. For instance, if a tooth has decayed, the ensuing toothache acts as a danger-signal, warning a man to go to the dentist : if he felt no pain, his teeth might be irretrievably ruined before he knew that anything was wrong with them. If all cancerous growths caused pain even in their very early stages, mankind would be, or should be, only too thankful, for then there would be a much better chance of a curative operation. As it is, a cancer may grow to such dimensions and attack the system in such a way before it causes noticeable pain that, when it is discovered, little hope of permanent recovery remains. Again, if putting one's hand very near the fire caused no pain, we might find children playing with the fire and burning themselves to death.   Physical pain, therefore, cannot be called an evil without qualification ; it is a useful ' provision of nature ', from the above point of view, at least.   Nor should we forget that a great deal of physical pain, and also mental suffering, is directly dependent on man's free-will.   Normally speaking, if man is to possess the gift of freedom in this life, then the power to choose the right and the truly good carries with it the correlative power to do wrong.   If a man deliberately chooses to form a drug-habit, it is no good blaming God if he afterwards suffers a painful craving and involves himself in misery. Similarly, if a man occupies a position of great power and chooses to pursue the path of worldly ambition and unbridled egoism, he may involve thousands in suffering, e.g. through a wantonly aggressive war.   Again, men *could*, by the use of reason and good will, remedy a great deal of the social injustice and evil that afflicts mankind ; if man is too short-sighted or selfish to do this, then it is he himself who is to blame. Nor should we forget that pain and suffering, though they may—and often do—embitter and sour a character, bringing out the worst in a man, may also, if borne bravely, develop and strengthen character in a way that the absence of all pain and suffering can hardly do.   Finally, according to Christian doctrine, though the capacity for suffering attends naturally on animal nature, in man and beast, God would, if man had not sinned, have preserved him in freedom from pain and suffering by *preternatural* means, and the action of divine grace would have developed and perfected his character with the co-operation of his free-will.

But, while the foregoing points should be remembered, it must be frankly admitted that they do not answer the difficulty in any complete fashion.   God, it might be replied, knew perfectly well when He created the world (such language is, of course, inaccurate, as spatio-temporal categories do not apply to God or the divine knowledge, but we have to use human language, for the very simple reason that we have no other to use) that man *would* sin : He, therefore, knew that by creating the world He was entailing the existence of all the suffering and pain that has in actual fact afflicted mankind.   He gave man moral freedom, but He knew that, by so doing, He was making it possible for a few men to bring misery to thousands. Again, though fortitude in suffering may contribute to the strengthening and deepening of character, it is difficult to see how the sufferings of children who die in very early youth can do anything towards this end. Moreover, a reasonable objicient might say, it is not that we demand that God should intervene to prevent suffering in individual cases by miraculous means, which would be a rather presumptuous demand, but rather that we cannot see how God can be freed from responsibility for suffering and evil, when He knew from all eternity what course human history would take, should He create the world. Now, God certainly did know what course human history would take (not because He predetermines its course, but because all is present to His eternity, there being no past or future in God's knowledge) ; but at the same time He knew that He would accomplish the redemption of the world in Christ, that He would suffer with man and for man, not in His Divine Nature (which is impossible) but in the human Nature that He freely assumed at the Incarnation, and that He would not only supernaturalize human sorrow and suffering, giving man the power to unite his individual suffering with the redemptive act of Christ and to make that suffering of value to himself and others, but would also restore all things in Christ, drawing to Himself the human brothers and sisters of Christ, purified and ennobled by suffering, united with Christ in some degree in His redemptive act, and ennobling them to attain, in heaven, a joy surpassing all experience on earth through the fullest flowering and the highest realisation of their potentialities, both natural and supernatural. It may be difficult to see how the sufferings of children, for example, can contribute towards this end ; but even they will recognize in heaven the place of their sufferings in the plan of Divine Providence and will, so to speak, ratify them, as the Holy Innocents do, who, though but infants, the Church acclaims as martyrs, as united to the Lamb of God.

Even these considerations do not, it is true, fully answer the difficulty : from the human viewpoint at least it would appear that there are sufferings which can be of little use to anyone and which, though not directly willed by God, are permitted by Him and for which He would appear to be responsible in that He created a world in which such suffering would take place. But, if we once admit that a world in which there is moral freedom is better than one in which there is no moral freedom, then we must also admit that a world in which there is moral freedom *plus* the consequences of that freedom is better than a world without moral freedom and without its consequences. The *possibility* of complete and final shipwreck is no real objection (the Church does not assert of any definite individual that he has lost his soul, nor will God demand of any man more than he has had it in his power to give), for what would be the good of freedom to choose God or reject God, if God were eventually to *force* all to choose Him, whether they wish to or not ? It is man's dignity that he can choose for or against God, and God will not infringe the liberty He has conferred. Yet, when all is said, there is a mystery in suffering and pain that the human mind cannot of itself fathom, and this is only to be expected. Granted the validity of Christian apologetics (we cannot argue for that validity now, and there are many good books on the subject available to all), there exists a loving, wise and almighty God and, when the human mind has done all that it can do to probe the mystery of suffering, it can only trust in God and believe that one day the full solution, which is denied it now, will become manifest. To the atheist it might appear that this is tantamount to an admission that the objection from suffering and evil against the existence of the Christian God, cannot be answered ; but it is really only an admission that it cannot be fully solved in this present life. If we know on other grounds that a Being of a certain character actually exists, then we must admit that an apparently real objection to the existence of that Being is capable of a complete solution, even if we cannot at present discern that complete solution. If a man really lives the Christian life, then, however much aware he may be of the existence of suffering in the world and however much he may deplore it and strive to alleviate it, this suffering will not disturb his faith, for he knows that God is mightier than man and that what seems impossible to man is not thereby impossible to God, that God will make all well and that what now appears to be a problem black as night and inscrutable will one day be seen to be no problem at all.

In the eyes of faith all things work together for good for those who love God. He Who brought all things into being and sustains them, Who in Christ has become the meeting-place of the Divine, the finitely spiritual and the material, Who would draw all men to Himself through incorporation with Christ, through a sharing in the life of the crucified and risen God-Man, moulds, as it were, and fashions the human beings that are to take their place as stones in great edifice, in the the Pleroma of Christ, and to those who submit themselves to the moulding hand of God, as He fashions them from within and from without, *all* things work together for good, whereas, to those who reject the moulding hand of God, this moulding, in so far as it involves suffering, inner or outer, of soul or body, is sheer suffering, mere pain, and easily turns to their hurt. This doctrine, that all things work together for good to those who love God, does not, of course mean that the Christian must take no steps to alleviate the sufferings of himself or others : on the contrary, he should do all in his power to reduce that which is, the Faith teaches, ultimately the consequence of sin, while at the same time, so far as he personally is concerned, he must be ready to discern the moulding hand of God and to accept positively the suffering which he has reason to believe that God wills him to accept, either because he *cannot* escape the suffering or because God impels him to seek a closer union with Christ in the sacrificial aspect of His life on earth. That all things work together for good is a belief of Christians ; but Christianity adds, ' to those who love God ' ; and we do not love God, if, under the pretext that all things work together for good and subserve the end of Divine Providence, we are blind and deaf to the sufferings of our fellow-men, inactive in face of the pain of the world. Yet both man's attempt to alleviate suffering and that suffering itself, suffering which cannot be fully alleviated in this world, enter into the Divine Plan, as creation moves forward to its appointed goal, as the fulness of Christ is realized in His mystical Body, until that day when the Divine Idea will be revealed to all the world.

In conclusion we may point out that, while Schopenhauer is justified in speaking of the incomplete and transitory nature of human happiness, he is wrong in his belief that real and lasting happiness is impossible for man. If man cannot find complete and lasting satisfaction in finite goods, this is not because happiness is inaccessible or even because finite goods are not goods at all (they are) ; nor is it because the human will is a revelation of the insatiable craving of the metaphysical

Will, but because man, so puny in the quantitative order, is yet too great to be fully satisfied with anything less than the Infinite Good. Discontent with finite goods, ennui, boredom and weariness, disillusionment, represent, as it were, the constant invitation of God, whereby He would lead men to realize their true vocation and to seek complete happiness in Him. He has called us *ut filii Dei nominemur et simus*, and the Father does not will that His children should mistake the passing for the abiding, the partial for the complete, the wayside hut for the home. ' Thou hast made us for Thyself, O God, and our hearts can find no rest, until they rest in Thee '.

CHAPTER V

THE PARTIAL ESCAPE : ART

OUT OF THE FUTILE life of desiring and willing and striving Schopenhauer offers two means of escape, the one affording a temporary respite from the slavery of the will, the other a lasting relief through the denial of the will. The former path of escape lies through art, the latter through ethical renunciation. With the philosopher's ethical doctrine I shall deal in another chapter : in the present chapter I shall treat of his metaphysic of art. I say ' metaphysic of art ' since Schopenhauer does not merely make critical observations on styles of art or on æsthetic appreciation, but welds his theory of art into his philosophical system in such a way that it forms an integral part of that system, the theory including a doctrine as to the metaphysical foundations of art. As with Schelling and Hegel, so with Schopenhauer, the æsthetic theory is not something extraneous to the system, something added to it, the fruit of a side-line or hobby on the philosopher's part, but rather a stage in the system's development. Yet this does not necessarily mean that all that Schopenhauer has to say on the subject of art stands or falls with the system as a whole : it may well be that individual observations and points of treatment are of intrinsic value in themselves, quite apart from the relation of the æsthetic theory as a whole to the philosophical system.

As this book, however, is an exposition of the philosophy of Schopenhauer and not a work of art criticism, it is necessary to dwell on the philosophical side of his æsthetic theory at the expense of its purely artistic aspect.

Will, as mentioned before, objectifies itself immediately in the Platonic Ideas. (I use this term because Schopenhauer uses it : it is Schopenhauer's theory that is being discussed, and not the historic Plato's.) These Ideas are the grades of objectification of the Will, considered as anterior to multiplicity ; they are the species, ' the original unchanging forms and qualities of all natural bodies, both organized and unorganized, and also the general forces which reveal themselves according to natural laws '[1] ; they stand to individual phenomena as archetypes to copies. The idea is itself beyond space and time, the forms of individuality and multiplicity, being eternal and unchanged. According to Schopenhauer, ' the principle of sufficient reason has for it no meaning '[2]. It is a little difficult to see how in this case the Idea can be related to Will on the one hand (as a grade of objectification) or to multiple phenomena on the other (expressing itself in innumerable individuals and particulars) ; but, as it is in any case very difficult to see how the Will, that eternal striving, could manifest itself objectively in the Platonic Ideas at all, it is perhaps best to leave the question of the possibility of the Ideas on Schopenhauer's premisses and proceed (*possibilitate data, non concessa*) to expound what he has to say about them.

The Idea is eternal ; but the species, taken empirically, endures throughout its succeeding individual members. The Idea is not, then, to be identified with the species of e.g., man or dog, as known in the succeeding individual phenomena of these species : the latter, the temporally enduring species, is ' the empirical correlative of the Idea '[3]. In this point, therefore, the Schopenhauerian Idea does indeed resemble the Platonic Idea, in that neither is simply the *forma substantialis* or *specifica* of the man Tom or the dog Fido, but is the eternal archetype. This indeed makes it all the more difficult to determine the exact status of Schopenhauer's Ideas. We have the metaphysical Will, the *Ding-an-sich* on the one hand and, on the other, the world ' as Idea ', the phenomenal world of multiple subjects and objects :

[1] I, p. 219.   [2] *Ibid.*, p. 220.   [3] III, p. 123.

what place remains for the Platonic Ideas? They are not the noumenon itself, for the latter is undivided unity and, though each Idea is itself undivided, there are many Ideas, being the grades of Will's objectification. Yet they cannot be said strictly to be phenomena, to belong to the world ' as idea ', for they are unaffected by the principle that governs the phenomenal world, the object for a subject. They constitute a sort of half-way house ; but the assertion of such an intermediary sphere seems to the writer quite unjustified. Still, as it is difficult to see how there could be *any* objectification of Will, we will refrain from pressing the point. Plato's idea of an exemplary Absolute is a profound and luminous theory ; but that does not mean that Schopenhauer was justified in importing Platonism into his philosophy of Will, though as this importation enabled him to develop a most interesting æsthetic theory, in which passages of great beauty occur, we may well forgive him this transgression.

' The Idea ', says Schopenhauer, ' is the species, but not the genus ',[1] for, while the former are nature's work, the latter are man's work, mere concepts. ' There are *species naturales*, but only *genera logica* '. Ideas may also be described as *universalia ante rem*, in distinction from mere universal concepts, which are *universalia post rem*.[2] The Idea as such is undivided, but it is broken up into the multiplicity of individuals, not in itself, but through the perception of the perceiving subject. The latter, if gifted with reason (i.e., man), then restores the unity through rational reflection in the form of the universal concept ; but this concept, though possessing the same extension as the Idea, is only *abstract*. The Idea as such exists anteriorly to the activity of reason, and it is not apprehended immediately by reason : it is perceived or intuited. It is object, object for a subject, but it has not yet assumed the subordinate forms of phenomenality, which are included in the principle of sufficient reason. It is thus the immediate and most adequate objectivity of Will, and, if we were freed from the conditions of knowledge that bear upon us as individuals, we should contemplate only Ideas : our world would be a *nunc stans*. ' Time is only the broken and piecemeal view which the individual being has of the Ideas, which are outside time, and consequently eternal '.[3]

[1] III, p. 123.   [2] *Ibid.*, p. 125.   [3] I, p. 228.

Obviously, then, if we are to apprehend the Ideas, we must transcend the conditions of knowledge which bear upon us as individuals. One might expect that this would be beyond the power of any human being ; but Schopenhauer is equal to the occasion and is ready to postulate a mode of immediate apprehension ' by virtue of which the subject, so far as it knows an Idea, is no more individual '.[1] Knowledge, as I said in an earlier chapter, is, according to its origin and nature, bound to the service of the will and proceeds in accordance with the principle of sufficient reason, apprehending objects as related to one another in space, time and causality, and apprehending them as related to the will of the subject as an individual. In the case of the brutes this subjection of knowledge to the will, to desire, is never, and never can be, transcended ; but in the case of man it is possible for him to transcend such ' interested ' knowledge. His knowledge may break free from the service of the will, and he then becomes the ' pure, will-less subject of knowledge, which no longer traces relations in accordance with the principle of sufficient reason, but rests in fixed contemplation of the object presented to it, out of its connection with all others, and rises into it '.[2] He ' ceases to consider the where, the when, the why, and the whither of things, and looks simply and solely at the *what* ', losing himself, as it were, in the object, forgetting his own individuality, and becoming the clear mirror of the object, or even fused into one with the object. In such ' perception ' he is no longer individual, but the ' *pure, will-less, painless, timeless subject of knowledge* '[3] :   the individual as such knows not Ideas. In other words, in this form of knowledge man no longer regards things as particular objects standing in a relation to one another and to his will, as related to desire, but contemplates only the essential in an object, the Idea ; and in this contemplation he no longer desires or hates, but only *contemplates*, as pure subject of knowledge. He is thus lifted out of the slavery of the will, of desire, and becomes the impersonal spectator or contemplator of the eternal Idea, manifested in the object before him. For the time being, therefore, for the duration of his objective contemplation, he escapes from the servitude of the will : but it is, as it were, an island on the river, where the voyager may disembark

[1] I, p. 228.   [2] *Ibid.*, p. 230   [3] *Ibid.*, p. 231.

for a short while, before continuing on his journey, or' an oasis in the desert, where the traveller may enjoy shade and cool and refreshment, before going on his weary way over the burning sands under the pitiless eastern sun. Science never rests in an attained end, a fresh goal, a new discovery always draws the scientist on ; history is unceasing and never reaches completion ; but art grasps finality, expresses the adequate objectivity of the Will ', plucks the object of its contemplation out of the stream of the world's course, and has it isolated before it ', ' is everywhere at its goal '.[1] Æsthetic satisfaction, which affords a partial and temporary escape from desire and which consists in the apprehension of the Ideas, is facilitated both by the fact that in the work of art the unessential is eliminated and by the fact that the perceived object, the work of art, is unrelated to desire and so does not rouse the will but enables the beholder to contemplate with pure objectivity. To put it crudely, a man who sees a fine ripe apple lying on a plate on the table may very well desire to eat it, but if he sees the table with the plate and apple depicted in a still-life painting, he is more easily enabled to contemplate purely æsthetically, withou reference to the apple as a desirable comestible. Of course, he could contemplate the real apple too from a purely æsthetic standpoint (the artist himself does this) ; but the fact that he knows that the apple in the painting is not a real apple and cannot be eaten, *facilitates* a purely æsthetic contemplation, facilitates his liberation from the slavery of the will.

Kant had spoken of ' the pure disinterested satisfaction in judgments of taste ' in the *Critique of Judgment*, and Schopenhauer developed what Kant had already noted and incorporated it into his philosophical system. The Kantian influence is an undoubted fact, and Schopenhauer, of course, was quite aware of the fact ; but it would be rash to conclude to an Hegelian influence on the purely verbal ground that both Schopenhauer and Hegel speak of the Idea in connection with art. The work of art, according to Schopenhauer, is the expression of the artist's apprehension of the Idea and for Hegel too it is the sensuous manifestation of the Idea ; but the term ' Idea ' has not the same meaning for the two philosophers. For Schopenhauer it is the specific

[1] I, p. 239.

archetype, the 'Platonic Idea', whereas for Hegel it is the
Absolute : for Schopenhauer the Idea is eternal and static ;
for Hegel it is self-developing, self-manifesting Reason : for
Schopenhauer there are many Ideas, for Hegel but one.
Though Hegel lectured on æsthetic at Heidelberg, the notes
of his lectures on æsthetic theory at Berlin were not published
until after his death, so that it would be hardly possible for
Schopenhauer to have borrowed æsthetic notions from Hegel,
even had he wished (which is most unlikely !). In any case
it was his Platonic studies that influenced Schopenhauer
and not any hints that he culled from his arch-enemy, Hegel.
It would, however, be idle to deny the influence of Schelling,
who had already utilized the Platonic theory of Ideas. For
Schelling, in his middle period, the Absolute, Pure Identity,
expresses itself immediately in an eternal world of Ideas,
which are the true things-in-themselves. It is the function
of art to represent these Ideas in the concrete, in the finite
and spatial production, the work of art, so that the artist
represents objectively and concretely the Ideas which are
represented only abstractly by the philosopher. In view of
the startling resemblance between the art theories of Schelling
and Schopenhauer in salient points we can hardly suppose
that the latter was uninfluenced by the former, even if
Schopenhauer had already been influenced by his early
Platonic studies. Kant's philosophical theories did not
permit his taking the 'absolute standpoint' in regard to art
and Schelling was the pioneer in this direction, with Hegel
and Schopenhauer as his followers, each developing his
theme in his own way. It is perhaps not fanciful to think
that Schopenhauer may have learnt something even from
Aristotle, for whom the poet represents the universal concretely and not abstractly, like the philosopher. Poetry
is more philosophical than history, said Aristotle, since history
deals with particulars, poetry *rather* with universals (though
not with the abstract universal), and Schopenhauer says
much the same in different language.

Art is the work of genius. What is genius ? Schopenhauer defines it as 'the completest objectivity', as 'the
faculty of continuing in the state of pure perception, and of
enlisting in this service the knowledge which originally existed
only for the service of the will' ; it is the power of leaving
aside one's own personal desires and wishes, in order to become

pure knowing subject, and that for a sufficient length of time, and with sufficient consciousness, to enable one to reproduce by means of deliberate art what one has apprehended in contemplation.[1] It is as though the genius had a super-fluity of knowledge, i.e., more than is required for the service of the will (cf. Schopenhauer's doctrine of the progressive detachment of cognition from will, mentioned in an earlier chapter). The presence of this ' superfluity ' of the power of knowing explains the fact that the genius is unsatisfied with the trivialities of daily life, whereas the common mortal finds a satisfaction in his everyday existence that the former fails to find. Genius, then, is the power, not merely of apprehending of the Ideas, but of reproducing them or expressing them in painting, sculpture, poetry, architecture or music, and so is, to all intents and purposes, equivalent to the power of the great artist. The prominent position accorded to genius, artistic genius, by Schopenhauer, illus-trates the philosopher's relation to Romanticism, linking him up, not only with Schelling, but also with the cult of genius in general, which characterized the Romantic School. His thought on this matter influenced the young Nietzsche, who wrote his *Birth of Tragedy* under the influence of Schopen-hauer's philosophy and who represented the State in an early essay as having the function of rendering possible and facilitating the flowering of genius.

Imagination is a necessary condition of genius, but it is not the same thing as genius. It is a necessary condition, because the perceived objects of the phenomenal world represent or express the Ideas only imperfectly and power of imagination is needed in order to see what Nature was, as it were, trying to express, the perfect archetype that is only imperfectly represented in the perceived object. It is, however, not the same thing as genius, since imagination may be used simply in the service of the will, to minister to egotism, as when a man indulges in day-dreaming, building ' castles in the air ', or writes down his fancies to form the ' ordinary novel '. In the case of the genius his power of imagination is enlisted in the service of pure objective know-ledge, but the non-genius will generally use his imagination to consider some imaginary object in its relation to other objects and to his own will, i.e., in accordance with the

[1] I, p. 240.

principle of sufficient reason. Thus, though ' extraordinary strength of imagination accompanies, and is indeed a necessary condition of genius ', strength of imagination does not of itself indicate the presence of genius and ' men who have no touch of genius may have much imagination '.[1]   Again, genius is not the same thing as mere talent, which ' lies rather in the greater versatility and acuteness of discursive than of intuitive knowledge '.[2]

But the man of genius is not always engaged upon that type of knowledge which is peculiar to genius and in the more or less lengthy intervals he is subject to the deficiencies, and advantages, of the ordinary man. (This helps to explain why the act of genius has been regarded as inspiration, as a kind of divine *afflatus*.) Nevertheless, the man of genius shows a marked disinclination to certain types of knowledge based on the principle of sufficient reason, namely, abstract and logical reasoning. ' Experience has proved that men of great artistic genius have no faculty for mathematics ; no man was ever very distinguished for both '.[3] (Was not Leonardo da Vinci an exception at any rate ?) Moreover, geniuses are seldom men of great reasonableness and are often subject to violent passion and emotion, partly because they have strong and energetic wills, partly because in them knowledge of perception preponderates over abstract knowledge, producing a susceptibility to impressions, which latter they tend to take as guides to action rather than abstract conceptions. Again, since in them knowledge is, to some extent, freed from the service of the will (though, this does not mean that they have weak wills), they are inclined in conversation to think more of the subjects on which they are speaking than of the persons whom they are addressing and are likely to show imprudence in their objectivity.

Since the genius is gifted with an abnormal superfluity of intellect (abnormal, because by nature cognition is simply the servant of the will and orientated to practical life), his intellect ' often leaves the will very inopportunely in a fix, and thus the individual so gifted becomes more or less useless for life, nay, in his conduct sometimes reminds us of madness '[4]. Schopenhauer dwells at some length on the kinship of madness and genius and, among other quotations, quotes

---

[1] I, pp. 241-2.   [2] III, p. 138.
[3] I, p. 245.   [4] III, p. 155.

Dryden (though he actually ascribes the lines to Pope) to the effect that—

' Great wits to madness sure are near allied,
  And thin partitions do their bounds divide '.[1]

The philosopher assures us that in ' a diligent search in lunatic asylums' he had found individuals whose genius distinctly appeared through their madness.[2] The madman, according to Schopenhauer, does not usually err precisely in the knowledge of what is immediately present, but rather in regard to what is absent and past, which he often confuses with the present, thus falsifying the present through a fictitious connection with an imaginary past, mistaking connections and relations. It is at this point that he comes into contact with the man of genius, since the latter also leaves out of sight the knowledge of the connection of things and of the relations which conform to the principle of sufficient reason, ' in order to see in things only their Ideas '[3]. This vivid concentration on the present may give rise to phenomena that resemble madness. (But absent-mindedness, due to concentration on an immediate object of thought, is not the prerogative of artists, cf. Socrates, St. Thomas Aquinas or Hegel.)

Yet, even if genius, in the full sense, the faculty of clearly apprehending the Ideas and expressing that clear apprehension in the work of art, is present only in a few men, it must also be present, in some degree at least, in all men, except in those, if any, who are utterly incapable of æsthetic appreciation and for whom a word like beauty has no meaning, except, of course, in relation to sensual desire. Otherwise men in general would be just as much incapable of appreciating works of art as of producing them, whereas it is quite clear that a man may have a deep appreciation of a symphony or poem, though he himself is no composer or creative poet. With the exception mentioned above, all men are capable of transcending the narrow circle of the ego and its desires for a short time and knowing the Ideas objectively, though the genius has this faculty in a far stronger and higher degree and can exercise it more continuously. The fact that he expresses the Ideal in a work of art, in which the unessential

---

[1] The right reference is to Dryden's *Absalom and Achitophel*, 163–4.
[2] I, p. 247.   [3] *Ibid.*, p. 251.

and purely accidental is omitted, enables the ordinary man
to exercise more easily the lower degree of the faculty he
possesses : ' the artist lets us see the world through his eyes '.[1]
That he has these eyes is an inborn gift of genius ; but that he
is able to let the rest of us see with his eyes is acquired, is
due to technical ability, for which training and practice
is required. Thus Schopenhauer does not mean to exalt
native genius at the complete expense of technique : technical
knowledge alone will not produce a great artist, but some
technical knowledge is requisite.

There might seem, to judge by the actual words he uses
in different passages, to be a certain ambiguity or inconsistency in Schopenhauer's theory of the relation of the genius
to the ordinary man. Sometimes he speaks as though genius
means the capacity not only of apprehending the Ideas,
but also of expressing them in works of art of one kind or
another, while at other times he seems to imply that genius
is simply the faculty of objective knowledge, of contemplating the Ideas, and that the faculty of expressing this
knowledge concretely is due to acquired technical ability.
On the first view the ' ordinary man ', if he is no productive
artist at all, would not possess the faculty of genius in any
degree, unless indeed we wanted to adopt an idea of Benedetto Croce and say that all æsthetic appreciation or intuition
involves expression, at least interior expression in the sense
of imaginative recreation, in which case the external expression
of the artist would appear to be something almost accidental
and there would be really no ' works of art ' in the sense of
external statues, pictures, etc. But this was not Schopenhauer's opinion, for whom expression does not mean simply
interior imaginative reproduction. On the second view
the ordinary man, at least he who is capable of some æsthetic
appreciation, would certainly share in the faculty of genius
and Schopenhauer might agree with Croce *on this point*, that
the difference between ordinary men and geniuses is purely
quantitative and not qualitative. But this would not agree
with the common opinion that the artistic genius is precisely
the man who can create great works of art in some external
medium and that the ability to do this is not at all a mere
matter of technique alone. Technical training may be
required in some degree, but it cannot by itself supply the

[1] I, p. 252.

place of native genius, and artistic genius includes not only the capacity for vision, intuition, but also the capacity for external expression. Other men may possess the vision, but, if they lack the capacity for external expression, they would not normally be called artists. Croce declares that the external expression is merely practical in function, the creation of a stimulus for further internal expression on the part of the artist himself or others, while Schopenhauer regarded the metaphysical function of the work of art as being to facilitate disinterested knowledge of the Idea ; but, whatever we assign as the function of art from the viewpoint of a general philosophical system, whether that of Schopenhauer or Hegel or Croce or any other thinker we fancy, it is surely true that the *external* expression of intuition (be that intuition supra-intellectual or infra-intellectual or what you will) belongs essentially to the activity of the artist as such. The artist regards the production of the work of art as his creative activity as an artist, as *the* expression which matters, not as a mere practical note, so to speak. But, whatever verbal incon-sistencies Schopenhauer may have been guilty of, his real view is doubtless that artistic genius comprises both the faculty of intuition and the faculty of creative expression (which latter is *aided* by technical and acquired knowledge), and that the non-genius, who is at the same time capable of æsthetic appreciation, shares to some degree in the first faculty, even though he is lacking in the second. In regard, therefore, to the first component element of genius the ordinary man might be said to differ only quantitatively from the man of genius, whereas, in regard to the second component element, he differs qualitatively. The specific difference of genius, the faculty of creative experience, would thus distinguish the artistic genius from the ordinary man. That this represents Schopenhauer's opinion is clear from the fact of his admission that the ordinary man is capable of pure objective know-ledge, not only through æsthetic appreciation of the work of art, but also through disinterested contemplation of, e.g., natural beauty, even if he can exercise this contemplative faculty only in a much weaker and less sustained manner than the artistic genius.

Leaving Schopenhauer's treatment of the particular fine arts to the next chapter, we shall now proceed to some con-siderations connected with the main theme of this present chapter, art viewed as a quietener of will, as a temporary escape from the slavery of desire and the struggle for existence. So long as consciousness is dominated by the will, the individual is the prey of thronging desires and can know no peace or happiness ; but when he rises above his personal interests and contemplates the object purely objectively, disinterestedly, apart from its relation to his own will or to other things, he enjoys ' the Sabbath of the penal servitude of willing ; the wheel of Ixion stands still '.[1] It does not matter if the object of contemplation be insignificant, provided that it is contemplated objectively, and Schopenhauer mentions in this connection the Dutch paintings of still life and the ' very insignificant country scenes ' of e.g., Ruisdael. In such æsthetic contemplation, whether of works of art or of nature itself, so long as the object that arouses the contemplation is simply the significance and distinctness of natural forms, it is ' *beauty* that affects us and the sense of the *beautiful* that is excited '.[2] Beauty, objectively considered, is, therefore, significant form, the Platonic Idea presented to perception concretely, not represented abstractly by reason.

If, however, the objects of æsthetic contemplation have a hostile relation to the human will in general (i.e., to the body, which is the objectification of will), if they are seen to menace the body by their power or greatness, the beholder is filled with the sense of the *sublime*, and the object that produces the state of ' spiritual exaltation ', in which the beholder perceives and recognizes the hostile relation, yet, in spite of this recognition, gives himself to objective contemplation of the Idea expressed in the hostile objects, is the *sublime*. What distinguishes the sense of the sublime from the sense of the beautiful is, therefore, this, that in the case of the latter pure objective knowledge gains the upper hand imperceptibly, without a struggle, whereas in the case of the former, the sublime, the state of pure objective knowledge is attained only through the conscious and forcible detachment of the attention from hostile relations which have been recognized as such, a detachment that must be not only consciously won, but also consciously maintained. The sublime is thus not something entirely different from the beautiful ; it is rather the beautiful seen as involving a hostile relation to man. For instance, a man in a small boat at sea in a storm

[1] I, p. 254. [2] *Ibid.*, p. 260.

when contemplating the height and sweep and fury of the waves, the tossed spray as they dash themselves against the towering cliffs, the flashes of lightning, the stupendous might and power of nature, is contemplating the sublime : he recognizes the might and power that could at any moment engulf him, but, forcibly detaching his attention from personal danger and from fear, he sees the sublime beauty in the scene before him. ' He perceives himself as an individual, as the frail phenomenon of will, which the slightest touch of these forces can utterly destroy, helpless against powerful nature, dependent, the victim of chance, a vanishing nothing in the presence of stupendous might ', he ' obtains a glimpse of a power beyond all comparison superior to the individual, threatening it with annihilation ', and yet he remains the peaceful, knowing subject, the timeless spectator.[1]   Of course, if he allows fear to master him, and concern for his personal safety, if he views the forces of nature in their relation to his own particular will, then he ceases to be the contemplative beholder and ceases to contemplate the sublime.

Following the nomenclature of Kant, Schopenhauer distinguishes the dynamical from the mathematical sublime. The storm-scene would be an instance of the former, while the impression of the latter is produced in another way, by the contemplation of mere immensity in space and time, by a high and vast dome, by the vault of the starry heaven, by the eternal mountains or the age-old pyramids of Egypt.   But, though Schopenhauer adopts Kant's nomenclature, he will not admit Kant's explanation of the impression of the sublime. According to Kant, the sublime is the ' absolutely great ', " what is great beyond all comparison ',[2] ' that in comparison with which everything else is small ',[3] ' that, the mere ability to think which shows a faculty of the mind surpassing every standard of Sense '.[4]   The sublimity does not reside in the things of nature, but in the judging mind.   For instance a man who contemplates the might of nature from a position of security and at the same time is conscious that man's rational and moral character renders him superior to mere nature, attains the sense of sublimity.   Beauty, which is the object of æsthetic taste, has to do with form ; but sublimity has rather to do with that which lacks form and the sense of the sublime

---

[1] I, p. 265.
[2] *Kritik of Judgment* (Bernard), p. 106.
[3] *Ibid.*, p. 109.
[4] *Ibid.*, p. 110.

depends, to some extent at least, on moral reflections. Sublimity is thus more subjective than beauty. Kant rather characteristically remarks that ' the wide ocean, disturbed by the storm cannot be called sublime ', but should be termed ' horrible ' [1]: the mind must have recourse to reflections, of a moralizing type, if such a sight is to produce a feeling of the sublime. In practice we would certainly speak of the mighty forces of nature as sublime ; but in truth this is an improper way of speaking since it is rather man himself that is sublime than the object he contemplates. We call the storm, the hurricane, the tumultuous ocean sublime ('provided only that we are in security '), because ' they raise the energies of the soul above their accustomed height . . . and give us courage to measure ourselves ' (i.e. our rational nature and moral freedom), ' against the apparent almightiness of nature '.[2] This attitude was unacceptable to Schopenhauer, and, though he adopted Kant's division of the sublime into the mathematical and the dynamical, he declared that he could allow no share in the impression of sublimity to ' either moral reflections or to hypostases from scholastic philosophy '.[3]

The opposite of the sublime is the charming, ' that which excites the will by presenting to it directly its fulfilment, its satisfaction '.[4] Sublimity involves the will only to this extent, that something which is recognized as hostile to the will is made into an object of disinterested contemplation, so that the feeling of the sublime arises precisely when the relationship of the object to the particular will of the subject is transcended and disregarded. The charming or attractive, on the other hand, draws the beholder away from pure contemplation by directly exciting the will. This being so, it is an abuse of language to speak of every beautiful object that is bright or cheering as charming, for the beautiful object as such is the object of pure contemplation and not of desire. The word ' charming ' should therefore, according to Schopenhauer, be reserved for that which necessarily excites the will. He finds two species of the charming employed by artists, both of which he condemns. The first species, ' a very low one ', is to be found in Dutch paintings of still life that represent objects of food. He allows painted fruit, since one may contemplate a painted apple, for instance, as a beautiful product of nature,

---

[1] *Kritik of Judgment* (Bernard), p. 103. [2] *Ibid.*, p. 125.
[3] I, pp. 265–6. [4] *Ibid.*, p. 268.

without being obliged to think of it as eatable ; but there are other edibles which are painted so realistically that they ' necessarily excite the appetite for the things they represent . . . which puts an end to all æsthetic contemplation of the object '.[1] Schopenhauer instances, rather amusingly, ' oysters, herrings, crabs, bread and butter, beer, wine ', and so on. He also condemns that kind of presentation of the naked human body which excites the passions of the beholder : the sensual is to be avoided in art.

The other species of the charming is a *negative* form (in fact, we would call it the opposite of charming) namely the disgusting or loathsome, a species even more reprehensible than the positive form. The disgusting or loathsome disturbs æsthetic contemplation by presenting to the will objects which it abhors and so is inadmissible in art, whereas the ugly, which is simply the defective objectification of Will at a particular grade, may have a place in a work of art. Schopenhauer is again adopting a theory of Kant, who declared that ' Beautiful art shows its superiority in this, that it describes as beautiful things which may be in nature ugly or displeasing ' (he gives as examples disease, the havoc of war, etc.), whereas that which excites disgust ' cannot be represented in accordance with nature, without destroying all æsthetical satisfaction '.[2] But though Schopenhauer adopted this and other æsthetic notions from Kant, e.g. his conception of the disinterested character of æsthetic contemplation and his recognition and division of the sublime, he developed these points in function of his general philosophic system, a system which would scarcely have commended itself to his eminent predecessor. Thus since æsthetic contemplation is looked on by Schopenhauer as affording a temporary liberation from the servitude of the will, he naturally emphasizes very strongly the disinterestedness of true æsthetic intuition and all that disturbs that contemplation by exciting the will, i.e. the charming on the one hand and the disgusting on the other, is condemned for precisely that reason. Yet though Schopenhauer lays such stress on the subjective effects of art, it remains true that his æsthetic theory is more objective than that of Kant, in this sense that his philosophy enabled him to give a metaphysical foundation to beauty in a way that Kant was naturally debarred from doing. In this respect Schopenhauer parts

[1] I, p. 269. [2] *Kritik of Judgment* (Bernard), p. 195.

company with Kant and takes his stand with Schelling and Hegel, however much he might dislike the thought of being in their company. Moreover, in another respect too Schopenhauer is more objective than Kant. The latter, following eighteenth century writers (largely English), spoke constantly of the 'judgment of taste', and this judgment was for him subjective, contributing in no way to knowledge proper (though it is true that Kant is inconsistent or rather tends to open the way to asserting the objectivity of the judgment, without explicitly asserting it in clear language). For Schopenhauer, however, æsthetic contemplation is definitely knowledge, involving intellectual activity, though of an intuitive, and not a discursive, type : through contemplation the Ideas, objectively manifested, are apprehended by the perceiving subject.

It may be worth while pointing out that, while Schopenhauer agreed with Plato as to the objective status of Ideas (though his metaphysic of the Ideas was certainly not that of Plato) and as to the comparatively unsubstantial character of the phenomenal world (though here again Schopenhauer, following Indian thought, and combining it with his metaphysic of Will, differed very greatly from the Platonic theory), he certainly did not agree with Plato's æsthetic theory. It is notorious that Plato held that the artist is at the third remove from truth, in that he copies natural objects, which are themselves imitations or participations of true archetypal reality, whereas on Schopenhauer's theory the artist perceives the Ideas and expresses them in his work. It is correct, therefore, to say with Croce that Plato ' is justified and condemned by Schopenhauer exactly in the same way as by Plotinus of old, as well as by Schopenhauer's worst enemy, the modern Schelling '.[1]

I have used the phrase ' significant form ' for the object of æsthetic intuition, as Schopenhauer himself speaks of significant forms in this connection ; but it should be remembered that the philosopher's use of the phrase implies a more intellectualist and ' scholastic ' meaning than is necessarily implied by the same phrase as used in some modern writings on æsthetic theory. The artist contemplates the Platonic Idea, i.e. the specific archetype, manifested to sense-perception in the concrete phenomenal object, which latter expresses the archetype only imperfectly. Thus, although the æsthetic activity

[1] *Aesthetic*, Trans. by Douglas Ainslie, p. 306 (London, 1929).

is not one of discursive thought, and though imaginative power is a necessary condition, it is predominantly intellectualist in character, rendered possible by man's ' superfluity of knowledge ', and its object is one which can only be grasped by the intellect. We quite agree with Schopenhauer that intellectual penetration is necessary in some degree for the appreciation of æsthetic values in art, and we agree too that the intellectual activity involved cannot be simply equated with rational discursive thought ; sensitive susceptibility is also involved, since the object apprehended by the intellect is essentially wedded to qualified matter. Æsthetic appreciation, properly so called, is not a pure activity of the intellect, nor yet an activity of the intellect that only accidentally depends on sensitive perception—which it perhaps would be, if the object of æsthetic contemplation were simply the specific form. We do not see how the object of æsthetic appreciation can possibly be the specific form, since we can very well apprehend the specific form in an object without at the same time apprehending the æsthetic character of an object. The ' significant form ' of a landscape or section of landscape may stand out before our eyes without our adverting to any substantial or accidental forms as such. Schopenhauer would doubtless reply (a) that he expressly stated that the æsthetic apprehension of specific form is not the same as a purely rational apprehension of specific form, and (b) that it is not so much the concrete specific form of a particular object that is apprehended in æsthetic appreciation as the eternal Idea imperfectly expressed in the object, the Idea for the apprehension of which power of imagination is also necessary. That this more or less represents Schopenhauer's view is true enough ; but then we do not believe in the existence of Ideas in the precise sense in which he used the term. There are indeed archetypal Ideas (to speak anthropomorphically) in the Divine Mind, but these we certainly do not directly apprehend, whether by intuition or not. If, therefore, the object of æsthetic contemplation were the specific form, it would have to be the specific form of the concrete object, since it is not, admittedly, the abstract concept, the universal idea. What then of artificial objects, which have no natural specific forms as such ? Cannot these be beautiful ? And what is the specific form of a group of objects, as in a picture of still life, or of a landscape ? Schopenhauer might point out that in a work of architecture, which, as he would agree, has no natural specific form, we contemplate the Ideas that are the lowest grade of the Will's objectification, in the interplay of natural forces, gravity, rigidity, etc., but this seems to be very farfetched. What we appreciate is surely rather the order and co-ordination of elements that unify the æsthetic whole and are the reason why we apprehend the union of variety as beautiful. In any case it would appear that external form is more relevant to æsthetic appreciation than specific form in the philosophical sense.

' Significant form ' is ' meaning ' in a sense, but it is scarcely a meaning which can be stated in so many words, since it is the object of æsthetic appreciation, and æsthetic appreciation is not a purely intellectual activity. If we reflect on some personal act of æsthetic appreciation of natural beauty, we shall probably become conscious that that which has been stimulus and object is a certain pattern or structure, a certain formal co-ordination of elements, with due subordination of the elements to the dominating form (*not* specific form), which gives life and meaning to the whole. This form or pattern is not apprehended merely as a geometric pattern of lines in abstracted isolation, but as essentially embodied in coloured surfaces, in the juxtaposition and harmony of coloured figures, which are united in an æsthetically appreciable whole. The coloured surfaces are part of the pattern and any attempt to shed them as irrelevant is doomed to sterility. The empurpled trunk of the pine tree, with its close-set cap of contrasting darkness, may embody a geometric pattern, but it is by no means the geometric pattern alone that arouses our appreciation : in the beauty of the varying and graded colours of a November sky the colours, though they be harmonized and juxtaposed in patterned structure, are essential. In the work of art too, the product of human reason, form is essentially wedded to the material, and it cannot be abstracted and expressed as an intellectual idea, without draining it of all content as an æsthetic form and turning it into a pale and bloodless ghost ; a bare skeleton or scheme, a mere caricature. Form, in the sense of pattern, may be more explicit in the work of some artists than in that of others, in El Greco more than in Murillo, in Gainsborough more than in Reynolds, yet it is always embodied form ; even in the Cubist and geometric pioneers, in spite of over-intellectualization, form cannot free itself from the embodying matter. Picasso in his cubist phase is still a master of colour, while we cannot but be struck by the delicacy and purity of colour in the work of Henri Matisse, in spite of the apparent simplicity of line and of representative elements (perhaps largely *because* of this simplicity). Pattern of line and form may be the factor which reduces component parts to due harmony and relative subordination, welding them into a significant whole ; but it is not everything in a work of art. What would be left of Monet's painting of the façade of Rouen cathedral, if it were reduced to a mere skeletonic framework of so-called significant form ? The form in a work by the sculptor Bourdelle or by Aristide Maillol is obviously the significant element, but equally obviously it cannot stand alone. The intellectual element in art is still but an element, even though it be the element which confers significance on an otherwise meaningless material.

Æsthetic appreciation of beauty in art is, therefore, not only intellectual in character, but also sensitive, and this not merely accidentally but essentially. Hence perhaps the reason why beauty, in nature as in art, does not fully satisfy the intellect, since the intellect is unable fully to grasp it and to fathom all its depth and its implications : significant form is not only significant of itself (in *nature* at least, as contrasted with art, in which meaning and significance are more apparent to us, since the work of art is a product of the human reason), but also of something else, behind and beyond it, supporting it and constituting the ground and origin of its existence. The philosophy of Arthur Schopenhauer cannot provide a metaphysical basis for natural beauty : it is impossible to see how natural beauty can be in any manner the manifestation of a senseless, empty striving, the metaphysical Will. It is true that the spiritual *Ens a se* cannot be the object of æsthetic appreciation in the strict sense, if the latter is essentially intellectual-sensitive in character, and that it cannot be beautiful in the primary (i.e. primary *quoad nos*) sense of the word ; but, if this phenomenal world is the visible (external) manifestation of God, the *explicatio Dei*, we must predicate Beauty of God in an analogical, and unimaginable, sense. We must indeed say that He is Beauty itself, That which lies behind all created beauty, that to which natural beauty points, that of which things of beauty in art and nature tell in silent allusion and hinted implication, the true αὐτὸ τὸ καλόν of Plato. St. Augustine maintained that we could have no knowledge that any given beautiful thing is but imperfectly beautiful or that one object is more beautiful than another, unless we had an inkling of Beauty itself, in comparison with which other objects are seen to fall short, to be imperfect. That we have no intuition of Absolute Beauty and no innate idea in the full sense, is clear ; but the human will (we speak, as St. Augustine did, of man *in the concrete*) is dynamically orientated towards the Absolute, and this may explain, in part at least, the elusiveness, secretiveness and suggestiveness of natural beauty and the dissatisfaction, or rather lack of complete satisfaction, experienced by not a few in regard to all concrete beautiful objects. ' I have been dreaming ', says Professor Storitsyn in Andreyev's play, ' I have been dreaming of beauty. It is perhaps strange, but I, a book-man, a professor in galoshes, a learned bourgeois, a street car traveller, I have always been dreaming of beauty '.[1]

CHAPTER VI

THE PARTICULAR FINE ARTS

SCHOPENHAUER CONSIDERS AND ARRANGES the arts, architecture, landscape-gardening, painting and sculpture, poetry (culminating, as we would expect, in tragedy) and music, not according to the medium employed in each, but according to the grades of Ideas expressed in each or the clear intuition of which they facilitate. His treatment of the arts is thus dependent on his general philosophical position. For instance, all the arts save music express different Platonic Ideas, different grades of the Will's objectification, whereas music expresses no Idea, but rather the Will itself, the *Ding-an-sich*, and so is the highest of the arts. If we are unprepared to accept Schopenhauer's doctrines of the Will and of the Ideas, it may, therefore, appear that his classification and treatment of the arts is unworthy of consideration, and indeed, in general, that attempts to arrange the arts in an ascending

---

[1] *Professor Storitsyn*, by Leonid Nikolayevich Andreyev, Act II. In the foregoing remarks the writer has utilized an article he contributed to *The Modern Schoolman* (St. Louis, Missouri), in March, 1937.

series constitutes little more than a game or harmless amusement. Yet, while his grading of the arts depends on his philosophical theories, and, to that extent, stands or falls with those theories, he makes many luminous and interesting observations by the way. His metaphysics of music, for example, may not commend itself from a strictly philosophical viewpoint ; but the passages in which he exalts his favourite art are full of beauty and can be read as literature, whatever one thinks of the philosophy.

' Matter as such cannot be the expression of an Idea ',[1] for matter is nothing but causality : moreover matter, as the common substratum of phenomena, is the connecting link between the Idea and the particular object. Again, matter as such is an abstract conception : it does not exist precisely as such and cannot be perceived, for we perceive only definite material objects. However, there are some low-grade objectifications of Will, the most universal qualities of matter, such as gravity, cohesion, rigidity, sensitiveness to light, which it is the function of *architecture* to express, i.e. architecture considered simply as a fine art, in precision from its application to useful ends. In regard to these latter it serves the will and not pure knowledge.

Architecture, therefore, brings into clear distinctness, some low-grade Ideas, ' such as gravity, cohesion, rigidity, hardness, those universal qualities of stone, those first, simplest, most inarticulate manifestations of will ; the bass notes of nature ; and after these light, which in many respects is their opposite '.[2] Now, we would commonly think and say that works of architecture exist to serve practical ends, as churches, temples, palaces, law-courts and so on, and the attribution of any such function as that attributed to them by Schopenhauer we would naturally be inclined to dismiss as fanciful. But, though we may not be prepared to admit that architectural creations exist *in order to* exhibit e.g. the qualities of stone, it does not follow that they do not in practice exhibit these qualities and forces or that the due exhibition of these qualities does not contribute to the æsthetic effect. In other words, impatience with Schopenhauer's philosophizing should not lead to our dismissing all his observations on æsthetic as worthless. Let

---

[1] I, p. 275. (Any reader who consults Haldane and Kemp for this passage should beware of the misprint, occurring more than once, of ' casuality ' for ' causality ' and ' casual ' for ' causal '.)

[2] I, p. 277.

us take as an example his assertion that ' properly speaking the conflict between gravity and rigidity is the sole æsthetic material of architecture ; its problem is to make this conflict appear with perfect distinctness in a multitude of different ways '.[1] Most probably we shall not be inclined to attach weight to Schopenhauer's notioh that this conflict of forces represents the conflict of low-grade Ideas, the latter representing in turn the conflict of the Will with itself ; but his observation that each part of a building, that is to be a truly beautiful and unified whole, must contribute to the stability of the whole building and not be a mere useless excrescence, is clearly not a foolish observation, even if it is a fairly obvious one. It is doubtful if we would have much admiration for interior columns in a Gothic church or for external flying-buttresses, had we real reason to believe that they were utterly useless and conventional ornament, that they had no part to play in preventing the force of gravity bringing the roof crashing down on to the ground. The supposition that flying-buttresses serve some useful purpose is probably at the back of our minds, even if we may be deceived on occasion.

The illustration of flying-buttresses, given by the author, must not be taken to imply that Schopenhauer had any great appreciation of Gothic architecture. On the contrary, he condemned Gothic architecture, partly because he considered that the action of gravity is unduly disguised in arches and vaults and that rigidity, expressed in numerous buttresses, towers, pinnacles, etc., is given undue prominence, partly because he disliked ornamentation, e.g. statues on the façade, as constituting an admixture of another art, as something superfluous. The Greek style was, therefore much more acceptable to his taste than the Gothic. ' If one could bring an ancient Greek before our most celebrated Gothic cathedrals, what would he say to them? βάρβαροι ! '[2] He did indeed admit some good points in Gothic architecture (it would be rather surprising if he did not, given Goethe's celebrated appreciation of it), but, generally speaking, he had little use for it and he ascribed the satisfaction taken in it by others as due to historical associations and not to true æsthetic perception.

That works of architecture are generally executed for practical, and not for purely æsthetic ends, was, of course, perfectly well realized by Schopenhauer, and he found the great merit of the architect in his ability to subordinate to an æsthetic end elements required for a practical purpose. But it is the very utility of architectural work that makes the existence of professional architects necessary and so enables a very costly form of art to subsist, whereas lack of utility and necessity prevents the 'artistic arrangement of water' from taking its place beside architecture as a sister art, a place which, in Schopenhauer's opinion, it has every right to occupy.[1] He thus recognized 'artistic hydraulics' as a genuine art, the function of which is to express and exhibit the Ideas of fluid matter, e.g. in leaping waterfalls, cataracts, fountains and so on, as architecture unfolds the Ideas of rigid matter. Similarly, following Kant, Schopenhauer admitted landscape-gardening or 'artistic horticulture' as a fine art, the function of which is to exhibit the Ideas of the 'higher grades of vegetable nature'.[2] Probably we would be prepared to admit as fine arts neither artistic hydraulics nor artistic horticulture, though it would seem rather difficult to give any hard and fast definition which would validly differentiate fine art from what is not fine art.

According to Schopenhauer, 'the great problem of historical painting and sculpture is to express directly and for perception the Idea in which the will reaches the highest grade of its objectification', i.e. man.[3] In animal painting (which is non-historical in Schopenhauer's use of the term) 'the characteristic' is entirely one with the beautiful, and the most characteristic lion, for instance, is the most beautiful lion, for animals have no individual character. In the case of man, however, the specific characteristic is distinct from the individual characteristic (the former being called beauty and the latter character or expression) and the problem of the painter or sculptor will be that of representing both elements at once in the same individual. For treatment of the various theories of 'the characteristic' (as found e.g. in Goethe or Hirt) we must refer the reader to a history of æsthetic theory; here it is sufficient to point out that Schopenhauer was somewhat hampered by his philosophical opinions. Thus, having said that the Ideas are specific and that the artist exhibits the Ideas, he should, we might reasonably expect, go on to say that the painter or sculptor depicts, or ought to depict, the ideal specific type, a view which is far too abstract and for-

---

[1] I, p. 281.   [2] *Ibid*, p. 282.   [3] *Ibid.*, p. 284.

malistic for us to accept. However, he modified this view (as he had to, unless he wished to talk nonsense), and justified the modification by declaring that ' to a certain extent every man expresses an Idea peculiar to himself '.[1] But this peculiar Idea is simply an aspect of the Idea of humanity, that aspect which is specially apparent in this or that individual. Thus the character which the artist expresses is at once *individual* and *ideal*, and Schopenhauer saves himself from having to say that the artist has to depict the specific type or ideal alone. He had too much sense to say this, but his philosophy of the Ideas compelled him to link up somehow the ' characteristic ' depicted by the artist with the specific type. On the other hand this theory happily prevented him from saying (not that he had any wish to say it) that the painting of a definite man must be simply a photographic representation. The artist, then, must express ' character ' (by which Schopenhauer means the peculiar ideal significance of the individual), but the character must not be emphasized to the exclusion of beauty, by which Schopenhauer meant the Idea of man in general, i.e. the specific type, completely expressed in sensible form.

We may regret that Schopenhauer associated beauty so exclusively with the specific type ; but this position is linked up with his philosophical theories, as we have seen. It may indeed appear a necessary association, since we think of ugliness as a defect, a literal ' deformity ', not, of course, in the sense that the ugly is without form (that would be absurd), but in the sense that the ugly does not possess the ' right ' external form. The beautiful would be that which is ' just right ', and the ' just right ' would refer to the due expression of the specific ideal in the individual. The specific *Idea* (even granting that there is such a thing) could not be beautiful in the ordinary connotation of the word, since it does not appear to sense-perception ; but it becomes beautiful when properly expressed in sensible matter. One great difficulty against such a view is this, that if the beautiful is to be found in the sensible expression of the specific type, we could not judge that a particular object, e.g. a particular man, was beautiful, unless we already knew the perfect specific type, with which to compare its particular embodiment. Schopenhauer tried to escape from the difficulty in the following way.

[1] I, p. 290.

He ridiculed (and rightly) the idea that the artist observes beautiful parts, distributed among many individuals, in x a beautiful hand, in y a beautiful face or foot, and then combines them into a beautiful whole. For one thing, how is the artist to know that just these parts are beautiful ; will not the same difficulty arise in regard to his knowledge of the beauty of the parts that has already arisen in regard to the whole ? But, being unwilling to say that we do have, or that the artist has, a clear knowledge of ideal beauty prior to experience and observation, he said that we have an *anticipation* of that which nature is striving to express, this anticipation being rendered possible by the fact that both we and nature are ultimately the same Will. The true artistic genius not only has this anticipation, but also recognizes the Idea in the particular phenomenon, thus understanding the half-uttered speech of nature and articulating clearly what she only stammered forth. ' He expresses in the hard marble that beauty of form which in a thousand attempts she failed to produce, he presents it to nature, saying, as it were, to her, ' That is what you wanted to say ! " And whoever is able to judge replies, " Yes, that is it ".'[1] We are inclined to agree with Schopenhauer that there is some *a priori* inkling of Beauty (not an 'innate idea'), though, as indicated in the last chapter, we would explain this on Augustinian lines and not as Schopenhauer explains it ; but it does not follow that beauty is to be exclusively associated with the specific type. If it were, then the adequate sensible embodiment of any and every specific type should be beautiful, a proposition which, even if it were true in itself, scarcely forms the basis for our actual judgments on beauty. It may well be that the adequate embodiment of *some* specific types is necessarily beautiful ; but beauty, if objective, would seem to stand on its own feet, and to be more directly a question of ' significant form ' (which is not precisely the same as substantial form), *splendor ordinis*, harmonious union in variety, etc. If the statue of a man by a great Greek sculptor is objectively beautiful, this is surely much more a matter of the formal arrangement, design, pattern and harmony of lines and curves than of the adequate embodiment of the specific type. For with what right do we say that a Greek is objectively more beautiful than a Chinese, a European than a Negro type ? ' If even the Gulf of Naples has its

[1] I, p. 287.

detractors, and if there be artists who declare it inexpressive, preferring the "gloomy firs", the "clouds and perpetual north winds" of northern seas, is it really possible that such relativity does not exist for the human body, source of the most varied suggestions?'[1] If we wish to affirm the objectivity of beauty in relation to the human body, for instance, and at the same time to avoid arbitrary judgments, it would seem that we must find the foundation of that beauty in formal elements which are not necessarily and exclusively connected with the specific type.

According to Schopenhauer, "in sculpture beauty and grace are the principal things : but in painting expression, passion and character predominate ; therefore just so much of the claims of beauty must be neglected ',[2] since the perfect beauty which is demanded in sculpture would, in painting, produce monotony. (Here again we see the unfortunate and exclusive association of beauty with the specific type, for Schopenhauer implies that the more the 'characteristic', in the sense of elements peculiar to the individual, prevails, the less beauty there is.) It is on this account that ugly faces and emaciated figures are acceptable in a painting (as in Domenichino's painting of the dying St. Jerome), while emaciation in a sculptured figure is repulsive. Linking this up with his philosophic views, Schopenhauer declares that sculpture is suitable for the affirmation of the will to live (and so was the art of the ancients), whereas painting is more suitable for the denial of the will to live (and so has been the art of the Christian era). It is hardly worth while discussing this theme, since, if one quoted a statue of a dying or tortured man, it would always be open to the philosopher to declare that, though the execution was masterly, the subject was unsuitable for sculpture (which he does declare in reference to the emaciated figure of St. John the Baptist by Donatello), or that the portrayal of the dying men exhibited his will to live. In any case, if there was truth in Schopenhauer's contention that some subjects are more suitable for painting, others for sculpture, it would be far more likely to depend on difference of medium and other factors intrinsic to art as such than on metaphysical considerations, however exalted.

However, in spite of his philosophy of art, Schopenhauer insisted that the Idea of man must be unfolded by the painter

---

[1] *Aesthetic*, Croce, p. 106.　　　　[2] III, p. 193.

through the portrayal of individuals in various scenes, events and actions, which, even if seemingly trivial on occasion, acquire significance through the very fact that they are the means whereby the Idea is exhibited to perception. It is a mistake, he says, to look down on the Dutch School, because its painters often represent events and objects of ordinary life, for an event may be outwardly insignificant (e.g. bearing no obvious relation to world-history), yet inwardly significant at the same time, in that it reveals in some way the Idea of man. The scenes and events that make up the lives of millions of men afford, by their manifold variety, a rich material for exhibiting the many-sidedness of the Idea of man. Indeed, ' to fix the fleeting, ever-changing world in the enduring picture of a single event, which yet represents the whole, is an achievement of the art of painting by which it seems to bring time itself to a standstill, for it raises the individual to the Idea of its species '.[1]

Since art exists for the direct presentation of the Idea to perception and has its root in intuition of the Idea, a form of art which starts with an abstract and non-perceptible concept and is designed to lead the beholder's mind to this abstract conception, is condemned by Schopenhauer as no true art. Sculptural and pictorial *allegories* are, therefore, rejected, as being ' nothing but hieroglyphics ' : ' the picture or statue is intended to accomplish here what is accomplished far more fully by a book '.[2]   That allegorical works of art (he instances, e.g. Correggio's ' Night ' and Poussin's ' Hours ') may be fine works of art, he does not deny ; but the artistic value they possess does not belong to them as allegories. Still more is *Symbolism* to be rejected, by which Schopenhauer means the employment of purely conventional signs to signify concepts, as yellow may be used to signify falseness, blue to signify fidelity.   However useful the employment of such symbols may be in ordinary life (as in the use of the sign of a bush to indicate a tavern), it is foreign to art.   Schopenhauer recognizes that Winckelmann held a contrary opinion, speaking in favour of allegory, but points out that a man may have a real appreciation for, and a sound judgment of, artistic beauty, without being able to give an abstract and philosophical explanation of the nature of the beautiful, just as a man may have a sound judgment in regard to particular cases of conscience, without

[1] I, p. 298.   [2] *Ibid.*, p. 306.

being really versed in moral philosophy. This is, of course, quite true, but it is a little amusing to find him ascribing Winckelmann's views on allegory to his ' peculiár metaphysic of the beautiful '. This may be quite true, but it is obviously a charge that could be brought against Schopenhauer himself, even if his judgment concerning the non-desirability of allegory in painting and sculpture was correct.[1]

Poetry also has as its aim the revelation of the Ideas. It is true that in poetry the words communicate directly only abstract conceptions, but the intention of the poet is to make the hearer or reader perceive ' the Ideas of life ' in the perceptible ' representatives ' of the concepts, i.e. in individual things. This necessitates the use of the reader's own imagination, and in the Supplement[2] he defines poetry as ' the art of bringing the imagination into play by means of words '. How does the poet arrange the abstract concepts, which are the immediate material of poetry as of prose, in such a way as to stimulate the reader's imagination? By means of the epithets he employs he narrows down, as it were, the universal concept towards the sphere of perception, thus enabling the reader, through the assistance of his own imagination, to apprehend the Idea in the perceptible object. Schopenhauer gives two examples, one from Homer, the other from Goethe. The text of the latter is :

> *Ein sanfter Wind vom blauen Himmel weht,*
> *Die Myrte still und hoch der Lorbeer steht.*[3]

Although he does not apply his principles to the quotations in detail, it is quite clear what Schopenhauer means. If the poet, for example, merely said ' heaven ' or ' sky ', it would not have the same effect on the imagination as ' blue sky ', the epithet ' blue ' immediately conjuring up before the imagination the Italian sky. Similarly ' wind ' or ' breeze ' by itself is obviously much more general than ' a soft breeze ' or ' a gentle breeze '. The two lines together bring before the imagination the sunlit Italian scene, with the breeze scarcely moving the myrtles and laurels under the cloudless blue sky. That the use of epithets aids the imagination in this way is undeniable, and the truth of Schopenhauer's

---

[1] He allowed allegory, metaphor, etc., in *poetry*, as poetry starts from the conception.

[2] III, p. 200.

[3] I, p. 314. Cf. *Goethes Werke*, I, p. 169 (Stuttgart, 1857).

contention is not vitiated by his extravagant notion that the ultimate aim is the apprehension of the Idea in the perceptible.

It is interesting to note in passing that Schopenhauer asserts as one of the functions of rhythm and rhyme that of producing a ' blind consent to what is read prior to any judgment ', which ' gives the poem a certain emphatic power of convincing independent of all reasons '.[1] This assertion may sound rather far-fetched at first hearing ; but reflection will show perhaps that there is something in it. The metre, the poetical form of Lucretius' *De Rerum Natura*, for example, carries us on, and, unless we are reading the poem from a strictly philosophical standpoint, we do not stop every moment to say to ourselves, ' He has not proved that point ', or ' How does he know that the soul is made of atoms ? ' or ' What brought about the collision of atoms ? ' Similarly, we can and do read Milton's *Paradise Lost* as a great epical work, without troubling much about the precise theological opinions displayed. It may be said, ' Well, one knows it is only poetry '. Precisely, and is it not the poetical form to a great extent that enables us to take a detached and æsthetic standpoint ?

From the fact that poetry has concepts as its immediate material, it follows that its province is very extensive, so that it can represent the Ideas of all grades of the Will's objectification ; but its principal object is the representation of man as he expresses himself ' through a series of actions, and the accompanying thoughts and emotions '.[2] History indeed also treats of man ; but it is concerned with the truth of the particular phenomena as such, whereas poetry is concerned with the truth of the Idea, which is found in no particular phenomenon, yet speaks for them all. ' The poet from deliberate choice represents significant characters in significant situations ; the historian takes both as they come '.[3] The historian's treatment follows the principle of sufficient reason and he only takes notice of connections, of what has results and consequences, whereas the poet comprehends the Idea, the inner nature of man, apart from all relations and without reference to time. The historian does not, Schopenhauer admits, entirely lose to view the inner nature and significance of the phenomena he considers : but, ' however paradoxical

---

[1] I, p. 314.   [2] *Ibid.*, p. 315.   [3] *Ibid.*, p. 316.

it may sound, far more really genuine inner truth is to be attributed to poetry than to history '.[1] The very character of Schopenhauer's metaphysic precluded him, of course, from attributing any great value to history ; the whole world is Maya and it is by no means the progressive development or manifestation of Reason, as Hegel, that ' intellectual Caliban ' and ' sophist ', fondly imagined. The attempt to comprehend world-history as a planned whole is the special contribution of the ' Hegelian pseudo-philosophy, everywhere so pernicious and stupefying to the mind ', and the Hegelians would do well to learn from Plato that the passing, transitory and essentially changing phenomena are not the object of philosophy.[2] Schopenhauer also quotes Aristotle's dictum in the *Poetics*, that poetry is more philosophic than history.[3]

The genuine poet can be recognized by the unforced and natural character of his rhymes, which appear as if by divine arrangement, his thoughts coming to him in rhyme, whereas the prosaic man seeks the rhyme for his thought, and the bungler has to seek the thought for the rhyme. As to classical and romantic poetry the distinction, says Schopenhauer, depends on this fact, that the classical poet chooses only natural and purely human motives, whereas the romantic poet loves also to introduce artificial, conventional and imaginary motives such as those which spring from the ' Christian myths ', from the ' chivalrous over-strained fantastical law of honour ', from ' the absurd and ludicrous Germano-Christian veneration of women ', or from ' doting and mooning hyperphysical amorousness '.[4] The distinction is in fact analogous to that between Greek and Gothic.

Lyrical poetry is distinguished by its subjectivity, by the fact that what is therein represented is none other than the representer himself. In the song, for instance, the poet perceives his own emotional state vividly and describes it, and since man's inner nature is unaffected by the passage of centuries, genuine lyrical poetry always retains its freshness and can be read with pleasure after thousands of years. We cannot dictate to the poet *what* states of mind he is to represent, for he may sing of voluptuousness just as well as of mystical experience : ' he is the mirror of mankind ', and brings to its consciousness what it feels and does.'[5] Thus, Schopenhauer

[1] I, p. 316.   [2] III, pp. 224–5.   [3] *Ibid.*, p. 220.
[4] *Ibid.*, p. 209.   [5] I, p. 322.

J

would doubtless agree, the poems of Catullus on the one hand
and of St. John of the Cross on the other will always retain
their freshness and appeal, though it must be confessed that
the former type will always have the wider appeal, since there
are comparatively few who have any real inkling, let alone
personal experience, of the states of soul expressed by the
Castilian mystic. Very often the subjective mood of the
lyricist will colour his perceived surroundings and the latter
the mood of the lyricist, and as the result we have such songs as
those of Goethe or of the *Wunderhorn*.

> ' I live not in myself, but I become
> Portion of that around me ; and to me
> High mountains are a feeling '.[1]

Epic poetry is more objective than lyrical, but a subjective
element remains, which finds expression in ' in the tone, in the
form of the delivery, and also in scattered reflections. We
do not so entirely lose sight of the poet as in the drama '.[2]
The most objective form of poetry is the *drama*. It is the
function of the epic and dramatic poets, as of all poets, to
exhibit the Idea of man, but they do so by true and profound
representation of significant characters and by the invention
of significant situations, in which the peculiar qualities of the
heroes will unfold themselves distinctly. It is the complete
significance of the situations depicted that should distinguish
epic and the drama from ' real life ' and the historical
narration of real life. Truth is, of course, required, in the
sense that the characters must be unified and contradict
neither themselves nor human nature in general, and gross
improbability in character or event should be avoided ; but
neither the epic nor the drama should be a literal transcription
of everyday life, for it is the function of the poet to weld all
the parts of his work into a significant whole, rejecting the
accidental and insignificant, in other words, the purely
irrelevant. Aristotle was quite right in insisting on the
dramatic unity of action, but the rigid insistence of French
critics on the other two ' unities ' is unnecessary : unity of
time and place are requisite only in so far as their neglect
would impair unity of action. (Schopenhauer's view on the
matter of the three unities is substantially that of Aristotle,

[1] Quoted from Byron. *World*, I, p. 324.
[2] III, p. 211.

who nowhere insists on any other unity than that of action, though he casually remarks, as a purely empirical observation, that dramatists, i.e. the Greek dramatists, the only dramatists he was acquainted with, generally observe a certain unity of time, i.e. one day. Whatever one may think of the demand for the three unities raised by Italian and French critics of the sixteenth century, it was certainly not Aristotelian, and Lessing is perfectly correct when he maintains that such critics and dramatists misinterpreted Aristotle and erected absurdly rigoristic rules, to which the Shakespearian drama certainly does not conform, whereas it could be shown to conform to all that is strictly demanded by Aristotle in the way of unity.)

Schopenhauer insists that subordinate characters must be real and natural, and that the ability to make them so is one of the hall-marks of a really great poet, who transforms himself, as it were, into each of his characters in turn and speaks out of each of them, whereas poets of the second rank (he instances Byron) transform the principal character into themselves, with the result that the other characters often remain lifeless and devoid of convincing reality. Elaborating his thought a little, we may point out that this many-sidedness, this extensive sympathy, is certainly characteristic of a really great dramatist like Shakespeare. In Othello, for example, it is not merely the Moor himself whose character is drawn distinctly and strikingly ; Iago, Desdemona, and others, are portrayed with equal care. Goethe too does not bestow all his attention on Faust in such a way that all other characters remain simply lay figures or marionettes.

The summit of poetical art is *tragedy*, ' both on account of the greatness of its effect and the difficulty of its achievement '. Given the pessimistic philosophy of Schopenhauer, we would expect him to exalt the type of drama which portrays ' the terrible side of life ' and presents to us ' the unspeakable pain, the wail of humanity, the triumph of evil, the scornful mastery of chance, and the irretrievable fall of the just and innocent.'[1] In tragedy we behold the Will's strife with itself objectified, and in some characters knowledge of the true nature of the world, a knowledge purified by personal suffering, leads them to see through the veil of Maya and the principle of individuation and so produces resignation and the surrender of the very

[1] I, p. 326.

will to live. Schopenhauer thought that he could discern
this surrender of the will to live, this final resignation, in
Goethe's Gretchen, Calderón's steadfast prince, Shakespeare's Hamlet, Voltaire's Palmira, who says to Mohammed,
'the world is for tyrants : live!' Tragedy thus awakens
the knowledge that life, as unable to provide any true
happiness, is unworthy of our attachment, and so leads to
resignation. Schopenhauer admits that this spirit of resignation seldom appears in ancient tragedy, in direct expression
at least, and is more apparent in Christian tragedy, which
'shows the surrender of the whole will to live, joyful for-
saking of the world in the consciousness of its worthlessness
and vanity'.[1] This being so, modern tragedy is to be ranked
as superior to ancient. 'Shakespeare is much greater than
Sophocles ; in comparison with Goethe's Iphigenia one might
find that of Euripides almost crude and vulgar'.[2]

But though Schopenhauer commends ' Christian tragedy '
in preference to ancient tragedy for the aforesaid reason, it
must not be thought that he evinced any sympathy at all
with the demand for ' poetical justice '. On the contrary,
such a demand springs from a misconception of the nature of
tragedy and of the nature of the world, the inner character of
which is portrayed in tragedy, and Dr. Johnson's lament on
the absence of poetic justice in certain plays of Shakespeare
is a piece of ignorant and dull criticism. It is certainly
absent ('for in what has Ophelia, Desdemona, or Cornelia
offended ? ') but the demand for its presence can only proceed
from ' the dull, optimistic, Protestant rationalistic, or peculiarly
Jewish view of life '. One may quite well be a believing
Christian and yet at the same time agree with Schopenhauer's
rejection of the demand for ' poetic justice ' in tragedy. As
far as this world is concerned it is obvious that not all wrongs
are righted, not all sufferings compensated by pleasures, not
all wickedness punished, and to demand a *deus ex machina*
(whether of the ancient variety or a modern equivalent) to
set things right and produce a happy ending is simply to
demand the abolition of tragedy. Those who look to the
drama simply for light amusement can keep away from
tragedy, while the moralistic demand for ' poetic justice ' is
futile and presupposes, as Schopenhauer hints, the non-
Christian view that great suffering must be the result of

[1] I, p. 214. [2] *Ibid.*

moral fault and that the sufferings of the innocent must be
balanced on earth or not at all. Schopenhauer himself, of
course, thought that the individual can *never* attain true and
positive happiness, untarnished by suffering ; but that does
not vitiate his criticism of the banal moralizing he condemns.
However, it would be foolish to labour the point, as few to-
day would maintain what Schopenhauer calls the ' peculiarly
Jewish view of life ', referring, of course, to that measurement
of life and virtue in terms of temporal prosperity which is
shown by some characters in the pages of the Bible (and which
is not in accord with the teaching of Christ).

It is essential to tragedy that it should represent a great
misfortune, but the author can accomplish this in several
ways. First, he can portray a character of great wickedness,
who is the cause of the misfortune. Schopenhauer gives as
examples, among others, Iago in *Othello*, Shylock, in *The
Merchant of Venice* and Creon in the *Antigone*, though one may
feel a doubt if Creon can rightly be termed a character of
' extraordinary wickedness, touching the utmost limits of
possibility ' ; bad he may well have been, but pig-headedness
and heartless pride are more in evidence than diabolic
wickedness. Secondly, the author can depict the misfortune
as coming about through blind fate (chance and error), as in
the *Oedipus Rex* or *The Bride of Messina*. Thirdly, he can
introduce the misfortune in such a way that it is due neither
to a great error nor to surpassing wickedness, but to the
ordinary relations of the *dramatis personæ* with one another, as
when ' characters of ordinary morality, under circumstances
such as often occur, are so situated with regard to each other
that their position compels them, knowingly and with their
eyes open, to do each other the greatest injury, without anyone
of them being entirely in the wrong '.[1] The *Clavigo* of Goethe,
is, says Schopenhauer, a perfect model of this type of tragedy,
while *Hamlet* can also be reckoned as belonging to the same
class (as far as the relation of Hamlet to Laertes and Ophelia
is concerned) and *Faust* (if we regard the events connected
with Gretchen and her brother.as constituting the principal
action). As one would expect, Schopenhauer looked on this
kind of tragedy as the best, even if the most difficult to execute,
inasmuch as the very ordinariness of the characters and

[1] I, p. 329.

circumstances bring the tragedy very near to us and show us that we too might be entangled in an analogous fate.

If the ultimate aim of tragedy is to turn us towards resignation and the denial of the will to live, *comedy* on the other hand represents an incitement to the continued assertion of that will. If it represents suffering to our gaze, it presents it as transitory and as turning to joy, while it makes material for laughter even out of life's adversities. Thus, whereas tragedy declares that life is evil, comedy declares that life is good and amusing. But Schopenhauer goes on to remark that the author must see to it that the curtain drops at the moment of joy, so that no one has a view of what comes after : in any case a serious reflection on the burlesque side of life will convince us that ' what so exhibits itself is something which had better not be '.[1] In this way the philosopher finds material for pessimism even in comedy and the lighter side of life.

Music stands by itself, apart from the other arts, for while they exhibit Ideas, different grades of the Will's objectification, music is a direct representation or copy of the Will itself, a fact which explains its incomparably powerful and penetrating effect. However, as it is the same Will that objectifies itself both in the Ideas and in music, there is an analogy between the Ideas and music, and Schopenhauer professes to find correspondences in music to the differently-graded Ideas. Thus in the deepest tones of harmony, in the bass, he recognizes the lowest grades of the Will's objectification, unorganized nature, while the fact that there is a limit of depth below which no sound is audible corresponds to the fact that no matter is perceivable without form and quality. In the complemental parts that make up the harmony between the bass and the leading voice singing the melody he recognizes the whole gradation of the Ideas, the melody itself, sung by the principal voice, representing the intellectual life and effort of man, for ' the melody has significant intentional connection from beginning to end '.[2] The inexhaustibleness of possible melodies corresponds to the inexhaustible fecundity of nature in regard to different individuals, faces and courses of life, while the transition from one key to another represents death.

However, these analogies (which the reader will most probably consider fanciful in the extreme) do not betoken a

---

[1] III, p. 219.　　　　　　[2] I, p. 335.

direct relation, for music expresses the Will itself and not the phenomenon. Moreover, since it expresses the Will itself, music should not be so closely allied to words that it is dependent on them to produce its effect, striving to speak a language which is not its own, and Schopenhauer commends Rossini on the ground that his music produces its full effect when rendered by instruments alone. (A similar dislike of the subordination of music to words was shown by Nietzsche in his reaction from the Wagnerian opera.) Music is thus itself a universal language and reveals the inmost essence of things. " This is so truly the case that whoever gives himself up entirely to the impression of a symphony, seems to see all the possible events of life and the world take place in himself, yet if he reflects, he can find no likeness between the music and the things that passed before his mind ".[1] In this way music goes straight to the inner reality, the Will, and the composer reveals the inner nature of the world, expressing it in a language which his reason does not understand. If, however, the composer attempts to imitate the phenomenon directly, as known in perception, he does not express the inner nature of the noumenon and produces but an inadequate imitation of the phenomenon. All imitative music of this type is to be rejected, and Schopenhauer condemns Haydn's *Seasons* on this score. (In showing a mistrust of purely imitative music, embodying, e.g. the singing of birds or the gurgling of streams, directly imitated, Schopenhauer showed sound judgment, with which we may agree, without having to agree with his rationalization of the judgment.)

Since music expresses the inner nature of reality, we should obtain a true philosophy, says Schopenhauer, were it only possible to give a perfectly accurate and complete explanation of music, extending even to particulars, i.e. were it possible to express accurately in concepts all that music expresses without concepts. He, therefore, parodies the saying of Leibniz, that music is *exercitium arithmeticæ occultum nescientis se numerare animi* (which is true of music only when regarded externally and apart from its æsthetic and inner significance) as *Musica est exercitium metaphysices occultum nescientis se philosophari animi*. [2]

[1] I, p. 339.
[2] I, p. 342. (Haldane and Kemp give the reference, *Leibnitii epistolæ, collectio Kortholti*, ep. 154. It may be noted that Leibniz states the same doctrine in section 17 of his *Principes de la nature et de la grace, fondés en raison*.)

But such a complete metaphysic of music is impossible in practice, and music itself, Schopenhauer insists, speaks to the heart : to the head it has nothing *directly* to say.   In ' programme-music ' there is such an appeal to the head and such music, as already indicated, is to be rejected.   ' For expression of the passions is one thing, painting of things another '.[1] Music should be allowed to speak directly for itself and should not be overloaded with accessory elements, as it is in grand opera, which ' is not properly a product of the pure artistic sense '.[2]   Schopenhauer remarks that ' the sung mass affords a much purer musical pleasure than the opera ', because the words are scarcely perceived or ' become a mere *solfeggio* ' by endlessly repeated alleluias, amens, etc.   Needless to say, the philosopher is not thinking of the Gregorian chant, but of High Mass as rendered in the Court Church at Dresden, for example.   ' Masses and symphonies alone give unclouded and perfect musical enjoyment ' : the opera adds to music ' shallow drama and its pseudo-poetry '.[3]

Schopenhauer says little of the novel, except to register his conviction that youth is given a false view of life through novel-reading.   In his essay *On Education* (*Parerga and Paralipomena*) he exempts *Gil Blas*, *The Vicar of Wakefield*, and, ' to some extent ', the novels of Sir Walter Scott from hostile criticism ;[4] but he evidently was unprepared to consider the novel, or indeed prose-work in general, as an art-form. Still, we may imagine that, were he living at the present time, he would have a word to say in favour of the more famous novels of Thomas Hardy—for obvious reasons.   In modern drama he would doubtless relish, as regards the thought if not as regards the presentation, the plays of Pirandello, and we can scarcely suppose that he would have refrained from commending August Strindberg for his anti-feminism.

From what I have said concerning Schopenhauer's views on the arts, it is clear that his judgment was often sound and his criticism to the point, but that, like anybody else, he was subject to prejudices (e.g. on the subject of Gothic architecture), while his rationalization of the judgments he made, based as it is on very largely *a priori* grounds, is too frequently fanciful, arbitrary and even extravagant and far-fetched.

---

[1] This (and the *following*) quotation comes from S's essay *On the Metaphysics of the Beautiful and on Aesthetics* (*Parerga and Paralipomena*), VI, pp. 462-3.
   [2] *Ibid.*, p. 464.   [3] *Ibid.*, p. 468.   [4] VI, p. 669.

Nevertheless, his treatment of art, like those of Kant, Schelling and Hegel (different though they may be from one another in many respects) helps to show that a philosophy of art has a genuine claim to exist. If Schopenhauer's philosophy of art and æsthetic was marred through its relationship to his philosophy in general, that was not because of the relationship as such, but because his general philosophy was so largely false. One can no more cover all the truth about art and æsthetic appreciation by a purely empirical treatment of art than one can cover all there is to say about the world in terms of physical science or about man in terms of biology. Music, for instance, can be studied in several ways, but a mathematical treatment, for example, though justified in its own sphere, would afford no complete explanation of a symphony and its function. Artistic creation is a permanent activity of the human spirit and any comprehensive philosophical system must contain a theory of art and æsthetic, integrated into the system. If individual philosophers have in the past approached art and æsthetic from a false standpoint or have applied false principles and argued from unproven premisses, with the result that they concocted a more or less fantastic philosophy of art, the conclusion is that the work must be done again, in a more careful, more objective and less arbitrary fashion, and not that it should never be done at all. The existence of false, or partly false, philosophies of art no more proves the impossibility of a philosophy of art at all than the existence of bizarre philosophies of religion proves the impossibility of any philosophy of religion. A permanent activity of the human spirit cannot be a matter of indifference to the philosopher.

CHAPTER VII

MORALITY AND FREEDOM

IN ÆSTHETIC CONTEMPLATION, as we have seen, the beholder is released from the slavery of the will ; his knowledge is pure objective knowledge, no longer the mere servant of desire. But this release is only temporary, for though the æsthetic beholder contemplates ' the play ', i.e., the objectification of Will, without desire, the time inevitably comes when he tires of the play and lays hold once more on the empirically real, the will to live reasserting itself. Art, therefore, is not a complete quieter of the will ; it does not, to use Schopenhauer's phrase, deliver a man for ever from life, but only at moments ; it is not a path out of life, but only an occasional consolation in life.[1] It is only through the resignation of the saint, the denial of the will to live through renunciation and self-denial that the final escape is achieved.

Before, however, going on to describe the achievement of salvation as depicted by Schopenhauer, it seems desirable to say something about his general position in regard to morality and particularly in regard to human freedom. He roundly declares the opinion ' that the world has merely a physical, and no moral significance ' to be ' the greatest, the most pernicious, the fundamental error, the true perversity of opinion, and may well be at bottom that which faith has personified as Anti-christ '.[2] Furthermore, he claims that it is he who has first shown the true operative foundation and goal of morality. How can the world, as portrayed by Schopenhauer, have any moral significance at all, and how can it afford any objective foundation for morality ? Is not the thing-in-itself a senseless, eternal, blind striving, so that, even if man is able to practise morality, his moral practice will be at variance with the inner nature of reality ? If ultimate reality is God, theistically conceived, then the world created by Him will have moral significance in that man's ultimate end will be Ὁμοίωσις τῷ θεῷ κατὰ τὸ δυνατόν,

---

[1] I, p. 346.
[2] On Ethics (Parerga and Paralipomena), VI, p. 215.

which will be partially realized by moral action. In other words, if there is a personal God Who created the world for a purpose and exercises Providence, the world will have a value and moral significance, whereas, if there were no God at all and nature in general were the *ens a se*, the world would have, of course, a physical significance, but we could not speak of it as having a moral significance, though man could set himself a τέλος, if he found it necessary or desirable. He could even perhaps practise morality as we know it, in the sense of doing those actions which we call right, but this morality would have no ultimate significance, even if *de facto* it increased the happiness of the human race. Now, in the philosophy of Schopenhauer there is no God, and ultimate reality, of which nature is the manifestation, is, at the very least, non-moral : how then can he justifiably claim that the world has moral significance and that it was reserved for him to expound the fact in any satisfactory manner ? Ultimate reality is, according to him, the Will to live and the Will to live expresses itself in its phenomenal objectification in the form of self-assertion and egoism. ' There really resides in the heart of each of us a wild beast which only waits the opportunity to rage and rave in order to injure others, and which, if they prevent it, would like to destroy them '.[1] This ' wild beast ', this ' radical evil ', is the manifestation of the metaphysical Will itself, ultimate reality : would it not then be more accurate, on these premises, to say that the world has *no* moral significance and even that ultimate reality is evil ? And is it not precisely to this conclusion that Schopenhauer's doctrine that ethics culminates in the *denial* of the will inevitably points ? If the supreme act of the moral man is to *deny* that which constitutes the core of all reality, the natural conclusion to be drawn is surely this, that ultimate reality is non-moral, or rather ' immoral ', so far as ethical categories can apply at all to an impersonal reality. In any case it can have no *moral* significance as such : it is simply indifferent to all morality, though its natural tendency would be to produce in man what we commonly call immorality, unbridled egoism, selfishness and self-assertion. That Schopenhauer did not view surrender to unbridled egoism as moral conduct certainly stands to his credit ; but it does not follow that he was justified

[1] *On Ethics* (*Parerga and Paralipomena*), VI, p. 230.

in stating or implying that the constitution of the world affords an objective basis for morality.

In the *Supplement* Schopenhauer says that his philosophy ' is the only one which confers upon ethics its complete and whole rights ' and declares that the problem of philosophy since the time of Socrates has been ' to connect the force which produces the phenomenon of the world, and consequently determines its nature, with the morality of the disposition or character, and thus to establish a *moral* order of the world as the foundation of the *physical* '.[1] The theistic solution is, in his view, childish and unable to satisfy mature humanity ; but pantheism is in no better plight, rather in a worse one. Theism does at least make God transcendent, whereas pantheism identifies the world with God or God with the world, making the world a ' theophany ' in the most literal sense. But in this case everything is divine, excellent and admirable ; nothing is censurable. Schopenhauer will not allow the theistic explanations of evil and suffering ; but pantheism cannot even recognize evil as such and is compelled to justify everything, descending to base sophistry in order to do so. As long as one looks only at the physical aspect of the world (as romantic, poetic pantheists are inclined to do) one may perhaps regard it as ' divine ' without seeming at first sight to be talking nonsense ; but if one considers also the *subjective* and *moral* side of the world, if one considers the misery and suffering and cruelty and wickedness there is in the world, it is inconceivable that such a world can be divine, can be a literal theophany. As Schopenhauer very rightly remarks, ' all pantheism must ultimately be overthrown by the inevitable demands of ethics, and then by the evil and suffering of the world '.[2] Although Spinoza gave a naturalistic account of the distinction between right and wrong, he then went on to build up his rational ethic culminating in the *amor intellectualis Dei*, but such an ethic is quite out of place in his pantheistic and deterministic system. Blyenbergh brought objections against Spinoza himself on these lines, objections which modern commentators, as the late Professor de Burgh observed, ' have almost with one voice dismissed, as those of an ignorant amateur, unworthy of the great philosopher's attention. But they remained unanswered, for the simple reason that no

[1] III, p. 403.　　　　[2] *Ibid.*

possible answer could be given to them. Moral experience is inexplicable on the basis of Spinoza's metaphysic '.[1] But, though Schopenhauer's criticism of pantheism is telling enough, is his own philosophy in a much better situation ? In one respect it certainly is, for in an atheistic philosophy there can be no ' problem ' of evil and suffering, since there is *ex hypothesi* no God, with Whose existence and nature suffering and evil have to be reconciled : the only problem that arises is how to reduce the suffering in the world, if its reduction is judged desirable. An atheistic philosophy is better off than a pantheistic system in this respect also, that, whereas the latter must, if it be logical, justify *all* human actions *sub specie æternitatis*, it is open for an atheist to say, ' There is no absolute moral law, but certain acts will promote human pleasure and general peace or are at least compatible therewith, while other acts are not. It is, therefore, only common-sense to prevent individuals disturbing the general peace and temporal welfare, if the majority are in a position to prevent them, and this can be done without passing any specifically *moral* condemnation on those whom one eliminates or incarcerates '. But, if there is question of the world having a moral significance, an atheist philosophy can afford no foundation at all for asserting any such significance, whereas a pantheistic philosophy can. If the world is God and if the term God means Supreme Value and Goodness (as a matter of fact a logical ' pantheistic ' system is simply monism and ' God ' is an unnecessary label or synonym), then the world is good and all men's actions are good and moral and contribute to the *explicatio Dei* ; but a Godless world has no particular significance at all, whether moral or immoral.

According to Schopenhauer, the world receives a *moral* tendency through the fact that the phenomenon of the Will must exactly correspond to the nature of the Will.[2] ' As the Will is, so is the world '.[3] If we want to know what men are worth from the moral point of view, we have only to look at their fate in the world. What is their fate ? Wretchedness, misery, death. Therefore they are morally worthless. Therefore eternal justice reigns. ' In this sense we may say, the world itself is the judgment of the world '. (cf. the famous saying of Hegel, *Die Weltgeschichte ist das Weltgericht.*) ' If

---

[1] *Spinoza*, by Prof. de Burgh. *Philosophy*, July, 1936.
[2] III, p. 405.   [3] I, p. 454.

we could lay all the misery of the world in one scale of the balance, and all the guilt of the world in the other, the needle would certainly point to the centre '.[1] The world, with all the many phenomena it contains, is *one* Will : consequently, if one man injures another, the inner truth of the matter is that the one Will is inflicting suffering on itself. ' The inflicter of suffering and the sufferer are one. The former errs in that he believes he is not a partaker in the suffering ; the latter, in that he believes he is not a partaker in the guilt '.[2] In short, the suffering in the world is the effect of guilt, of wickedness. Of whose guilt ? Of everybody, of the Will itself ? What does this guilt consist in ? In existence.

> *Pues el delito mayor*
> *Del hombre es haber naçido.*

' Calderón has merely expressed in these lines the Christian dogma of original sin ', says Schopenhauer.[3] Our ' original sin ', then, is the crime of existence itself and we pay for this crime by suffering and death, thus vindicating ' eternal justice '. ' Why should it not be a crime, since, according to an eternal law, death follows upon it ? '[4]

Our existence is, therefore, a crime. But who commits this crime ? The Will, which produces us and which *is* each one of us, according to our inner nature. Similarly the Will, in and through us, pays for its crime by suffering. This inevitable retribution is eternal justice and consequently the world has a moral significance. Now, in the first place we might ask how the Will can possibly be guilty or commit any crime. Crime is presumably an offence against a law and, in spite of his talk about ' eternal justice ', Schopenhauer certainly did not mean to admit the existence of Law or Justice transcending the Will. If he had admitted this, he would have had to change the whole character of his philosophy. Guilt, in the moral sense, presupposes freedom, but the Will is not free. Schopenhauer admittedly declared that it *is* free, but all he meant by this was that it is self-determined and acts under no external constraint, for the very simple reason that there is nothing outside itself to constrain it. The Will acts according to its own nature, and that nature is blind and irrational, it has no moral free-

---

[1] I, p. 454.
[2] *Ibid.*, p. 457.
[3] *Ibid.*, p. 458.
[4] *Ibid.*

dom, therefore, and cannot possibly be 'guilty' or commit a crime. (If it were free and had committed a crime and were guilty, Schopenhauer would be attributing the world to a devil or demon, which was certainly not his intention.) In the second place, it may be pointed out that it would be senseless to say that the individual man is guilty of his own existence, since he is not responsible for his own existence : it is the Will, which objectifies itself in the individual phenomena, that is ultimately responsible, as Schopenhauer admits. Very well, but who is it who suffers, who pays the price of guilt ? It is the individual. It is no good saying that it is the Will that suffers in the phenomena and that all these are one, for, if the individual is phenomenon, the suffering, which the individual undoubtedly undergoes, is also phenomenon : in so far as suffering is real at all, it is the suffering of an individual and of no one else. It would be ridiculous to suggest to Herr Himmler that he is suffering in all the unfortunate victims of the German concentration camps ; it is merely playing with words. But if it is the Will that is guilty of the crime of the world's existence and it is the individual alone that pays for that guilt, where is the 'eternal justice'? However, it is not worth while discussing the point at all, since it is perfectly clear that Schopenhauer's world has no 'moral significance' at all : either the individual pays for a crime for which he is not responsible (and then it is absurd to speak of 'eternal justice'), or every suffering is the result of personal guilt, a position which it is obviously impossible to maintain (and which no sane theist, it may be remarked, would ever dream of asserting).

It might be objected that by taking literally words such as 'guilty' or 'crime', I have made Schopenhauer's doctrine into an easy victim. Very well, let us eliminate such phrases and see what remains. The primitive Force or Energy has evolved into the world as we know it, a world in which evil and suffering predominate (the last point Schopenhauer most certainly held). Suffering and evil follow on existence. What else can this mean but that the sensitive organism is naturally capable of pain and that, while a good deal of pain and suffering are unavoidable owing to the physical nature and conditions of the world and of man, and while man sometimes causes pain and suffering to his fellows unconsciously, at other times he does so consciously. But, as man is not free but is determined by character (a doctrine which Schopenhauer emphatically asserted), no given pain or suffering are really avoidable. Hence all pain and suffering are a direct result of the existence of the world and of man within the world. I fail to see how this theory could possibly supply any 'moral significance' to the world, though it might make a man hate the world and desire his own personal extinction.

The world, then, has no moral significance on Schopenhauer's premises and all that he is entitled to say, or might at first sight seem entitled to say, is that the world is a valueless and even 'bad' world, but that man can rise to ethical heights by denying the world. But there can be little talk of moral conduct, still less of moral obligation, if man is not free. Who would accuse a hen of being immoral or of doing wrong in an ethical sense, because it strayed outside the run, when it was supposed to be inside ? And who would suppose that a mouse is under a moral obligation not to attack the cheese in the cupboard, if it got the opportunity ? Schopenhauer taught that the individual man is *not* free and that there is no 'categorical imperative', and it is only just to admit that he accordingly disclaimed any intention of *exhorting* anybody to do anything. A man's character is something given and it determines his actions. Virtue cannot be taught, and it would be 'just as absurd to expect that our moral systems and ethics will produce virtuous, noble and holy men, as that our æsthetics will produce poets, painters and musicians '.[1] In other words, just as artistic genius is a gift of nature, so is a virtuous character, and just as it would be absurd to exhort a man to become a great artist, so it would be absurd to exhort a man to become a saint. If a man has it in him to become a great artist, then he will become one in act or, if he does not, this is due to some unalterable element in his character : if a man has it in him to become a saint, he will become one or, if he does not, that will be because of some interior or exterior circumstance beyond his free control (which is much the same as saying that he had *not* got it in him to become a saint). In either case exhortation would be quite out of place. This is, of course, quite logical on a deterministic hypothesis ; but facts of life cannot well be bypassed altogether and we find Schopenhauer often

[1] I, p. 350.

speaking of ' ought ' in practice and showing moral indignation which may do him credit but hardly fits in with his
theories. Thus apropos of a book on negro slavery in America
(1841) he declares that the account given ' inflames all human
feeling to such a degree that with it in the hand one could
preach a crusade for the subjugation and punishment of
the slave-holding States of North America. For they are a
disgrace for all humanity '.[1] Even if Schopenhauer attempted,
as doubtless he would attempt, to reconcile this indignation
with his own brand of determinism, his judgment on the
treatment of the slaves would appear to express the conviction that such things *ought not* to be, i.e., that the slave-
owners *ought not* to behave in that way or that others *ought*
to stop them. But there is no room for an ' ought ' in
Schopenhauer's system : he is only entitled to register the
fact that some people act in this way, others in that. What
is the standard in reference to which we can determine that
one course of action is better than another, and, if there is
a standard, how can it have any objective foundation ?

I turn now to consider Schopenhauer's views on freedom
in more detail. First of all, the Will, i.e., the noumenal
or metaphysical Will, is free. Since it is the thing-in-itself,
it is not subordinated to the principle of sufficient reason,
is not determined as a consequent, knows no necessity. ' The
concept of freedom is thus properly a negative concept, for
its content is merely the denial of necessity '.[2] But this negative
freedom, which Schopenhauer attributes to the Will-in-
itself, is no more than absence of external compulsion, and
this is not freedom but spontaneity. The Will is irrational ;
it cannot choose between *x* and *y* : it cannot even choose *x*
consciously. If it wills *x*, it wills it because it must will it
— not from external necessity, it is true, but from internal
necessity, because the Will is what it is. If Schopenhauer
chooses to call this ' freedom ', we can hardly deny him the
right to use the word in his own chosen sense ; but to call
necessity ' freedom ' is merely to find a synonym (and a very
bad one, since it is generally applied to something quite
different) for necessity ; it does not change necessity into
freedom from the objective standpoint, any more than it
would turn my pen into a cat, if I chose to call all pens ' cats '.

[1] *On Ethics* (Parerga and Paralipomena), VI, p. 227.
[2] I, p. 370.

But this ' freedom ', such as it is, which belongs to the metaphysical Will, does not appear in the phenomenon. ' Our individual acts are in no way free '.[1] Why is this? Because they proceed from our characters, which are given and fixed, so that a man ' can never do anything else but precisely what he actually does on any occasion. The entire empirical course of a man's life is accordingly, in all its events, great and small, as necessarily predetermined as that of a clock '.[2] Man's individual will certainly follows motives, but the way in which a man reacts to motives presented by the intellect is determined by his unalterable inborn character : the motives call forth his actions with necessity according to the nature of that inborn character. It is true, says Schopenhauer, that knowledge varies and motives vary with it ; but different motives, though affecting the will, do not change it. ' All that they can do is thus to alter the direction of its efforts, i.e., bring it about that it shall seek in another way than it has hitherto done that which it invariably seeks '.[3] Thus the root-tendency of a man's will, the kind of things he wills, is fixed once and for all by his inborn character ; new knowledge and fresh motives can only affect him to this extent, that they may influence him to seek what he *must* seek in a different way from that in which he has hitherto sought it. An example will make clear what Schopenhauer means. A man may, out of egoism, refuse to give money. After a time he becomes persuaded that he will be rewarded a hundredfold in a future existence if he gives money now. He then gives, but his giving is now determined by precisely the same egoism that determined him formerly not to give. *Velle non discitur.*

Schopenhauer draws a distinction between the *intelligible* and the *empirical* characters, adapting for his own purpose, as on other occasions, Kant's terminology and distinctions. The intelligible or noumenal character is ' the will as thing-in-itself so far as it appears in a definite individual in a definite grade ', and the empirical character is ' this phenomenon itself as it exhibits itself in time in the mode of action, and in space in the physical structure '.[4] This may sound very mysterious and obscure ; but his meaning is as follows. The metaphysical Will objectifies itself in individual wills

---

[1] *On Ethics* (Parerga and Paralipomena), VI, p. 242.
[2] *Ibid.*, p. 243.   [3] I, p. 380.   [4] I, p. 373.

and the individual will, considered as an act of the metaphysical Will, i.e., considered *anteriorly* to the particular acts of the individual will, is the intelligible character. The particular acts of the individual will enter into consciousness, are known empirically, but the will considered in *itself*, apart from its particular acts, does not enter into consciousness, cannot be known empirically : it is noumenal or intelligible, a necessary presupposition of the particular acts which is known only gradually through its particular acts and never directly in itself. The intelligible character, therefore, in so far as it is regarded as an act of the metaphysical Will, may be said to partake of the latter's 'freedom' (Kant's noumenal freedom !), but this does not mean that it can change or be altered any more than the metaphysical Will can change its nature. Every man's intelligible character is, therefore, ' indivisible and unchangeable ', but it manifests itself, expresses itself in particular acts of the will. This manifestation of the intelligible character is the whole conduct and life of a man as known by experience and constitutes his empirical character. The empirical character is determined by the fixed intelligible character and flows necessarily from it, the latter, as it were, fixing the unalterable direction of a man's acts of will, so that, if his intelligible character is of this particular type, all his particular acts will be of this particular type, and if his intelligible character is of that particular type, all his empirically-known acts will be of that particular type, the manifold acts being called forth by intellectually-presented motives, but always in accordance with his fixed intelligible character.

It is by means of this distinction between the intelligible and empirical characters that Schopenhauer explains (i.e., explains away) the conviction of personal freedom. The intelligible character of a man is not known directly to him : he only knows directly his particular acts of will and he knows them only *a posteriori*, not *a priori* : i.e., he does not know beforehand what they will be, but only knows them when they have happened and so have entered any consciousness. It is as though a man knew only the conclusion without knowing the premisses and without seeing directly that the conclusion follows necessarily from the premisses. Hence he imagines that he might have acted in a different manner to the way in which he actually has acted and believes that he is free, that he possesses *liberum arbitrium indifferentiæ*. This belief is, however, a delusion, and the delusion results from his ignorance of his intelligible character and of the necessary link between the latter and his empirical character. It is only by subsequent reflection on his actual conduct that he can come to know that his empirical character is the necessary unfolding of his intelligible character and that all his particular acts are determined. Moreover, man, although a *determined* phenomenon of the Will, is a phenomenon of the Will which is ' free ' and this inner identity of himself with the eternally ' free ' Will gives him an *a priori* conviction of freedom, an original feeling of freedom, which he extends even to his individual acts. It is only *a posteriori*, from experience and reflection on experience, that he comes to realize ' that his actions take place with absolute necessity from the coincidence of his character with his motives '.[1]

The doctrine of an empirical freedom of the will, of a *liberum arbitrium indifferentiæ*, agrees, says Schopenhauer, with the doctrine of the *soul*, as pre-eminently an *intellectual* subject. According to this doctrine man becomes what he is through knowledge : he, e.g., first knows something to be good and then chooses it as such, the will following the judgment of the intellect. According to Schopenhauer on the contrary, Will is first and original and knowledge is added to it merely as an instrument : a man does not first know something to be good and then will it, but first wills it and then calls it good. Therefore every man is what he is through his original will, and knowledge merely leads him to learn in the course of experience *what he is*, i.e., his character, from which his particular acts of will follow with necessity. ' Therefore he cannot resolve to be this or that, nor can he become other than he is ; but he *is* once for all, and he knows in the course of experience *what* he is. According to one doctrine he *wills* what he knows, and according to the other (i.e., Schopenhauer's) he *knows* what he wills '.[2]

From the intelligible character and the empirical character Schopenhauer distinguishes a third kind, *acquired* character, which is more or less what we understand by character when it is said of someone, ' he has character '. The empirical character is in itself naturally consistent, but until a man attains to clear knowledge of what he wills and of what he

---

[1] I, p. 372.   [2] *Ibid.*, p. 378.

can do, ' his path will not be a straight line, but wavering and uneven '.[1] He sees what is attainable by man in general, but does not yet know what part of that general field of possibility is suitable for him and can be realized by him. Accordingly he may envy another his position and circumstance, although these are really only suitable to the other's character and, if he found himself in the other's position and circumstances, he would be unhappy, at least, if he did not find the circumstances absolutely unendurable. ' For as a fish is only at home in water, a bird in the air, a mole in the earth, so every man is only at home in the atmosphere suitable to him '.[2] From deficiency of proper insight into this fact a man may make all sorts of abortive attempts to do violence to his own character, and we would call him a man without character, i.e., a vacillating man, who does really know what he wants or wants to do what he cannot do. When a man has acquired a clear knowledge of his own individuality, of his unalterable character, his mental and physical powers, and carries out deliberately and methodically the role which properly belongs to him in particular, he has acquired character, is a ' man of character ', of strong character. He will not allow himself ' to be led by the passing mood or by solicitations from without to resolve in particular cases what is contrary ' to his will, his empirical character as a whole : he will endeavour to cultivate, employ and make use of those talents which he really possesses and which are specially pre-eminent in him. (Considered in itself all this is true enough, of course ; but whether it fits in exactly with the deterministic doctrine of Schopenhauer is another matter.)

It might be thought that the phenomenon of repentance would constitute a serious objection to Schopenhauer's character-determinism, as implying a conviction on the part of an individual that he might have acted otherwise than he did ; but the philosopher has an explanation ready. ' Repentance never proceeds from a change of the will (which is impossible), but from a change of knowledge '.[3] A man cannot repent of what he has *willed*, but he can repent of what he has *done*, inasmuch as he was led by false conceptions to take the wrong means to achieve the object of his will. To take an example we have already used. The man

---

[1] I, p. 392.   [2] *Ibid.*, p. 393.   [3] *Ibid.*, p. 382.

who formerly refused to give money, but afterwards gives it, in consequence of a belief that the giving of money now will result in his gaining a hundredfold in another existence, may repent of his former refusal to give money, because he now believes that another course would have paid him better. He does not repent of what he formerly willed, namely, the satisfaction of his egoistic desires, for it is precisely the same will that makes him sorry that he previously took such short-sighted measures to satisfy it. He does not repent of his egoism, which is his unalterable character, but he repents, is sorry for, the fact that he took less satisfactory means to gratify his egoism. He remains the same man, with the same character and root tendency of will that he was before. A man's character is his fate, then, as Herakleitos remarked.

Although in general a man's conduct is determined, Schopenhauer admits an exception to the general rule, an ' entirely exceptional case '.[1] What is this exceptional case? It is seen in the ' transition from virtue to asceticism ', when a man has thoroughly penetrated the principle of individuation, seen through it, realized the horrible nature of the thing-in-itself, of which all individual beings are but phenomena, and *denies the will to live*, renounces himself, practises asceticism and abnegation. He ' ceases to will anything, guards against attaching his will to anything, and seeks to confirm in himself the greatest indifference to everything '.[2] This denial of the very principle which constitutes a man's inner nature is a *free* act, and it is found only in exceptional cases. By that surrender and denial of the will to live, ' which fills everything and strives and strains in all ', the Will ' first gains freedom here in him alone '.[3] The thing-in-itself, the metaphysical Will, is free, as we have already seen, since it is not subordinate to the principle of sufficient reason, while in its manifestation, in phenomena, it is always subject and bound ; but in this one case of the denial of the will to live, the essential freedom of the thing-in-itself becomes manifest in the phenomenon. The Will, manifest in the phenomenon, denies itself, denies what the phenomenon expresses, and therefore this exceptional act of freedom takes the form of a self-contradiction, as Schopenhauer frankly admits. In self-renunciation there is ' a contra-

[1] I, p. 372.   [2] *Ibid.*, p. 491.   [3] *Ibid.*, p. 498.

diction of the phenomenon with itself'.[1] (That the self-renunciation of an ascetic is a free act, we willingly admit ; but it is only self-contradiction in this sense, that the ascetic denies himself the satisfaction of certain impulses and desires, while at the same time he affirms himself according to other capacities and desires. If man were nothing but a phenomenon, an illusory manifestation of a unitary Principle, which is essentially the will to live, it is very difficult to see how this Principle could deny and contradict itself in man. If it did do so, it would not be only the Will to live, while, if man denies the will to live, man must be something *more* than the will to live. Hence, either the one Principle is wrongly defined as the will to live or man is wrongly said to be a mere phenomenon of the Will to live. In other words, Schopenhauer is unable to explain, in terms of his system, how this 'self-contradiction' comes about or is possible.)

In conclusion, I shall make some remarks on character-determinism in general. The doctrine of character-determinism can certainly be presented in a very plausible manner. If a man has a certain character (and everyone obviously must have a character of some sort, strong or weak, good or bad, etc.) certain motives will appeal to him, and it is, at the very least, probable that he will act in a certain way, respond to events, circumstances, persons, ideas, in accordance with his character. An individual is not simply man-in-general, he is a particular man with a particular character. But not only is it *probable* that a man will act in accordance with his character (which everyone would admit without difficulty), it is also *necessary*. A human act is not a detached entity, it proceeds from a man, a definite man with a definite character: his act is an expression of himself, his character : it must have a *ratio sufficiens*, a reason why it is what it is and that reason must be sought in the man himself. But when we say ' in the man himself', we cannot mean anything else but ' in that man of that character ', for it is absurd to make a dichotomy between the man and his character, as if the character were a sort of hat that he can put on or take off as he chooses. Moreover, do we not always assume character-determinism in ordinary life ? If we know a man well, we are pretty sure how he will act in a given situation ; if we know him very well indeed, we are certain how we will act. If we

[1] I, p. 371.

have a great friend whose probity we admire, we are certain that, if the opportunity arises for him to execute some shady transaction, he not only *will not* take advantage of it, but *could not* take advantage of it. ' So and so could not do that ', or ' I could not do such a thing myself '—are not such phrases common and do they not pre-suppose the conviction that a man necessarily acts in accordance with his character ? If someone unexpectedly does an unworthy act, of which we would not have thought him capable, we say, ' there must have been some flaw in his character, some weak spot, which I had not observed ', assuming that, if we had known his character perfectly, we would have known beforehand how he would act, that he would yield to that particular temptation and commit that unworthy act. Similarly, if someone of whom we had a poor opinion unexpectedly does a heroic deed, we may say, ' there must be more in him than I ever realized ', or ' he must have a stronger character than I realized after all '.

Now, that we can be pretty sure how a man will act in a certain situation, if we have a good knowledge of his character, is undeniable ; but that does not necessarily mean that he is *determined* to act in that particular way. Self-training and development of one's character is undertaken indeed partly in order to ensure, so far as such a thing can be ensured, that we will react to circumstances in a certain way, in accordance with certain principles perhaps ; but do we not feel that there is need of constant guard over ourselves, constant watchfulness, precisely because we cannot be absolutely sure that we shall in fact really act as we would wish to act ? It is a fact of experience that good men may deteriorate or inferior characters become better, but this is inexplicable if character is fixed and determines a man's acts necessarily, since it is only through his acts that he can improve or worsen his character. If his character is now good, how, on a deterministic hypothesis, could he ever perform those actions which will produce deterioration of his character ?—and yet some good men do deteriorate. Conversely, if a man's character is now bad, how, on a deterministic hypothesis, could he improve that character by his acts ?—and yet some men do in fact improve their characters.

The thorough-going character-determinist would probably say that the apparent change in a man's character is no more than the unfolding of the original character in an apparently fresh direction, in response to new stimuli, so that we speak of a ' change ' in the man's character only because we did not formerly realize all that his character contained and implied. For example, a bad man is converted to a better way of life ; instead of neglecting his wife and children, he now cares for them and looks after them. We might say ' how he is changed ! ' implying that his character has been changed. ' No ', the character-determinist might reply, ' the character is the same ; all that has happened is that in response to certain events or fresh circumstances or fresh ideas a real side of his given character has unfolded itself necessarily. You think it something new, but it was really there before ; owing to change in external circumstances that hitherto dormant side of his character now reveals itself in action '. But what does such a reply mean ? It means that a man's character is given from the start. By what or by whom ? By his parents ? But the parents can only transmit *physical* predispositions, they cannot transmit a soul, since the soul is spiritual and cannot be passed on by generation : they cannot, therefore, transmit the child's character. That the human soul is spiritual we cannot undertake to prove here : we will content ourselves with pointing out that if anyone asserts that the psychical character of a child is transmitted by its parents he is implying the truth of an unproven, and unprovable, hypothesis, namely that the soul is material or that it is a mere epiphenomenon or efflorescence of matter. In point of fact, however, no sane determinist would assert that the *entire* character is transmitted by the parents : he would say that it is also formed by education, environment, social contacts, etc. But is it credible that a character is developed and built up merely *passively*, as if it were a bit of clay that is kneaded and moulded ? Whatever the effect of the influence of education, environment, etc. (and no one denies their influence), the acts of a child or a man have an effect too in moulding his own character. They cannot porceed merely from his character, for it is quite unproven that his character is already fully formed. And is it ever fully formed, in the sense that it is unalterable and completely stereotyped ? Hardening of character certainly takes place, but the soul is not a material object that can be moulded into a fixed and unalterable form. To explain an apparent change of character by referring it to the response of an already fixed character to new stimuli, without any reference to a man's own acts, is sheer dogmatism : it is to *assume* precisely that which the determinist should prove. No one really supposes, unless he is imbued with a theory that blinds him to actuality, that a man's character is ever irrevocably fixed in this life, and much less that it is fixed from the beginning. Phrases like those we have already mentioned, which seem to support determinism (e.g. ' he must have had a flaw in his character which I had not observed '), imply indeed that a man had a disposition, towards, e.g. cowardice, which one had had no previous opportunity to observe ; but they do not necessarily imply that the act whereby a man surrenders to that predisposition, to that temptation, is a *determined* act. If people would only ask themselves what ' given ', ' fixed ', ' unalterable ' really imply, when applied to character, they would be less ready to assert the existence of any such thing, for they would see that they are surreptitiously importing quantitative notions into a sphere where they do not apply and are looking on the human soul and its will, as if they were bits of clay or marble or bronze.

Finally, let us clear up one or two pieces of sophistry. It has sometimes been asserted that the strongest motive always prevails and determines choice. But how does anyone know what ' the strongest motive ' is ? Only by looking at the actual motive under which a man acts. In other words, all they are saying is, ' the prevailing motive is the prevailing motive ' or ' the motive under which a man acts is the motive under which he acts '. If a man were very given to consuming his wages in drink and then one Saturday took them home to his wife, they would presumably say that the stronger motive had prevailed. Leaving out of account the fact that they speak as though motives were bricks which hit a man in the ribs, and pushed him to one side or the other, we may point out that if a man turned his attention away from the pleasures of drink and applied it to considerations concerning his wife and family, that direction of attention was his own free act. If the determinist cares to say that the motive of supporting his family or avoiding friction with the wife was the strongest motive, he must at the same time admit that it was the man himself who *made* it the strongest motive. It would be simply ridiculous to speak as though two detached motives had a

fight between themselves, after which the winner gave a kick
to the man's will or pulled it towards itself.

A second bit of sophistry. If a man pursues money and then
one day gives up the pursuit of wealth and turns to laying up
for himself 'treasure in heaven', the character-determinist
may say with Schopenhauer that the man's character remains
the same, but that a fresh conception has suggested new means
of achieving the same end : the man is still determined by
self-interest. Well and good, but pursuit of self-interest is a
very wide term, which in its most extended application may
mean choosing *sub ratione boni*. Now, the upholder of free
will does not, if he has any sense, deny that a man chooses
sub ratione boni, nor will he deny that a man who deliberately
aims at laying up treasure is pursuing his best interests ; but
what he does deny is that the man is determined to choose any
particular kind of good, any particular way of satisfying his
self interest. If a man abandons avarice for asceticism under
the influence of fresh conceptions, it is *he himself* who fixes his
attention on those conceptions and allows himself to be influenced by them. In other words, if *bonum* is the natural
object of the will, then a man will choose *sub ratione boni* ;
but that does not mean that he is determined to choose this or
that particular *bonum*. Schopenhauer talks as though the
object which the will chooses made no difference to the
character of the will ; but, though a man who desires union
with God because he can find no true peace and happiness
elsewhere, is seeking his own good, there is a world of difference,
not only in object but also in character, between the man who
seeks his happiness in God (and we might add, in 'forgetting
himself' in service for others) and the man who seeks his
happiness in sensual excesses. To pretend that the characters
are the same, because each man is, in a sense, self-seeking, is
sheer sophistry ; nor did Schopenhauer really think that they
are the same, as is abundantly clear from his works.

CHAPTER VIII

RIGHT AND WRONG : THE STATE

THE WILL IS WILL to live, will to existence, and this Will is present, whole and undivided, in every man. Consciousness (unreflective and immediate) of this fact and also of the fact that he is the condition of the object, that all Nature, including other human beings, are his ' idea ', expresses itself in *egoism*, ' which is essential to everything in Nature '.[1] The microcosm, the individual man, finds himself to be of equal value with the macrocosm : he therefore makes himself the centre of the world, has regard for his own existence and well-being before anything else and would be ready to annihilate the whole world, could he, by so doing, maintain himself in existence a little longer. This egoism is based on a truth, that the individual *is* the one Will ; but, in so far as it shows itself in the conflict of individuals, it is based on a delusion, the delusion of individuality, the failure to realize that individuality is only phenomenal and that all are *one*. If we prescind from the extravagances, we may say, then, that Schopenhauer finds the fundamental disposition or tendency of man in *egoism*, which is a consequence of the biological impulse to self-preservation and, if need be, to self-assertion at the expense of everything else. In this way his thought is akin to that of Hobbes and Spinoza. In passing we may point out the inadequacy of this theory. An impulse to existence, continued existence, even to self-assertion, the ' will to power ', certainly appears in man, in some individuals more strongly and prominently than in others ; but equally certainly there is, as the Adlerian School has shown, a will to community. Man is an individual certainly, but he is not merely a detached individual, for he is by nature a social being, a ζῷον πολιτικόν and the so-called will to community is as fundamental to man as the ' will to power '. We do not mean to imply that Adler's psychology is in itself an adequate account of man ; we simply choose out one point which suits our present purpose, a point in which it shows itself superior to the psychology of Hobbes, of Spinoza or of Schopenhauer.

[1] I, p. 428.

The conflict of different egoisms, of different individuals, expresses the inner conflict of the Will with itself. ' We see ' its terrible side in the lives of great tyrants and miscreants, and in world-desolating wars ', ' its absurd side . . . as self-conceit and vanity '.[1] Both history and personal experience reveal it to us, but it shows itself in its most distinct form in anarchistic revolution, when each one grabs for himself all he can get and recks not of his neighbour's happiness. Then we see the *bellum omnium contra omnes* ', which Hobbes has so admirably described in the first chapter of *De Cive* '.[1]

The simplest assertion of the will to live is the assertion of one's own body, which, in its inner nature, is the Will ; it is objectified will. But, on account of the egoism peculiar to every individual, this assertion of one's own body very easily extends to the *denial* of the same will expressed in another's body, either by destroying this latter or by compelling it to serve one's own will, instead of allowing it to serve the other's will, which is its natural function. This breaking through the limits of one's sphere and encroaching on that of another is *wrong* or what we denote by the concept of wrong. According to Schopenhauer, both the doer of wrong and the sufferer of wrong recognize instantly, always and obscurely (i.e. not in abstract reflection) the fact of wrong, the former recognizing it through the vague feeling of remorse (or wrong committed), the latter through ' a direct and mental pain ', different from the accompanying physical suffering.

Wrong expresses itself most completely and palpably in cannibalism, which exhibits the greatest conflict of the Will with itself, and that in man, the highest objectification of Will. After cannibalism it expresses itself most distinctly in murder, which ' is followed instantly and with fearful distinctness by remorse '.[2] (Dostoevsky relates, in *The House of the Dead*, that among the criminals with whom he had to associate in Siberia he had been unable to discern any sign of remorse at all, still less of repentance.) Mutilation, says Schopenhauer, is to be regarded as differing from murder only in degree. Next to murder comes enslavement, and finally theft or seizure of another's goods. In so far as these are the fruit of a man's own labour, to seize them is much the same as to enslave him, and so theft is related to enslavement as injury to murder.

[1] I, p. 428. [2] *Ibid.*, p. 432.

A right to property is acquired by expending one's labour upon it, by incorporating one's labour, as it were, in the object (an object, of course, that is not already the property of someone else). The moral right of property is thus based by Schopenhauer on work and he rejects Kant's view of 'first occupation' as foundation of the right of property. 'To me this is only explicable on the supposition that his powers were failing through old age'.[1] It may seem that Schopenhauer too bases the right of property on *occupation*; for, if a man cuts down a tract of forest and ploughs the land, he has 'occupied' it. But Schopenhauer would point out that this is an instance, not of *mere* occupation, but of *effective* occupation, through the incorporation of labour in the thing occupied : it is this expenditure of labour that gives a moral and natural right to the object, not its mere occupation. 'How should the mere avowal of my will to exclude others from the use of a thing at once give me a *right* to it ? ' he asks, apropos of Kant's view. It is not mere occupation, but effective occupation through labour that confers a moral title to property, so that if a family has hunted a district for many years but has never done anything at all for the improvement of the land, it has no moral right to exclude a stranger from the land. It has a moral right to the animals it has killed, for it has expended labour on them by the very fact of catching them, but it has no moral right to the *land*, unless it has done something to improve it, e.g. by cultivating it : it cannot simply say, 'That land is ours', and then exclude everyone else. It is not a question of the amount of labour expended by an individual, for if a man plucks or picks up from the ground wild fruit (Schopenhauer's language is reminiscent of Locke's), he has not expended much labour, but he has expended some, and that is enough : it is proportionate to the object at least. Schopenhauer quotes with approval an ancient saying to the effect that ' a cultured field is the property of him who cut down the wood and cleared and ploughed it, as an antelope belongs to the first hunter who mortally wounds it '.[2] Of course, a man may part with his property by voluntary arrangement, if he wishes ; but he can acquire no natural moral right to anything upon which labour cannot be expended, either by improving it or, at least, preserving it from harm. He can acquire a right to possession of the

---

[1] I, p. 433.   [2] *Ibid.*, pp. 432–3.

latter type of object, only through ' a voluntary surrender on the part of others, as a reward for other services '[1] ; but this presupposes a community already in existence, a comunity regulated by agreement, i.e. the State.

The doing of wrong occurs either through violence (murder, etc.) or through craft. If I lie to another, I do violence to another through craft, presenting illusive motives to his mind, in order to influence his will, either out of simple self-interest or out of sheer wickedness, i.e. seeking enjoyment in the painful consequences to another of my lie. Every lie (the mere refusal of information is not, of course, a lie) aims at extending the authority of one's own will to other people, at asserting one's own will through the denial of theirs, and is accordingly wrong. (The most complete lie is the *broken contract*.) Wrong through craft, of which lying is an example, is more shameful at least than wrong through violence, for it uses subterfuge and betrays weakness, lowering man as a physical and moral being : a liar's victory rests on the fact that men credit him with an honesty which he does not possess, whereas the use of sheer physical force is frank and open. Good faith and honesty are the bonds which unite together externally the multiple phenomena of the one Will and limit individual egoism ; but treachery and faithlessness break the bond and afford unrestricted scope to private egoism. (Schopenhauer's own character undoubtedly shows itself in his hatred of lying, for he himself never hesitated to say what he thought. Similarly we can trace the influence of his own character in his concern to find a moral basis for private property.)

The concept of *wrong* is the original and positive concept (whatever the form of the word might seem to imply) and the concept of *right* is derivative and negative, being merely the negation of wrong. This notion leads Schopenhauer to the extraordinary conclusion that e.g. to refuse to help a starving man is not wrong, because the action of refusal does not positively encroach on the sphere of assertion of another's will. Now, if right be merely the negation of wrong, we would expect him to admit that the refusal to help another in great need is *right ;* but Schopenhauer does not explicitly say so, and, though he says it is ' not wrong ', he admits that it is ' cruel and fiendish ' and tries to get out of the difficulty by

[1] I, p. 434.

observing that a man who acts in such a manner would certainly commit all manner of wrong, whenever he felt inclined, granted the opportunity. In other words, Schopenhauer boggles at the logical conclusion of his theory of right, and this goes to show either that right is *not* something merely negative or that Schopenhauer explained the concept of wrong too narrowly, through a desire to found it on his metaphysical theories, and that the refusal to help another in great need (when one *can* help him, of course) is wrong. As a matter of fact, it is the concept of right that is positive and original : wrong can have no meaning unless it be the transgression or omission of right.

Schopenhauer finds the principal application of his theory of right as the negation of wrong in the justification of self-defence. To ward off violence cannot be wrong : therefore it is right. If another denies my will through violence, i.e. through aggression, I can legitimately oppose violence to violence, I may use compulsion ; more than that, I may employ craft to defend myself. Hence it follows that a promise extorted by violence is no binding promise, and one who has been compelled to make such a promise, may deceive the other party. " If some one plays with me for money he has stolen from me, I have the right to use false dice against him, because all that I win from him already belongs to me '.[1] Now, Schopenhauer is quite correct in asserting a right to self-defence against wanton aggression ; but the way in which he establishes that right is most unsatisfactory. If self-defence is right because it is not wrong, then, if refusal to help a starving man is not wrong, it must be right. Does not Schopenhauer himself say that the whole province of possible actions is divided into such as are wrong and such as are right ?[2] The trouble is that there can be no positive moral obligation in Schopenhauer's system, so that ' right ' must be negative, the negation of wrong, the concept of which is justified by appeal to metaphysical notions that, as interpreted by Schopenhauer, lead to a too narrow view of wrong, with the inevitable consequence that right includes actions generally esteemed as wrong, though, as we have seen, Schopenhauer shies at the application of the logical consequences.

Whatever one may think of the way in which Schopenhauer establishes right and wrong, it is clear that on his theory the

[1] I, p. 439.   [2] *Ibid.*, p. 437.

distinction is anterior to the foundation of the State and is prior to positive law. 'Therefore the concepts right and wrong, even in a state of nature, are certainly valid and by no means conventional'.[1] One may not be able to enforce right and prevent the suffering of wrong in a state of nature, and it is true that the protection of right is ensured only in the State, but right itself exists independently of the State and, though force may suppress right in a state of nature, it cannot abolish it. 'Those who, with Spinoza, deny that there is a right apart from the State, confound the means for enforcing the right with the right itself'.[2] The moral law, then (so far as one can consistently speak of a moral *law* within the framework of Schopenhauer's philosophy) is, as regards the distinction between right acts and wrong acts, a *natural* law and not a creation of the State : the latter does not establish right and wrong by its positive law.

As man possesses reason, he can see that the pleasure of inflicting wrong is counterbalanced by the suffering of wrong, while experience teaches many people that they are more likely to suffer wrong than to inflict it or at least that they are always in danger of suffering it : he thus comes to conclude in the course of time that he can free himself from the pain of suffering wrong only by renouncing the pleasure of inflicting it. Men accordingly agree together to renounce the pleasure of inflicting wrong, and this agreement is the origin of the State. The State, therefore, is the creation of enlightened egoism, and it exists simply in order to prevent the *suffering of wrong :* it does not exist primarily to prevent wrong-doing. If it were possible, says Schopenhauer, to conceive an infliction of wrong without a correlative suffering, it would not be the function of the State to prohibit that wrongdoing. It is not the function of the State to enforce the doing of right, but to enforce the not-doing of wrong ; yet in order to to do this effectively, it has, by positive legislation, to lay down rights, which are not to be transgressed, and, by affixing penalties to the infringement of law, to provide the egoistic individual with sufficient motives to prevent his infringing those rights, in order that wrong may not be suffered by others. From the purely ethical viewpoint the concept of wrong is primary and the concept of right is its negation, but from the juridical standpoint the concept of right is primary and positive and

---

[1] I, p. 440. [2] III, p. 409.

the concept of wrong negative, so that it is as though the State borrows the concepts of right and wrong from ethics and then makes them juridical by inverting them. All the same the State does this with a view to preventing the suffering of wrong, and not in order to ensure ethical action, so that it is an erroneous view which looks upon the State as an institution for furthering morality, an institution which consequently attacks egoism. On the contrary, the State ' has sprung from egoism and exists only in its service—an egoism that well understands itself, proceeds methodically and forsakes the one-sided for the universal point of view, and so by addition is the common egoism of all '.[1] The State, therefore, springs from enlightened or rational egoism and exists in its service : it is not a moral educator.

The first aim of the State is protection of its members from external aggression, principally, of course, from aggression on the part of other nations. In the relations between the States the ethical distinction of right and wrong holds good, since it is wrong if one State asserts its will through the denial of that of another State ; but there can be no positive law, since there is no effective international tribunal. (By talking of the ' will of the State ' I do not mean to imply that Schopenhauer held an ' organic ' theory of the State : I use the term simply for the sake of convenience.) The second aim of the State is protection within itself, i.e. protection of the members of the State from aggression by other members, and this it does by positive legislation, backed up by penalties, and by bringing the force at its disposal to prevent the suffering of injury on the part of individuals.

But there is always the danger that the State may exceed its powers, so that there must also be ' protection against the protector ' : public right must be guaranteed. This is best attained by separating from one another the legislature, the judicature and the executive.[2] Depotism is simply the establishment of a positive wrong, while republicanism tends to anarchy : constitutional monarchy indeed tends to government by factions, but, until we can attain the perfect State, constitutional monarchy is the preferable form of government, since the good of the royal family (the monarchy should be hereditary) is so bound up with the good of the

---

[1] I, p. 445.
[2] III, p. 410. Cf. Kant's *Treatise on Perpetual Peace*.

country that the one can never be advanced without the
other.[1] Schopenhauer, therefore, opts for constitutional
monarchy, with the separation of the legislature, executive
and judicature, as the form of State best calculated to ensure
' protection against the protector ', i.e. to prevent the growth
of despotism or excessive State-control.

Schopenhauer gave a good deal of consideration to the
subject of punishment[2] and I shall set down his opinions in
brief. The real aim of punishment is to *deter* others from
committing a like offence. The one end of the law is deterrence from the infringement of the right of others and the law
is fulfilled in the punishment of such infringement, so that
' the law and the fulfiment of it, the punishment, are essentially
directed to the *future*, not to the *past* '. (We would naturally
understand by ' fulfilment of the law ' obedience to the pre-
scription of the law ; but Schopenhauer is thinking of the
law, backed by sanctions, as essentially deterrent in character,
so that, when the deterrent penalties of the law are realized in
fact, the law can be said to be ' fulfilled '.) That punishment is retributive in character, Schopenhauer will not allow.
Retributive punishment is, in his eyes, simply *revenge :* it is
the requital of wrong by the infliction of pain, with the aim
of obtaining consolation for the suffering one has borne by
the sight of the suffering one has inflicted on another.
' This is wickedness and cruelty, and cannot be morally
justified ', for wrong which some one has inflicted upon me
by no means entitles me to inflict wrong upon him '.[3] Jurists
may speak of the expiation of crime or the neutralization or
abolition of a crime, but no man has a right to set himself up
as a moral judge and requiter in this way. ' Vengeance is
mine : I will repay, saith the Lord '. Man has, however, a
right to care for the safety of society, and this can only be
realized by instituting penalties for those who disturb the
safety of society and executing those penalties with a view,
not to requital, but to deterrence.

Kantians object to this that, if punishment be merely
deterrent in character, the criminal is used simply as a *means*,
whereas no man should be used merely as a means. Schopenhauer answers that it is perfectly right to use the murderer,
for example, as a means, by putting him to death, to deter
others ; it is right because the murderer was a citizen and

[1] I, p. 443.   [2] I, pp. 448 ff. III, pp. 412–14.   [3] III, p. 449.

therefore, implicitly at least, a party to the contract, whereby, in order to secure his own life, freedom and property, he pledged his life, his freedom and property for the security of all, which pledge he has now forfeited by committing murder. The view that all citizens are party to a contract is, of course, difficult to maintain, for if you say, as it is obviously necessary to say, that the contract is entered into implicitly (except in the case of those who deliberately seek and obtain naturalization) the difficulty remains that most citizens are quite unable to do anything but live as citizens of the State in which they have been born. In the present world, moreover, there are few localities to which they can go, if they do not want to live in a State : they can hardly go and live at the North or South Pole. However, this difficulty attends all ' conventional ' theories of the State, i.e. all theories that base the State and membership of the State on a contract, explicit or implicit. On the other hand, to say that the State and membership of the State rest on force and violence, while no doubt often historically true (e.g. many people originally became subjects of ancient Rome through the use of force, members of the Pontifical States became Italian citizens through annexation of those States, etc.), affords no moral basis for the State at all, so that recourse to a ' conventional ' theory of some sort is necessary. But it would be out of place to discuss this matter further : I may just point that anyone who is born into a State, i.e. in a family whose members are citizens of a State, enjoys from his or her very earliest years the benefits of the State, so that, unless in later years they seek naturalization in another State or depart to the North Pole, they must be considered to have duties towards the State. They may, therefore, be said to have made an ' implicit contract ', for they cannot go on enjoying the benefits and protection afforded by citizenship without at the same time discharging their duties as citizens. They cannot have it both ways : if they continue voluntarily to enjoy the benefits, they must be understood as voluntarily bound to the discharge of duties, so that, if they will not discharge their duties they render themselves liable to penalties. In this way the ' contract ' is made into the *logical*, rather than the *historical* foundation of the State.

Aristotle said centuries ago that man is a political or social animal, and that he who has no need of society must be either a beast, infra-human, or a god, supra-human. This is not a mere empirical observation of the fact that human beings tend to live together, but it expresses a naturally-implanted tendency of human nature, answering to a natural need of man. As human nature is the work of God (here, of course, we proceed beyond Aristotle), as the natural law, expressed in man's natural tendencies, reflects the Eternal Law of God, and as man is rational and free, man is under a moral obligation to form society : the formation of society is not something purely ' conventional '. This moral obligation bearing on man-in-general does not mean that every single individual is always and everywhere bound to be an ' active ' member of a political community, any more than the obligation to propagate the species means that every single man must marry and attempt to found a family. The supernatural invitation of God may lead a man into the wilderness, as it may lead a man to choose the life of celibacy ; but even then he cannot legitimately endeavour to cut himself off altogether from society spiritually as well as physically, he is bound to his fellows by the law of charity or love and through the very fact of incorporation with Christ. So, even if he, for supernatural reasons, lives the life of a hermit in the wilderness, he is spiritually bound to his fellows and must, in that sense, be an active member of society.

Yet obligation to form society does not imply that man is bound to form any particular society or any particular type of society. Empirical considerations such as community of speech, of locality, etc., will dispose men to form a definite political entity ; but one could not say, for example, that all men inhabiting a certain geographical locality are morally bound to form one State. Nor could one say that they are bound to choose a particular form of government, monarchy, for instance, or republicanism. All authority comes ultimately from God, but it comes to the government *via* the people, and the people are entitled to choose any form of government which is consonant with the moral law or to change the existing form of government, given sufficient reasons for doing so. To state, therefore, that man is under a moral obligation to form society, does not mean the entire exclusion of the contract theory. The general obligation to form society is primary, but an explicit or implicit consent of the members is *logically* presupposed in the foundation of a *particular* political society. Once it is formed, then all children are born into that society, receive benefits from it, enjoy rights and should, throughout their lives, discharge their duties towards the community (unless, of course, an individual ceases to be a citizen of the State in which he was born by becoming a naturalized member of another State by an explicit act).

To return to the subject of punishment. We have seen that Schopenhauer rejects the Kantian theory of punishment as retributive in character : what does he say of the theory that the function of punishment is to *reform* the criminal or to reform the criminal *and* to deter others ? In the first place, as he does not believe in the alterability of character, he is led to say that ' moral reformation is really not possible, but only determent from the deed through fear '.[1] In the second place, it is always doubtful if we can attain two different ends by one means, and this is especially the case when the two ends are opposite ends. Now, ' education is a benefit, punishment ought to be an evil ; the penitentiary prison is supposed to accomplish both at once '.[2] The upholder of the reformatory or educative view of punishment would, of course, remark that punishment ought *not* to be an evil. If it were an evil, then we should be returning evil for evil, which is to make two evils instead of one. Punishment, he would say, is, or ought to be, for the good of the criminal, by reforming him, and for the good of others, by deterring them from crime. In so far as *both* these ends are put forward together Schopenhauer answers that a man who is tempted to crime by want and misery will not be deterred by the sight ' of the palatial prisons which are built by honest men for rogues '. He also observes that if penitentiary prisons are to be regarded as educational institutions, it is a matter for regret that one can only obtain entrance through crime—to which it might be retorted that one can hardly send people to prison on the possibility of their one day committing a crime and that, in any case, a penitentiary prison is an ' educational institution ' for *criminals* and not for the population at large.

With respect to the kind of punishment Schopenhauer declares that, as the right of punishing depends on the contract and the pledge made therein, the character and amount of punishment should be proportionate to the value of that for which the pledge is made. Thus a man is justified in demanding the pledge of another's life as a guarantee for the

---

[1] III, pp. 412–13.   [2] *Ibid.*, p. 412

security of his own life, but not for the security of his property, for which a lesser pledge is sufficient. In his view, therefore, capital punishment is ' absolutely necessary ' for the security of the lives of the citizens, but to impose the death penalty for theft of property is excessive and unjustified.) ' In general the injury to be guarded against affords the right measure for the punishment ', so that the law may rightly impose hard labour for smoking in a forest during the summer (because of the danger of conflagration), while permitting it in winter.[1] He also says that, whenever possible, the apparent severity of a punishment should exceed the actual severity, and draws thence an argument against solitary confinement, on the ground that, while a very severe punishment in actuality, its great severity has no witnesses, is not anticipated by any-one who has not experienced it, and so does not act as a deterrent. (In answer to the objection that punishment cannot act as a deterrent, if man is not free, we must recall Schopenhauer's thesis that, while the will is not free, it is determinable by motives, so that, although the intending criminal cannot become non-egoistic, knowledge of the penalties attending on crime can induce him to seek the satisfaction of his egoism in another direction.)

The State, then, is the creation of enlightened egoism, and, under the guidance of this enlightened egoism, ' each promotes the well-being of all because he sees that his own well-being is involved in it '.[2] In practice the State is still far from the achievement of this end, an end which might appear to be something approaching a Utopia ; but, even if it did attain to it, suffering would still remain, and, even if sufferings were removed, ' ennui would at once occupy every place they left '. Moreover, when strife is banished from within the State, it reappears in the form of war, under a far more bloody and destructive guise ; and, even if war were abolished, we should be faced by over-population of the planet, ' the terrible evil of which only a bold imagination can now realise '.[3] In short, life is essentially a life of evil and suffering, and the only way of salvation is a path out of life, the character of which I shall presently describe.

[1] I, p. 414.   [2] Ibid., p. 451.   [3] Ibid., p. 452.

CHAPTER IX

VIRTUE AND HOLINESS : THE WAY
OF SALVATION

THE BAD MAN, as we would expect from the preceding chapter, is he who not merely asserts his own will to live, but also, in asserting it, goes so far as to deny the will of another as appearing in that other's body. Filled with a vehement and egoistic will to live, unable to see that the difference between individuals is but phenomenal, he seeks exclusively his own interest, regardless of others, who mean nothing to him at all. He is termed bad, then, in virtue of his egoistic opposition to the will of others. (Schopenhauer defined the ' bad ' as that which lacks conformity with a definite effort of the will, just as ' good ' signifies ' the conformity of an object to any definite effort of the will '.[1] He thus made the concepts of good and bad relative concepts.) The good man, on the contrary, will be he who does not assert his will in such a way that he denies that of others and who realizes that all individuals are truly one, this realization producing sympathy instead of egoism. But between the bad and the good proper Schopenhauer recognizes an intermediate grade, which is the mere negation of the bad : this grade is that of *justice*, which we will now consider. It is indeed a little difficult to see how there can be any grade that is purely negative, for if it exists at all and is not bad, it would seem that it must be good. However, let us pass over this terminological difficulty.

The man who observes and respects the natural distinction of right and wrong, even when this distinction has not been fortified by the State through the establishment of sanctions, is the *just* man. He asserts his own will, but he never asserts it to such an extent that he denies or aims at destroying the will appearing in another. He does not disregard others completely, as the bad man does, or treat them as if they had a nature quite different from his own, as though they were mere instruments to minister to his gratification or obstacles to be eliminated, he abstains from injuring them, and he desires to render to others what he has received from them.

[1] I, p. 465.

The just man has penetrated the principle of individuation, the veil of Maya, to the extent of setting others so far on a level with himself that he does them no injury ; but he has not risen to the height of looking on others as one with himself ; his penetration of the illusion of individuality is as yet very limited. Schopenhauer thus relates the distinction between the bad man and the just man, and between the just man and the positively good man, to degrees in the penetration of the principle of individuation. The bad man is so thoroughly enmeshed in the veil of Maya that he asserts his own individuality to the exclusion of that of others ; he is the thorough egoist, the hyper-individualist. The just man penetrates the veil to a certain extent, for he abstains from that egoistic self-assertion that injures others and, to that degree, places others on a level with himself ; but he has not penetrated the veil as far as the positively good and virtuous man who sees that individuality is illusion, that all are one, who places others on a level with himself by practising benevolence and love. It is only he who has penetrated the veil of Maya, who can say to himself, in reference to all other individuals, *Tat twam asi* ('This thou art !'), that is on the direct road of salvation. If it be objected that very few just men or good men would recognize Schopenhauer's description of their knowledge, of their incomplete or complete penetration of the veil of Maya (since very few of them are Schopenhauerians !), the philosopher answers that he does not mean to imply that they have abstract, reflective knowledge of this penetration : he is stating abstractly what they realize only by a dim, obscure, immediate conviction. They might explain their conduct, just or good as the case may be, in other terms, ethical or theological, according to their preconceptions ; but it is the fact of their conduct which shows him, Schopenhauer, that they do have this obscure consciousness. This answer pre-supposes, of course, the truth of the philosophy of Schopenhauer, which we do not admit ; but, metaphysics apart, the distinction between the bad man, the just (i.e. merely just) man and the good man is that between the purely egoistic individual, the man who orders his conduct according to the principles of strict justice but goes no further, and the man who practises love towards all. On the one hand we have the ethic of justice and on the other hand the ethic of love (which for Schopenhauer means sympathy).

Goodness of disposition proper is, therefore, a pure or disinterested love of others, which proceeds from a degree of penetration of the principle of individuation higher than that attained by the merely just man and which shows itself in the placing of other individuals and their fate completely on a level with oneself and one's own fate. ' Further than this it cannot go, for there exists no reason for preferring the individuality of another to its own '.[1] Yet if a number of individuals are threatened with death or misery, this may outweigh regard for one's personal well-being, and the man who has attained the highest goodness and nobility will sacrifice himself, even his life, on their behalf. Those who sacrifice themselves for the maintenance of something very precious and beneficial to mankind, e.g. fundamental truths, are on the same high level. (One might have thought the number would make no difference, if it has been once realized that *all are one* ; but it would be ungracious to carp, when Schopenhauer is discoursing on such sublime themes as self-sacrifice.)

In accordance with his principle, discussed earlier in the book, that happiness is simply negative in character, Schopenhauer asserts that all that the good and noble man can do for others is to *alleviate their sufferings*, the motive being the knowledge of the suffering of others, which is placed on a level with his own. ' It follows from this that pure love ($\dot{\alpha}\gamma\dot{\alpha}\pi\eta$, *caritas*) is in its nature sympathy '.[2] The philosopher therefore rejects the notion of Kant that all true goodness and virtue must proceed from a rational principle, from the idea of duty and the categorical imperative, and that the feeling of sympathy is weakness. On the contrary, says Schopenhauer, ' all true and pure love is sympathy, and all love which is not sympathy is selfishness. $\text{"}E\rho\omega\varsigma$ is selfishness, $\dot{\alpha}\gamma\dot{\alpha}\pi\eta$ is sympathy '.[3] The two may be, however, and indeed frequently are, combined, as in genuine friendship, which is always a mixture of selfishness and sympathy.

After a digression on the subject of weeping, which he defines as ' sympathy with our own selves ', due to the repetition in reflection of the pain we experienced,[4] Schopenhauer proceeds to discuss the denial of the will to live. This proceeds from that same penetration of the principle of individuation which produces goodness, love and true nobility, but is a

[1] I, p. 484.
[3] *Ibid.*

[2] *Ibid*, p. 485.
[4] *Ibid.*, pp. 486-8.

volence, betrays its insufficiency even in the fact that so miserably little real and pure morality is found among men '. He is not referring, he tells us, to the absence of the sublime virtues, such as self-sacrifice, for these are found practically only in novels and plays, but to the absence of virtues that ' are the duty of every one '. If an old man reflects on those with whom he has had to do, ' how many persons will he have met who were merely really and truly *honest* ? '[1] (Schopenhauer would doubtless have been gratified, had he lived to see the erection of monasteries and convents by members of the Anglican Church.) But, if he tilted against the Protestants, he tilted also against those ' open enemies of Christianity ', who denoted the ideals of perfect chastity, self-renunciation, asceticism, ' anti-cosmic ' (a very proper word to use, of course, on Schopenhauer's theory) and, by so denoting them, meant to *condemn* them. Such obscuration of the mind can only be the result of the fact that these people, like so many more in Germany, have been completely spoiled and led astray by ' miserable Hegelism, that school of dullness, that centre of misunderstanding and ignorance, that mind-destroying, spurious wisdom ', the veneration of which ' will soon be left to the Danish Academy '.[2] (It will be remembered that Schopenhauer failed to secure the prize, when he sent an essay to the Danish Academy.)

But if Schopenhauer found his theory of the denial of the will to live exemplified in the lives of Christian saints and ascetics, he found it still more vividly represented among the Hindus and Buddhists. This is but natural, since asceticism with a view to deliverance, i.e., deliverance as understood by Schopenhauer, is much more apparent in Hinduism, with its doctrine of Maya, or in Buddhism, with its doctrine of Nirvana, than in Christianity, which is a religion of *life* and which teaches that ultimate reality is a Personal God and that human persons survive death in their individuality. Moreover, Schopenhauer's ethic of sympathy, which is predominantly (though not entirely) passive, is more akin to traditional Hindu and Buddhist ethics than to the more dynamic ethic of Christianity. In the teaching of Vivekananda, for example, or the Bramah Somaj we do indeed find emphasis placed on the active aspect of love ; but Schopenhauer, of course, was not acquainted with these

[1] III, p. 465.   [2] *Ibid.*, p. 437.

modern developments of Hinduism. Moreover, such men as Ramakrishna (who died in 1886, at the age of fifty) and Vivekananda (who died in 1902, at the age of thirty-nine) were certainly influenced, to a varying extent, by Christianity. In any case, in Schopenhauer's eyes, the great fundamental truth, ' which is contained in Christianity, as in Brahmanism and Buddhism ', is ' the need of deliverance from an existence which is given up to suffering and death ', and ' the attainableness of this by the denial of the will '.[1]

Now, leaving out of account the Brahman and Buddhist philosophies and confining ourselves to Christianity, it is quite clear that the Christian Saints and ascetics would by no means describe their conduct and experiences in terms of the Schopenhauerian philosophy. Schopenhauer is equal to the occasion and has his answer ready. The saints and ascetics all had an intuitive, concrete knowledge of the truth (i.e., the truth proclaimed by Schopenhauer), though they had no abstract, philosophical knowledge of that truth and expressed themselves in terms of their preconceived ideas or traditional dogmas. Thus a Christian saint would give a different account of his conduct from that which a Hindu ascetic would give of his, but their different language and abstract explanations are of no importance : their conduct is the same, their lives are similar, their immediate and intuitive knowledge is the same, though they bring this knowledge to explicit, rational consciousness in different ways. ' A saint may be full of the absurdest superstition, or, on the contrary, he may be a philosopher, it is all the same '.[2] His sanctity is guaranteed by his conduct alone, conduct which proceeds from an intuitive knowledge of the world and is expressed in dogmatic terms only for his personal satisfaction. ' It is therefore just as little needful that a saint should be a philosopher as that a philosopher should be a saint ; just as it is not necessary that a perfectly beautiful man should be a great sculptor, or that a great sculptor should himself be a beautiful man '.[3] (Schopenhauer is doubtless here thinking of criticism that might be levelled against himself, for he adds : ' In general, it is a strange demand upon a moralist that he should teach no other virtue than that which he himself possesses '.) The saints and ascetics have, therefore, an *intuitive* knowledge of the world ; but to express

[1] III, p. 452.   [2] I, p. 495.   [3] *Ibid.*

this knowledge abstractly, in universal and conceptual form, is the task of the philosopher, and Schopenhauer claimed to have discharged this task, to have interpreted philosophically the immediate, unreflective knowledge of the ascetic and saint.

The author of this book writes from the Christian standpoint : he is firmly convinced of the truth of the rational basis of the Christian religion, i.e., of natural theology and Christian apologetic, which form the logical basis for the acceptance of Divine Revelation.   This necessarily means that he adopts in regard to Christianity an analogous position to that which Schopenhauer adopts in regard to his philosophy.   Thus, whereas Schopenhauer interprets the experiences and conduct of mystics, saints and ascetics in terms of the Schopenhauerian philosophy, the Christian will interpret all genuinely religious experience and all genuinely saintly conduct in terms of Christian dogma.   This is obvious and must be taken for granted : it would be impossible to give a Christian apologetic here, nor would it be desirable to include the very long digression necessary for this purpose in a book devoted to expounding and criticizing the thought of a particular philosopher.   But we do desire to make this clear, that the adoption of the Christian standpoint does not mean that one rejects *a priori* the genuinity of all religious experience or saintly conduct on the part of men or women who do not explicitly accept the Christian Religion : it does mean, however, that one will understand all genuine religious experience as experience of the one God Who has revealed Himself in Christ and all genuinely saintly conduct as inspired by the grace that comes from Christ alone.   As to assessing in particular cases what is genuine mysticism or genuine holiness, there is normally no means of doing so : we can attain to some degree of moral certainty perhaps, but it is only in the case of those whom the Church has canonized that we know for certain that they are, in the fullest sense, saints.   Still, conduct, as Schopenhauer remarks, is the best guide, and, just as the lives of some may show their mysticism to be but pseudo-mysticism, so the lives of others, even outside the Christian fold, may show that they were ' not far from the Kingdom of God '.

The foregoing remarks obviously presuppose the possibility of supernatural mysticism in a man who has not received sacramental baptism. Not all would agree on this point, perhaps ; but it is difficult to see how the *possibility* can be excluded altogether *a priori*. Supernatural experience of God, such as is enjoyed in the mystical state, clearly presupposes the presence of *gratia sanctificans* and so presupposes 'justification'. Now, since supernatural faith is necessary for 'justification', even for *baptisma in voto*, it might seem that a Hindu, for example, can be 'justified' only if he turns to Christ and explicitly accepts the Christian revelation and that he cannot be 'justified' as long as he continues in Hinduism, even if he is a Hindu *bona fide*. If one were to adopt the theological opinion that *explicit* faith in the Incarnation and the Blessed Trinity were necessary to 'justification' and salvation, then it is clear that a man who did not have that faith, could not be in a state of grace and *a fortiori* could not enjoy supernatural mystical experience. But the Church has never defined the doctrine that *explicit* faith in the principal mysteries of the Christian religion is necessary to salvation, and, as long as this is not defined, one is at liberty to accept the other theological opinion that implicit faith, *fides virtualis*, may be sufficient. It is indeed certainly true that *supernatural* faith is requisite, but God offers sanctifying grace to all men (*Facienti quod in se est Deus non denegat gratiam*) and, as this is certain, we cannot see why a man or woman should not receive this grace effectively, even if they do not belong visibly to the Church, provided, of course, that they are *in bona fide*. The man or woman would then have supernatural faith, would be ready to accept *all* that God has revealed, were they to know it, but would have implicit, and not explicit, faith in the Incarnation and Blessed Trinity. There is no question of 'natural' faith being sufficient, for supernatural faith is required ; the question is, 'Can one who is not visibly a Christian effectively receive sanctifying grace?' If this is possible, then he or she would obviously receive the virtues and gifts that are linked with sanctifying grace, and, if this is the case, how can we exclude the possibility of that grace being so increased in the soul that supernatural mystical experience of God is enjoyed? I do not propose this as the only possible view, as I have no wish to dogmatize in such a matter : I only put it forward as a possible and legitimate view.

But, even if we grant the possibility of supernatural mysticism

in the spiritual life of one who has not been visibly linked
to Christ by the bond of sacramental baptism, it does not
follow that all apparent cases of mysticism are cases of *supernatural* mysticism. Where there is loving experience of the
Object, we would indeed suspect the existence of supernatural mysticism, and the latter may well have existed in
such authentic experiences as originated in or were inspired
by the Hindu doctrine of *bhakti*. Loving experience of the
Object which postulates a distinction between subject and
Object, may be mingled with or overlaid by or may alternate
with experience of a different type, which is probably predominantly intellectualist in character (where it is not ' pathological ') and which is interpreted as union with an impersonal
Absolute beyond all differentiation ; but where the first
element is present, it does not seem to be out of the question
to suppose a genuine mystical experience on the supernatural
level. It is difficult to suppose that a man who led such a
life as Ramakrishna seems to have led, was devoid of any
supernatural experience of God, however he may have interpreted it. But when there is no loving experience of the
Object but only an intellectualist and metaphysical apprehension of the Absolute, there may be room (i.e., leaving
out of account pathological cases and cases of self-deception,
self-induced hypnosis, etc.) for a ' natural mysticism ', the
existence of which is championed by, e.g., Jacques Maritain
in his extremely interesting essay on *The Natural Mystical
Experience and the Void*.[1] The existence of such a natural
mystical experience would probably be challenged by many ;
but, as there appear to be cases, especially in Hinduism, of an
authentic experience which can hardly be regarded as supernatural mysticism and yet cannot be dismissed as charlatanry,
the theory of such a natural mystical experience would fill
a gap that can hardly otherwise be filled, since, if we deny
the possibility of such an experience, we shall be forced
either to multiply the cases of supernatural mysticism so
as to cover instances where it can hardly have been present
or to dismiss out of hand as charlatanry or self-deception
experiences of even high-minded and noble men. According
to Jacques Maritain, whom no one can accuse of lack of
fidelity to the principles of Thomism, the natural mystical
experience is the result of a metaphysical self-stripping whereby

[1] *Redeeming the Time*, pp. 225 ff. (London, 1943.)

the soul attains *negatively* its substantial *esse* and, at the same time, without any duality of act, though only indirectly, God in His aspect as the Absolute. There would thus be ' an experience of God *inquantum infundens et profundens esse in rebus*, indirectly attained in the mirror of the substantial *esse* of the soul '. Sometimes indeed this natural mystical experience may be mingled with purely philosophic elements or with poetic elements (or even, on occasion, with supernatural elements), and then we get those atypical cases, which are so baffling and hard, at first sight at least, to explain.

If this is correct or acceptable, it still remains true that the mystic, whether genuine supernatural mystic or ' natural mystic ', may subsequently explain or rationalize his experience in terms of an ' apperceptive complex '—one man in terms of Neo-Platonism, another in terms of the Vedanta. Nor is this surprising, since all mystical experience, even merely ' natural ' mystical experience, if there really is such a thing, is, by the very fact that it is mystical, ineffable and incommunicable in itself. It must then be judged and interpreted according to certain truth, i.e., the Christian revelation. Even the ' rationalization ' of a Christian mystic is not self-guaranteed : we do not support the truth of Christianity merely by the testimony of mystics ; rather do we support Christianity by sound apologetic and judge the explicit rationalization of their experience given by the mystics by the test of Christian doctrine. Schopenhauer was thus quite right when he said that the rationalization of experience given by mystics cannot simply be taken at its face value : as he points out, ' the experience itself is " only attainable " in one's own experience and cannot be further communicated '[1] : so far as it can be described, it will be described in terms and language familiar to the mystic, which may or may not be adequate. But though Schopenhauer was correct on this point, he was wrong in thinking that his own philosophy was the standard by which the truth of such description or rationalization should be tested.

We admit, then, that Schopenhauer was correct in his assumption that the mystics' rationalization of their experience cannot *simply* be taken at its face value, for the very simple reason that mystical experience is in itself ineffable and,

[1] I, p. 530.

if the mystic himself tries afterwards in reflection to ' mediate ' that state, the genuinity of his experience is not by itself a guarantee of the truth of the philosophical or theological mediation. That is why a natural theology cannot be built simply on religious experience, for we cannot legitimately be called upon to accept without question the interpretation given by a mystic of an experience which is comparatively rare and which is in itself incommunicable. Suppose, *for the sake of argument*, that two men, the one a Christian and the other a Brahman, enjoy mystical religious experience, concerning the genuinity of which, as a psychological state at least, there can be no reasonable doubt. The Christian will afterwards interpret his experience as an experience of the Personal God, the Brahman may interpret his as a realization of union with ultimate impersonal Being. We cannot suppose that both are right in their interpretations, since both men claim to have had an experience of ultimate Reality (which can only be *one*) and yet give opposed statements concerning the nature of that Reality : if we are going to choose between their interpretations, we must have some other criterion than their own mediation of that experience. We do not, however, mean to imply by this that no use can be made of religious experience in natural theology, for it would seem that we can be morally certain at any rate that what we call mystical experience has been an empirical fact which cannot be adequately accounted for by purely naturalistic psychological interpretation or ' explaining-away '. Nevertheless, even if consideration of mystical experience as an empirical fact led us to conclude, with at least a very high degree of probability, that there is an ultimate Reality, which can be the Object of mystical experience, that would not tell us the character of that Reality or the relation of the phenomenal world to that Reality. Of course, one of the main reasons why certain Protestant theologians lay such stress on the argument from religious experience is that they imagine that the traditional rational proofs of God's existence have been ' shown up ' by Kant or at least that the latter's *Critique* has rendered their apodeictic certainty very doubtful. We do not believe that the Transcendental Dialectic has done anything to undermine the proof from contingency, for example, and if we can, as we can, establish God's existence and something concerning His Nature by means of rational abstract argument, the conclusions to which we come must serve us as a test for the accuracy or inaccuracy of a mystic's mediation of his experience. (As I have said, should we come to the conclusion that a given mystic's interpretation of his experience is inaccurate, that does *not* necessarily imply that we must reject the genuinity of the mystic experience itself, since that is something immediate and incommunicable.)

There have been plenty of ascetics, however, who denied themselves, and many truly virtuous men and women, who showed sympathy and love towards others, but who had no mystical experience at all so far as we know. It is even probable that there have been men and women who never enjoyed any ' extraordinary ' mystical experience, but who at the same time led lives of such purity and self-sacrifice that their lives were more meritorious in the eyes of God than the lives of some others who did enjoy mystical experience. Now, in regard to such persons it is quite unjustifiable for Schopenhauer to assert that the dominating motive of their lives was other than they themselves considered it to be. Mystical experience is not a work of the discursive reason and its subsequent mediation in reflection may be inaccurate ; but when there is no mystical experience but simply conduct based on certain rationally-conceived motives, one cannot legitimately separate the conduct from the motive and ascribe it to a quite different motive. One is speaking only of sincerely pure and good souls, of course, for it is obvious enough that there may often be a discrepancy between a man's professed motive and his actually operative motive, e.g., if a preacher professed to be preaching for the glory of God and the profit of the congregation, but was really preaching for his own glory, to make a name for himself. The preacher would, in practice, be hardly conscious perhaps of the discrepancy between his professed motives and his actually operative motive (fully conscious hypocrites are doubtless rare), he would in practice, be influenced by a *mixture* of motives ; but his behaviour and reactions, to failures for instance, might lead external observers to conclude that a self-regarding motive had far more weight with him in actuality than he supposed. These cases do not concern us here, for Schopenhauer is speaking of truly virtuous men and women, who do not give themselves to the alleviation of the sufferings of others for what they can get out of it, in the way of a reputation for philanthropy, for example. But if someone practises love towards his fellowmen because they are the children of God, his brethren, the redeemed of Christ, it is quite illegitimate to state that he is actuated by a motive that springs from intuitive knowledge of the illusion of individuality and the identity of all individuals in the one Will. Real Christian love is based on a rationally-conceived ground (it is indeed supernatural in character, but we prescind here from that theological fact) and is not equivalent to ' liking ' : one cannot, therefore, separate the conduct from the motive and still speak of the conduct as moral : moral conduct is the conduct of an individual and an individual, in his fully human acts, always acts for a motive, that motive being by no means irrelevant to the morality of his conduct. To take a crude example. If a man believed that the soul of his late father had entered his own dog, then, if he treated the dog in an appropriate manner, he would be acting morally ; if he maltreated the dog, he would be acting immorally, even though his belief, that his father's soul was in the dog, was void of objective foundation. In the first case the extreme attention he showed to the dog's welfare would be moral, not in itself, apart from his motive, but precisely because he thought that through that attention he was benefiting his father : if you abstract from the motive altogether, then his conduct towards the dog would have to be regarded as stupid or as maudlin sentimentality. Moreover, it is no good saying to the man, ' You are really bestowing all this care on the dog, because you recognize that it is identical with yourself' : he might very justifiably reply, ' I know much better than you do why I am bestowing all this care on the dog : I have a perfectly clear idea of my reason and motive ; I believe that my father's soul is in the dog and the motive for my care of the dog is to benefit my father : if I did not believe this, I would not go to so much trouble for a brute animal '. Similarly, it may be that there are in fact people who believe that all individuals are ontologically one and who show kindness to others for this motive ; but if a man shows sympathy and love towards others for another motive, because they are children of God, for example, or because they are rational persons, then we must admit that his conduct is based on *that* motive and not say that it is *really* based on quite another *Weltanschauung*. If a man's conduct springs from feeling, e.g., sensible affection, or, at the other end of the scale, from immediate mystical experience, he may indeed rationalize it inaccurately ; but if it springs from clearly-conceived, rationally-apprehended motives, as it often undoubtedly does, then it springs from those motives and not from others. If the non-mystic Christian acts from one clearly-conceived motive and the non-mystic Buddhist acts from another clearly-conceived motive, it is absurd for Schopenhauer to tell the one or the other or both that he or they are not acting from the motives they think they are acting from, but from motives expressed in the Schopenhauerian philosophy, of which they have an obscure knowledge. If he thinks that the motive of either of them is an improper or inadequate motive, he can tell them so and try to get them to change their motive ; but he cannot legitimately claim that they are really acting from a motive other than that which is the clearly-conceived mainspring of their conduct.

One cannot deny a certain sublimity in Schopenhauer's ethical ideal ; it is certainly not the ideal of a ' Philistine ' or mere comfort-lover ; but it is scarcely an ideal which, as presented by Schopenhauer, is likely to induce much in the way of practice. A thoroughly pessimistic conception of ultimate reality is not likely to induce many to strive after sanctity and holiness, nor will many be encouraged by having the goal of absolute nothingness held out before them. The Christian Faith directs the attention of man to the Beatific Vision of God, the philosophy of the Vedanta (or one form of it, at least) to re-absorption into the Absolute, the philosophy of Plotinus to union with the One ; but Schopenhauer holds out as the highest and final goal, not union with God with retention of individuality, not even unconscious identity with Will, but absolute nothingness. His philosophy is thus, in this respect at least, consistently pessimistic, and most people, if in any case death meant extinction of the individual consciousness, would see no reason to pursue the lonely path of suffering asceticism, with nothingness at the end of it, when they could follow Schopenhauer himself in living as comfortable a life as possible as long as they could and then going down into the inevitable oblivion. It is useless to say that this is a self-seeking view of things and that the good and heroic ideal is to deny evil, i.e., the Will to live, for, if existence *itself*, ultimate reality, is evil, there is not, and cannot be, any good at all. ' Before us there is certainly only nothingness ' ; behind all virtue and holiness we discern the final goal, ' which we fear as children fear the dark ', but which we must not evade like the Indians, ' through myths and meaningless words, such as re-absorption in Brahma or the Nirvana of the Buddhists. Rather do we freely acknowledge that what remains after the entire abolition of the will is for all those who are still full of will certainly nothing ; but, conversely, to those in whom the will has turned and has denied itself, this our world, which is so real, with all its suns and milky-ways—is nothing '.[1] This utter pessimism robs of all meaning and value the ideals of virtue and of holiness which Schopenhauer himself admired and proposed to the admiration and veneration of mankind.

Life as we know it is the manifestation of the Will to live, said Schopenhauer, and, since the manifestation of Will is full of suffering and evil and conflict, we must conclude that the Will itself, though a constant urge to life and more life, is itself bound to frustration, is caught, by its very essence, in the toils of suffering and self-diremption. For the human being, therefore, the phenomenal manifestation of Will at its highest grade, the only way of salvation can be a path out of life, a path which is in the end a path out of existence. Mere cessation of phenomenal individuality is not enough, for the inner nature persists, in identity with the one self-conflicting Will : if there is a final salvation, it can only be complete extinction, the abyss of nothingness. As the individual proceeds on the way of self-denial, life in him becomes weaker and weaker, until the final goal is at length achieved through death, when he in whom the will has turned and denied itself achieves, not simply phenomenal, but also total annihilation. If we wish to call the philosophy of Schopenhauer a philosophy of life, we must acknowledge that, though a doctrine of life, it is a condemnation of life : in fact it is a philosophy, not so much of life as of anti-life. In a sense Schopenhauer admits and even emphatically asserts certain values, virtue and ' holiness ' ; but in his philosophy these can be understood only negatively, for, if the existent is evil, it follows that value must be sought in a tending away from the existent. Thus the supreme value

[1] I, pp. 531–2.

will be—paradoxically enough—*nothingness*. Thus did Schopenhauer provide a counterblast to his hated enemy, Hegel. Instead of optimism, pessimism and the worst possible world ; instead of Reason, irrational Will ; instead of the manifestation of the Idea, the goal of nothingness.

CHAPTER X

SCHOPENHAUER, OTHER THINKERS, CHRISTIANITY

IF ONE READS *Die Welt als Wille und Vorstellung* as a work of literature, one certainly finds oneself compensated for the energy expended in covering so many pages by passages of striking beauty, while, if one reads it as an extreme theoretical expression of the pessimistic mood with which not a few are now and again afflicted, it has a certain impressiveness and appears to possess a simple consistency ; but, if studied from the strictly philosophical standpoint, internal inconsistencies very soon reveal themselves and the total system appears bizarre and fantastic in the extreme, so that one feels tempted to dismiss it as a mere imaginative creation or even as the product of a disordered mind. The thought may then occur to the reflective mind that the work of so celebrated a man as Schopenhauer cannot possibly be devoid of real philosophical value and that if one stripped away the terminological and rhetorical extravagances, one could discover underneath the husk a kernel of deep import. The author of this book acknowledges that he himself resolved to make this attempt, not in the course of the exposition itself but after its completion (since one is scarcely justified in presenting as a man's philosophy what one thinks he was ' getting at ', without paying any attention to the way in which the philosopher himself presented his thought, and so running the risk of reading into his thought what was not there or treating as irrelevant what he would by no means have considered irrelevant). Further consideration, however, convinced him that it is not possible to do this in any systematic way, for reasons which will presently become apparent.

At the same time it is quite clear that various theories of Schopenhauer reappear in later, and sometimes less imaginative, philosophers, so that it would appear worth while to draw attention to some, at least, of these theories in the present chapter, though first of all the author proposes to justify his conviction that it is not possible to give a systematic, coherent and consistent ' esoteric ' philosophy, which could legitimately be attributed to Schopenhauer or accepted as what he was really ' getting at '. We must remember that Schopenhauer professed his sure belief that his philosophy was *true*, and he undoubtedly meant that it was true *as he presented it* : he did not regard what we might consider mere fantastic extravaganzas as irrelevant to the system or as unimportant overloading.

It might easily occur to someone that by changing the term ' Will ' to ' Energy ' or ' Force ', one might present the philosophy of Schopenhauer as an evolutionary system more or less according to pattern ; and it might justifiably be pointed out that, although Schopenhauer had a special reason for employing the term ' Will ', he never meant to postulate a willing subject : the metaphysical Will was for him entirely impersonal, a fundamental energy, that lies at the base of, and forms, the world. A little reflection, however, will suffice to show that, even if one thought that an evolutionary system was the philosophic notion underlying the mythology of the Will, it is impossible to bring the Schopenhauerian philosophy within the framework of any such scheme, not at any rate without leaving out of account parts of the philosophy that were by no means unimportant in the mind of their creator. In the first place, are we to think of Schopenhauer's Will as material or immaterial ? To say that it is material would be scarcely accurate, since matter, in so far as we can attach any intelligible meaning to the term, is dependent on the *subjective* forms of space and time : the Will objectifies itself in material objects only in dependence on the *a priori* constitution of the human consciousness. It objectifies itself immediately in the Ideas ; but these are, in themselves, outside space and time and cannot be called material in any ordinary sense ; they are certainly not conceived as extended. Moreover, Schopenhauer called them the ' Platonic Ideas ', and the latter at least were not material, so far as their own essence was concerned.

On the other hand, although the Will is not extended in space and does not endure in time, it cannot be termed spiritual, for it is in itself irrational, and how can it be spiritual, if it is irrational, without intellect? As non-spiritual, therefore, the Will cannot be conceived as God (and Schopenhauer repudiated any such interpretation by his utter rejection of both theism and pantheism), while, as non-material, it cannot be consistently interpreted as material force or energy. Moreover, even if we did identify the Will with material force or energy, how could we go on to extract a consistent evolutionary doctrine out of Schopenhauer's philosophy? The Will is said to objectify itself, it is true : but the individual objectifications of Will are Maya, illusion. The Will manifests itself, objectifies itself, at various grades ; but the individual objectifications are the ' idea ' of an individual subject, are dependent on consciousness. The first book of the *World*, i.e., the doctrine that the world is *Vorstellung*, ' my idea ', renders impossible any realist evolutionary interpretation of the philosophy as a whole. We may say that the idealistic side of the philosophy is out of place and can be dismissed ; but Schopenhauer certainly did not think that it was irrelevant or of little importance, and it would be a queer evolutionary philosophy in which the whole phenomenal world was declared to be ' my idea '. Again, one would naturally suppose that change, motion, duration, were essential to an evolutionary system ; but time is *subjective* according to Schopenhauer.

Supposing that we choose to interpret the metaphysical Will as Life, as an *élan vital*. Immediately we come up against Schopenhauer's doctrine that the Will is not itself Life, but the Will to live : life as we know it is indeed the manifestation of Will, but it is illusory, Maya. And how can we reconcile any theory of ' creative evolution ' with Schopenhauer's philosophy? Even if we were prepared, in despite of the philosopher, to regard the ' Platonic Ideas ' as no more than abstractions or formulæ, as it were, of the various succeeding evolutionary grades, we should still come up against the theory that time is subjective and the fact that ' evolution ' for Schopenhauer is ideal rather than real ; the empirically real is Maya, and one grade cannot develop into another in real duration, apart from the perceiving subject. The *Origin of Species* was published in 1858 and shortly before his death Schopenhauer, judging the Darwinian theory according to an extract in *The Times*, déscribed it in a letter (March 1st, 1860) as ' downright empiricism '. He meant, of course, that Darwin left out of account the inner and hidden force that manifests itself in the struggle for existence and that adaptation to environment, natural selection, etc., are nothing but external conditions ; but, if one were to tack on empirical Darwinism to the metaphysic of the Will, what would one do with the idealism of Schopenhauer and the doctrine of Maya, factors which would scarcely fit in either with Darwinism as such or with the emergent evolution of, e.g., Lloyd Morgan ? As for Henri Bergson, the idea of real duration is essential to his philosophy of the world and, whatever may have been his precise position in regard to *space*, he did not accept the Kantian doctrine of *time*, which Schopenhauer certainly did. Moreover, it is clear from the later developments of Bergson's thought that the *élan vital*, considered biologically, is an effect of Creative Life itself, God, whereas for Schopenhauer, the Will is not the ' cause ' of life nor is it God, so that, to put it very crudely, we have to get the rabbit out of the hat without any recourse to the conjuror. The Will objectifies itself, but its objectifications are Maya : the Will is blind and irrational, but it knows itself, as it were, through its phenomenon ; it objectifies itself in a multiplicity of individuals at various grades, yet the multiplicity of individuals are but the ' idea ' of an individual subject that is itself a phenomenon ; it is not Idea, yet it manifests itself in Ideas : it is not itself Life, but the Will to live, and it denies itself, destroys itself, through the phenomenon. How is it possible to present a clear, consistent and systematic account of the Will that would bear any near resemblance to the system of Herbert Spencer or the empirical evolutionism of Darwin or the creative evolution of Bergson or the materialistic emergent evolution of the Marxists and which would at the same time be recognized by Schopenhauer as in any real sense a faithful transcription of his doctrine ?

Similarly, it is difficult to obtain any coherent and systematic psychology from the pages of Schopenhauer. The intellect is declared to be essentially the servant of will : in other words, the biological function of intelligence would seem to be stressed. At the same time, however, intelligence is supposed to be capable of formulating a conceptual philosophy, which is true and objective, whereas one would expect to find all the emphasis laid on the biological value of ' fictions ' and an anticipation of the theory of the late Professor Vaihinger. One cannot have it both ways : either intelligence is essentially practical in function, essentially the servant of will, and objective philosophical truth is unobtainable (at least, it could never be *known* to be the truth), or the intelligence has *ab initio* a speculative, as well as a practical function. That it has a practical or biological function, no one, of course, if he has any sense, would deny : but, if you start out by saying that the intelligence comes into being originally simply to serve a biological function, that it is in origin essentially and exclusively the servant of will, then, whatever ' superfluity ' it may develop in the course of evolution, you could never be certain that any one of its conclusions or formulated theories was any more than a biologically-useful fiction—in fact you could never be sure that the doctrine that the intellect is the servant of will is itself anything more than a biologically-useful fiction. Moreover, the discursively and rationally expressed philosophical system of Schopenhauer is not supposed to be the mediation of a supra-intellectual intuition, but rather of an infra-intellectual ' intuition ', an immediate consciousness that is common to all, and which can scarcely be differentiated from instinct : yet instinct, one would think, is essentially biological and practical in function. Schopenhauer may refer the ways of instinct, as seen in insects, for example, to the cunning of the Will to live ; but how can the mere Will to live have any ' cunning '? In any case, how is it ever going to be demonstrated that the whole intellectual life of man, including that of Schopenhauer, is any more than the result of the Will's cunning, that objective truth is not simply a *lusus imaginationis* ?

Nor, again, can we obtain any coherent ethic or theory of value from the philosophy of Schopenhauer. It is quite true that he speaks with respect of what he regarded as true virtue and holiness, and that in this sense he asserted values, sanctity and virtue, and held up an ascetic ideal ; but, as I remarked at the close of the last chapter, these values are negatively conceived and, given his metaphysic and characterization of the Will, the supreme value should be non-existence. With

Plato the supreme value, the Idea of the Good, was the supremely real, and indeed, if values are not in some sense objective and real, it is very hard to see how they can be values. Yet with Schopenhauer all is either Will or objectification of Will, and the Will, together with its manifestation, is evil, is that which should be denied. He asserted that the world had an ethical significance, an assertion that implies a positive theory of value ; but at the same time his pessimistic philosophy left no room for a positive theory of value. Moreover, while many philosophies of conduct have stressed self-denial, this has meant self-denial of lower impulses, e.g. control of the passions, in order that man's true nature may be asserted and developed without hindrance. If Epictetus counselled control of the passions, he insisted at the same time on a positive ethic ; if Spinoza regarded the power of the ' passive emotions ' as constituting man's servitude, he emphasized the ' active emotions ' and the supreme attitude of the *amor intellectualis Dei ;* if Plato urged men to curb the headstrong and recalcitrant steed, he insisted on the positive tendance of the soul and the integration of man's faculties in the service of his true end ; above all, if Christianity inculcates the necessity of the ' denial of self ', it certainly does not mean to imply that man should deny his inner self, that man should renounce his being as an individual man, for self-denial is not an end in itself, but is to be practised with a view to attaining a positive end, the highest possible perfection of man's being and activity, first of all in the supernatural order, yet also, if subordinately, in the natural order. For Schopenhauer, however, self-denial means denial of one's inner nature, not only denial of one's phenomenal individuality, but also denial of one's innermost essence, identity with Will, and the highest peak of holiness is the completest denial of one's own being and of ultimate reality, so that value increases and holiness increases in proportion as complete frustration is approached —truly a paradoxical position. Again, Schopenhauer, as we have seen, asserted a doctrine of character-determinism, a doctrine which, if consistently maintained, is incompatible with ethical discrimination and moral judgments based on a standard of value. Yet, after asserting determinism, he admits freedom, as a *deus ex machina,* in exceptional cases. Moreover, if character-determinism were true, would it not, at the very least, cast doubt on the objective validity of the Schopenhauerian philosophy and *Weltanschauung* ? That philosophy is a philosophy of pessimism, and presumably, on Schopenhauer's own theory, it would be the outcome of his pessimistic character, would stand in direct relation to his character and could not be considered as expressing absolute truth. In any case, it would seem impossible to obtain any real theory of value on Schopenhauer's premisses. I do not wish to affirm that his moral theory is entirely worthless, of course, for he does at least evince respect for disinterested sympathy and love and for the ascetic life and this respect does him credit, even if his reasons for showing that respect and his explanation of virtue and holiness are unacceptable : it is not everyone who has an ideal of conduct as lofty and sublime as that of Schopenhauer. Moreover, even if there were no God and theology were void of all objective foundation, the unprejudiced mind would have to admit that the world would be the poorer without the lives of St. Francis, St. Peter Claver, the Curé d'Ars. A ' philanthropic ' millionaire is not exactly the same thing as a saint. But, while I am far from saying that the ideal of conduct depicted by Schopenhauer is entirely worthless, I do affirm that his system gives no adequate foundation to the implied positive values and is incompatible with them, for sanctity is *in fact* something very positive. In the *Two Sources of Morality and Religion* Henri Bergson speaks of the saints and mystics as great men and women of action, as those who have a *prise de contact* with the Source of Life and who radiate and express in action the life and love with which they have been filled ; but, while for Bergson the supremely real is positive Life and Love, and sanctity implies a full measure of participated life and love, for Schopenhauer sanctity cannot but mean *less* life, since life is suffering and evil. In other words, although he exalted sanctity, Schopenhauer misunderstood it, and his picture of it is a distorted picture, inevitably so, if one considers his metaphysic. From the philosophical standpoint we can consider neither the metaphysic nor the ethic of Schopenhauer as showing any real interior similarity, whatever may be the superficial resemblance, to the metaphysic and ethic of the late Henri Bergson. Although the latter was never formally received into the Catholic Church, he said himself that he would have become a convert, had it not been for the persecution of the Jews that he anticipated, being unwilling to separate himself by a definitive act from his own people in their hour of trial, and he was led, partly at least, through his philosophical reflections to recognize the truth of Christianity : Schopenhauer, however, could scarcely be led to Christianity through his philosophy, for it was his very philosophy that caused him to misunderstand the Christian saints whom he admired, and a philosophy that is fundamentally anti-life is diametrically opposed to the religion, the Founder of which came that ' they might have life and might have it more abundantly '.

But enough of these strictures on the philosophy of Schopenhauer : let me now suggest a few of his doctrines that have reappeared in the thought of later philosophers. I do not mean to assert that these later philosophers have all consciously undergone the influence of Schopenhauer and have deliberately borrowed from his philosophy, for, unless a man makes an explicit avowal of the fact that he has borrowed some theory from another thinker or unless the historical connection is so clear that it cannot well be questioned, it is very difficult to ascertain the precise origin of any philosopher's doctrines. After all, the fact that some philosophical notion is found in x and later found in y does not of itself prove that y borrowed that notion from x, for what is there to prevent y thinking it for himself? If x could do so, why not y? Those who are possessed by the mania for discovering influences, sometimes forget this simple fact and, with all their learning, make themselves rather ridiculous. If it is necessary to suppose that all a thinker's views came from previous thinkers, then the latter's views presumably also hail from previous thinkers : where are we going to stop ? We can hardly ascribe to Adam all the various philosophical theories that have appeared in the course of human history ! So if I say that a theory of Schopenhauer, or something like it, appears in the philosophy of a later thinker, that should not of itself be taken to mean that, in my opinion, the later thinker actually borrowed the theory from Schopenhauer.

It is hardly necessary to say much about *Eduard von Hartmann* (1842–1906), retired army officer and author of the *Philosophy of the Unconscious*, since the influence of Schopenhauer upon his thought is obvious and von Hartmann was never so foolish as to attempt to deny it, though he protested against being regarded as a mere continuator of Schopenhauer. Many essential elements of the latter's system reappear in the system of von Hartmann, e.g. the unconscious character of the ultimate reality, teleology, pessimism, also the (professed, at least) use of the inductive method in contrast to the *a priori* method of Hegel ; but he rejected the doctrine of Schopenhauer that the ultimate reality is simply unconscious Will, for the reason that there can be no will tending towards an end, unless there is also an idea presenting that end to the will. ' Wherever we meet with a volition, a representation must be united with it, at the very least that which ideally represents the goal, object, or content of the volition ', and ' every *unconscious volition* also which actually exists must be united with ideas '.[1] Will without idea can never determine itself, so that will and idea must be correlative ; idea cannot be given that subordinate place which Schopenhauer attributes to it. Von Hartmann accordingly speaks of ' the singular defectiveness of the system of Schopenhauer, in which the Idea is by no means recognized as the sole and exclusive content of Will, but a false and subordinate position is assigned it, whilst the maimed and blind Will nevertheless altogether comforts itself *as if* it had a notional or ideal content '.[2] (Here indeed von Hartmann criticizes a really weak point in Schopenhauer's theory.) In this way von Hartmann brought together Will and Idea, and this enabled him to claim that his own philosophical system was a synthesis of Schopenhauerianism and Hegelianism.

But, though he made Idea correlative to Will, von Hartmann, who kept the unconscious metaphysical Will of Schopenhauer, had to make the metaphysical Idea unconscious too. Following the example of Schelling, he invented a new theory of identity, according to which there is an unconscious Absolute, one principle that possesses, however, the two coordinate functions of Idea and Will. Just as the Will of Schopenhauer could never determine itself to an end without Idea, so the Idea of Hegel could never attain to real existence without Will : the one-sided philosophies of Schopenhauer and Hegel must therefore be united. The unconscious Idea of Schelling was thus placed by von Hartmann alongside the unconscious Will of Schopenhauer, as metaphysical principles of equal value, which are identified in the unconscious Absolute. He admits that Schopenhauer, by postulating the

[1] *Philosophy of the Unconscious*, I, p. 123.
[2] *Ibid.*, p. 120.

Platonic Ideas, afforded an opening for the assertion of the unconscious Idea ; but he objects (and rightly) that Schopenhauer was quite unjustified, on his premisses, in asserting the existence of these metaphysical entities. Schopenhauer taught that the Will in itself is without Idea at all, but his observations on instinct, the life of the species, etc., depict the Will as acting ' precisely *as if* it were bound up with unconscious representation ', so that he had ready to hand, so to speak, the material which would enable him to drop the doctrine of the first book of the *World* and to take that step to objective idealism, which Schelling had taken before him. That he did not do so was due, according to von Hartmann, to the fact that he had not the courage to disavow his inheritance of subjective idealism and was unduly prejudiced against Schelling. Thus for von Hartmann consciousness is phenomenal and secondary and there can be idea without consciousness ; but there is no will without idea and idea, unconscious Idea, is metaphenomenal.

The world is the creation of the unconscious Absolute, existence being due to Will, essence being due to Idea or unconscious Reason. Left to itself, Will would have produced a meaningless world and the meaning, order, of the world, the arrangement of the world as we know it, is due to Idea, to Reason. Von Hartmann gave us as an explanatory sub-title of his chief work, ' Speculative Results according to the Inductive Method of Physical Science ', and he went to great pains to demonstrate the activity of the unconscious in the spheres of animal instinct (where we see action in view of an end, which is not apprehended in reflective consciousness), man's reflex movements, the formation of language, artistic creation, and so on. I have no intention of suggesting that his *empirical* observations on this matter are devoid of value, but it is hard to see how the ' *speculative* results ' follow from the empirical observations. An unconscious Absolute could not possibly have brought the world into existence : if such a monstrosity as an unconscious Absolute had really existed anteriorly to the world, it would presumably have gone on existing for ever in its splendid, unconscious isolation. Creation is unthinkable apart from a conscious creating Being, and to speak of creation by an unconscious Absolute is simply to string together words which do not fit. In fine, from the metaphysical standpoint, von Hartmann, in spite of his shrewd criticism of Schopenhauer (e.g. regarding the incompatibility of the first book of *The World* with the rest of the doctrine) offered the world one more fantastic dream, that passes under the name of philosophy.

Just as in his speculative metaphysics von Hartmann adopted a great deal of the theory of Schopenhauer, while at the same time he endeavoured to correct the one-sidedness of that theory, so, in regard to human life, he adopted Schopenhauer's pessimism to a great extent, while at the same time—strange to relate !—maintaining with Leibniz that the world is the best of all possible worlds. Both propositions are founded on experience, the latter on the observation of finality in the world and the progress towards consciousness, the former on the fact that consciousness reveals to us a world that is filled to overflowing with suffering and evil. The dark side of the world reveals the irrationality of Will, the teleology and progress in the world the nature of Idea. Pleasure is not, as Schopenhauer thought, entirely negative in character, for artistic and intellectual pleasures are positive ; yet such pleasures are the prerogative of but a few superior natures and they have to pay for their superiority by a greater capacity for suffering. It follows that the uneducated classes and primitive peoples are happier than the highly civilized and cultured. It is true that men may have a great capacity for suffering and yet remain attached to life ; but this is to be explained by the fact that the Unconscious cunningly deludes them, in order that humanity may continue to exist. Von Hartmann distinguishes three principal forms of illusion to which human beings have been subject in the course of history. In the first form of illusion they think that happiness is obtainable in this life, and this is the illusion of the pagans. In the second form, while recognizing that happiness is unobtainable in this life, they hope for it in another life, and this is the illusion of Christians. When both these forms of illusion, that of immediate personal happiness in this life and that of happiness in the hereafter, have been recognized as illusion, men fall into the third illusion of expecting the realization of Paradise on earth through continual progress. This also is illusion, for disease, old age, death and all the other ills that afflict humanity will be ever present apart from the fact that the progress of civilization serves to increase evil and suffering, e.g. by increasing material well-being at the expense of the spiritual or by the levelling-down of values and the decadence of real genius.

This being so, true wisdom, as Schopenhauer saw, lies in renunciation of life ; but this should take the form, not of asceticism on the part of a few individuals, but of a ' cosmic-universal negation of will ', ' after which there shall be no more volition, activity, or time '.[1] Schopenhauer was quite inconsistent (he certainly was) in declaring that an individual can, by his own denial, attain annihilation ; there must be a kind of cosmical suicide. Meanwhile the individual should not pursue a life of ascetic self-isolation, but rather work positively for the greatest possible development of consciousness in all, that all may realize the folly of volition, may yearn after peace and a state of painlessness and may, at length, by a common and simultaneous effort deny volition and so achieve the complete victory of the logical over the illogical (will). Von Hartmann, therefore, though differing from Schopenhauer as to the role of the individual, agrees with him that the redemption of the world—and so the redemption of the Absolute—is to be accomplished by man and not by the Absolute itself. ' The logical principle guides the world-process most wisely to the goal of the greatest possible evolution of consciousness, which being attained, consciousness suffices to hurl back the total actual volition into nothingness, by which the *process* and the *world ceases*, and ceases indeed without any residuum whatever whereby the process might be continued. The logical element therefore ensures that the world is a best possible world, such a one, namely, as attains redemption, not one whose torment is perpetuated endlessly '.[2] The notion is, apparently, that one day the major part of the actual volition of ' Unconscious Spirit ' will be manifested in humanity (after all, as von Hartmann remarks, man is ever suppressing animal and vegetative life other than that required for his own use !) so that, if humanity then denies volition by a common effort (presumably by simultaneous suicide), the world will cease to be and the Unconscious Spirit will have achieved ' redemption ' through man. If anything more bizarre than the theory of Schopenhauer could be imagined, surely von Hartmann succeeded in imagining it. By maintaining monism he made it impossible for him to say that God redeems man and conquers evil, and

[1] *Philosophy of the Unconscious*, III, p. 131.   [2] *Ibid.*, III, p. 142.

so he said that man redeems ' God ', by hurling the world into nothingness. Is this the substitution of philosophical truth for ' theological fable ' ? One needs indeed a sense of humour to appreciate such a philosophy.

To treat of the immediate disciples of Schopenhauer is not to our purpose, since it is obvious that the thought of the Master would be echoed in the writings of his ' missionaries ' ; nor do we wish to repeat here what we have already said elsewhere concerning the relation of Richard Wagner and Friedrich Nietzsche to Schopenhauer.[1] We would, however, recall to mind the fact that Nietzsche changed Schopenhauer's Will to live into the Will to power, *Der Wille zur Macht*. At the end of the second volume of the *Will to Power* there is a passage which no doubt was intended by Nietzsche as a sort of counterblast to the closing words of Schopenhauer's *World*. ' Do you also want a light, ye most concealed, strongest and most undaunted men of the blackest midnight ?—*This World is the Will to Power—and nothing else* ! And even ye yourselves are this will to power—and nothing besides ! ' It would indeed be inaccurate to make any sharp dichotomy between the Will to live and the Will to power, for the reason that the former shows itself, according to Schopenhauer, in egoism and in the struggle for existence, in conflict, which necessarily involves a fight for power ; but the great difference in this respect between Schopenhauer and Nietzsche is that, whereas the former hated and condemned the Will to live and the conflict engendered by it and exalted pity, sympathy and the denial of the Will, Nietzsche adopted the very opposite attitude, affirming, instead of denying, the Will to power and rejecting the Schopenhauerian ethic. Similarly, Nietzsche came to transform his admiration for the artistic genius as nature's highest product, an admiration that was originated, or at least confirmed and developed, by his reading of Schopenhauer and which he at first applied to Richard Wagner, during the halcyon days of their friendship, into the doctrine of the Superman, as the highest emodiment of the Will to Power. Nevertheless, although Nietzsche rejected the pessimism of Schopenhauer and put in its place a (false and foundationless) optimism, there was always a good deal in common between him and Schopenhauer, as may be seen

---

[1] See my *Friedrich Nietzsche* (Chap. VII, *Schopenhauer and Nietzsche*). B.O.W., 1942.

from one or two examples.   For Schopenhauer the body is
the objectification of Will, consciousness and cognition being
originally the servants of will, i.e. the human body.   He thus
gave a naturalistic explanation of consciousness, making will
prior to idea, body prior to mind.   Now, although Nietzsche
denies the existence of a distinct will in man and also the
transcendentalism of Schopenhauer's metaphysic, he insists
on the priority of body and the biological function of consciousness.   'The belief in the body is more fundamental than the
belief in the soul ',[1] 'perhaps the whole of mental development is a matter of the *body* ',[2] 'Knowledge works as an
instrument of power '.[3]   'To what extent is our *intellect* also
a result of the conditions of life ?—We should not have it did
we not *need* to have it, and we should not have it *as* we have it,
if we did not need it *as* we need it—that is to say, if we could
live otherwise '.[4]   'The purpose of 'knowledge—the concept
must be regarded strictly and narrowly from an anthropo-
centric and biological standpoint '.[5]   On the other hand,
whereas Schopenhauer, though affirming the biological
function of intellect, maintained the possibility of a progressive
emancipation of intellect from will, an emancipation that
results in the peculiar activity of the artist, the true philosopher
and the moral personality, Nietzsche did not, of course,
accept the notion that progress meant a progressive emancipation from, and finally denial of, will : on the contrary, 'I
value a man according to the *quantum of power and fulness of his
will :* not according to the enfeeblement and moribund state
thereof '.[6]   It is not emancipation from will that characterizes
Nietzsche's higher man, but emancipation from 'moral
prejudices '—the opposite view to that of Schopenhauer.
(As for Eduard von Hartmann, Nietzsche declared, probably
rightly, that his system is a 'philosophical joke '.)   Atheism
is, of course, common to both Schopenhauer and Nietzsche,
though both recognize the necessity of religion for the *plebs*,
yet the atheism of Nietzsche was far more consistent than that
of Schopenhauer, who tried to retain 'holiness ' without God.
Without tracing any further similarities between points in
Nietzsche's thought and points in the system of Schopenhauer,
I would point out that, though the former recognized the

[1] *Will to Power*, II, p. 18.   [2] *Ibid.*, p. 150.   [3] *Ibid.*, p. 11.
[4] *Ibid.*, p. 22.   [5] *Ibid.*, p. 12.   [6] *Will to Power*, I, p. 304.

latter as a precursor, he used those doctrines which he borrowed from Schopenhauer or which he formulated under the influence or stimulus of Schopenhauer's writings, in a different way from that in which they were used by the Pessimist himself and and in a different setting. Nevertheless, by his voluntaristic doctrine, put forward in opposition to Hegelian rationalism (an opposition shared by Nietzsche) and by his insistence on vitalistic biology, Schopenhauer stands in some way at the head of the continental *Lebensphilosophie*, even though the direct ancestry of the latter might be more justifiably found in Nietzsche and in Kierkegaard. For Schopenhauer and for Nietzsche, man and his destiny stand in the centre of the picture, occupy the centre of the stage ; for them it is not an ' unearthly ballet of bloodless categories ' that is at the root of the world and of human life, but Will and Life.

Mention of biological philosophy naturally leads one to think of the philosophic work of the late Henri Bergson. The influence of Schopenhauer was felt by other modern French thinkers, e.g. by Lachelier and Fouillée ; but we will confine ourselves to noting some examples of similarity of doctrine between Bergson and Schopenhauer, without, however, attempting to settle the question how Bergson arrived at those doctrines. First of all, Bergson, as is well known, emphasized the theory that the intelligence has a practical function, being directed primarily to action. For example, if we are to live a social life, we must have fixed and ' static ' concepts that can be expressed in words, in language. The inner nature of the self is ' pure duration ', unceasing creation, it does not consist of states, ranged alongside one another in a quasi-spatial manner ; but if we are going to speak to others about ourselves, we have to break up the inner flow of our lives, taking, as it were, snapshots which can be shown to other people : we have to speak of our states of anger, joy, sorrow, pleasure, etc., as though our souls were like the chain of a rosary and the states like the rosary beads. If we take a photograph of an arrow in flight, the flight is arrested, as it were : similarly, for practical purposes, for purposes of communication, we arrest the flow of our inner lives and form those static mental snapshots, which we call concepts. If I say to someone that I am in a state of anger or of joy, I treat my state as though it were a thing apart, a sort of quantitative object that can be handled and surveyed in abstraction, passed over to another for inspection ; I also express it by means of a universal concept which omits the personal shades and nuances that make the state peculiarly mine ; I divorce it from my inner life and universalize it, in order that I may be able to communicate with others. Intelligence, then, says Bergson, is characterized by a natural inability to comprehend life : it is intuition that really grasps the pure duration which is life. Intuition is supra-rational, supra-conceptual : it is vital experience, immediate consciousness of the object in its inner reality : it is disinterested, contemplative, and, as such, differs from instinct. The latter, instinct, is a kind of infra-conceptual, infra-rational intuition, an intuition which is lived, which is turned towards practice, and is not disinterested, self-conscious or contemplative. The insect that instinctively provides for its young in a marvellous manner, does so by instinct, unconsciously and instinctively prolonging the work of life : in practice, of course, we cannot avoid speaking as though the insect had a kind of entomological knowledge, but really it discerns the right thing to do without any reflection at all. Rational and discursive intelligence, therefore, stands between instinct on the lower level and true intuition on the higher level.

Now, this doctrine of Bergson bears a marked resemblance to that of Schopenhauer, who had stressed the importance of intuition and the inadequacy of merely conceptual and abstract knowledge for apprehending reality. Abstract reasoning serves to make knowledge distinct, by bringing it under abstract concepts : it puts us in a position to impart this knowledge and explain it to others. What Schopenhauer calls ' perception ' is immediate, unreflective and incommunicable in itself : but, for practical purposes, we have to express perceptual knowledge abstractly. If ' perception ' is akin to instinct, is common to men and brutes, there is, we remember, the higher intuition of the artist, whereby he apprehends the Platonic Idea and that immediate consciousness whereby some people at least apprehend the true nature of ultimate reality, Will, that reality which is abstractly expressed in philosophy. Moreover, Schopenhauer's doctrine of the superiority of direct perception to discursive reasoning is strikingly re-echoed by Bergson, e.g. in one of the lectures which he gave at Oxford. Schopenhauer declared, as I mentioned in an earlier chapter, that syllogisms are ' only a makeshift '[1] : ' Bergson affirmed at Oxford that, *Concevoir est un pis aller quand il n'est pas donné de percevoir, et le raisonnement est fait pour combler les vides de la perception ou pour en étendre la portée,*[2] a statement with which Schopenhauer would have fully agreed. Again, in the same lecture Bergson maintained that, though perception is directed to action and isolates, from the general field of reality, the objects that interest us, i.e. (in Schopenhauerian terms) appeal to the will, from time to time, by a happy chance, *des hommes surgissent dont les sens ou la conscience sont moins adhérents à la vie.* ' Nature has forgotten to attach their faculty of perceiving to their faculty of acting. When they contemplate something, they regard it for itself, and not for themselves '.[3] Is not this analogous to Schopenhauer's theory of the artist and of the æsthetic beholder, who enjoy a ' superfluity ' of intellect, a plus of intellect, more than is required for the service of the will ?

It is quite true that, in *La Pensée et le Mouvant*[4] Bergson explicitly distinguishes his intuition from that of Schelling and Schopenhauer, on the ground that, whereas their intuition is an immediate quest for the eternal (*une recherche immédiate de l'éternel*), his intuition is an apprehension of true duration (*la durée vraie*) ; but it must not be forgotten that in the *Two Sources* intuition *par excellence* appears as the immediate apprehension by the mystic of ultimate reality. Bergson certainly did not regard ultimate reality in the same manner as Schopenhauer did, for from the *Two Sources*, when interpreted in the light of statements he made elsewhere, it becomes evident that he came to believe in God, theistically conceived, Who is the Source of life and Who manifests Himself in life as known in this world ; but it can hardly be denied that there is some resemblance between the operation of the *élan vital*, as described in *Creative Evolution*, and the operation of Schopenhauer's Will to live or Eduard von Hartmann's Unconscious Absolute. There can be little doubt that Bergson learnt from, or at least received stimulus from, previous and contemporary French philosophers, psychologists and biologists, besides making personal investigations of his own, so that I am very far from suggesting that he took his ideas of intuition, conceptual knowledge and *élan vital* from Schopenhauer (this would certainly be quite false) or even that he developed them under

[1] I, p. 88.
[3] *Ibid.*, p. 173.
[2] *La Pensée et le Mouvant*, p. 165.
[4] pp. 33-4.

the direct influence of Schopenhauer's writings : nevertheless, the fact that Bergson mentions Schopenhauer, even if it is to disagree with him, would seem to indicate some sort of influence, however tenuous, though, as I have said, if we want to discover direct and positive influence on the development of Bergson's ideas, we have to go to French thinkers rather than to German. In any case my object is not to discuss the question whether or not Bergson was influenced by Schopenhauer, but rather the question whether or not there is similarity between certain views of Bergson and certain views of Schopenhauer, and that such a similarity does exist is an undeniable truth, even though the peculiar flavours of the two philosophies (so far as we are entitled to speak of ' a Bergsonian philosophy ', when Bergson expressly disclaimed the intention of forming any system) are very different. Schopenhauer's philosophy is, as we have seen, radically pessimistic and atheistic, with a nihilistic goal, whereas Bergson's philosophy is sanely optimistic, is, or became, theistic, and expresses the value rather than the disvalue of life. Schopenhauer's ' saints ' deny life, whereas Bergson's saints affirm life and draw fresh life and higher life, the life of love, from the Source of all life. We must bear this radical difference in mind, when asserting, as we have good reason to assert, similarity of view on the part of the two philosophers in regard to certain topics.

When one looks at the philosophy of Schopenhauer as a philosophy of development, of ascent to consciousness, and passes over those elements in his system which would seem to render objective duration and process impossible or to clothe them with the cloak of illusion, it is seen to look at once backwards and forwards. It looks backwards, first of all, inasmuch as it takes its place in the general line of German metaphysical philosophy of which the notion of historical becoming is a leading characteristic. By his dynamic conception of substance, Leibniz stands at the head of that line, in spite of his relation with the so-called Enlightenment. The Leibnizian system, it is true, may be looked at as a conclusion from certain logical premises, but to look at it exclusively from this viewpoint, to see it as no more than an application, and an unsuccessful one at that, of formal logical axioms, as several commentators have done, is to miss altogether that conception of dynamic unfolding, of historical development, which was one of Leibniz's chief contributions to philosophy. It was not Christian Wolff, with his substitution of arid rationalism for the ideas of development and finality, who was the true successor of the great Leibniz, but rather men like Herder, like the German Romantics and metaphysicians. In the systems of Fichte and Schelling this idea of development, of self-unfolding, of process is evident : neither the subjective idealism of the one nor the objective idealism of the other could be characterized as ' static '. But it is in the system of Hegel above all that the notion of becoming is given particular prominence. In spite of the aprioristic, logical and schematic character of his system, Hegel was through and through an historical thinker and he embodied in the logical scheme of the system a wealth of knowledge drawn, even if indirectly, from experience. The dialectic may be a logical and abstract scheme ; but it was certainly not merely abstract to the mind of Hegel and it was dynamically conceived, this dynamic conception being taken over afterwards by the Marxists, though they applied it in a different way and gave it a setting which was even less favourable for its objectivity than that of Hegel. Now, Schopenhauer, despite his doctrine of time, despite his idealism and phenomenalism, despite his pessimism and theory of renunciation, of denial of the Will, despite his violent opposition to Fichte, Schelling and Hegel, undoubtedly derives from the German romantic movement in philosophy and remained in close relationship with it. The whole doctrine of the Will, which is essentially dynamic in character, an urge to self-objectification, the doctrine of the degrees or grades of the Will's objectification, of the unceasing self-conflict of the Will manifested in the phenomenal world, of teleology whereby the unconscious ' design ' of Will is realized, is an undeniable link between him and his predecessors, and not all his abuse of Schelling and Hegel, not all his depreciation of the value and importance of human history, avail to sever that link. It is a mistake to insist so much upon the voluntarism of Schopenhauer that one sees him merely as an antithesis to Hegel.

But, if it is true to say that the philosophy of Schopenhauer looks back, in the sense of standing in organic relation to the immediate past, it is equally true to say that his philosophy looks forward. By its insistence on Will or Energy, by its theory of the subordinate or secondary position of consciousness, by its doctrine of the evolution of consciousness as a biological function, by the central position accorded to the concept of life, of the struggle for existence, it looks forward to those realistic and vitalistic philosophies, which would lay stress on life and evolution, on the priority of life to consciousness, to Eduard von Hartmann and Nietzsche and Georg Simmel, to Fouillée and Guyau and Bergson, to Belfort Bax and Lloyd Morgan. I do not mean to imply that all these thinkers were consciously or in any way directly influenced by Schopenhauer (von Hartmann and Nietzsche certainly were, while we have no knowledge of any direct influence at all on Lloyd Morgan, for example), but only to point out the forward-looking aspect of Schopenhauer's philosophy. His philosophy represents, in some of its aspects, ideas which were to become more or less current coin and which, through varied channels, influenced even thinkers who had perhaps never read a page of Schopenhauer when they adopted these ideas or who had rejected him as a romantic dreamer.

One or two final remarks on the Schopenhauerian philosophy and Christianity. Some eccentric people have professed to discern in Schopenhauer's philosophy an ' esoteric ' version of Christianity ; but superficial resemblances should not mislead anyone into supposing that the Pessimist is really, as has been asserted, the *philosophus christissimus*. For orthodox Christians Mind is prior to matter (not in the sense of subjective idealism, but in the theistic sense), Nature is an external phenomenon of God, life has value and purpose, human life in particular, human history, though its course is not predetermined, subserves teleology and is subject to Divine Providence, the world is not evil in itself but good, as created by God, Who is infinite Goodness, and as sanctified and, in a sense, elevated through the Incarnation. There is indeed evil and suffering in the world, but these are not the last word about life and are themselves subordinate to Divine Providence: the final goal is not nothingness, but the positive vision and possession of the Supreme Good, not the denial of life, but the fullness of life. These are doctrines essential to Christianity and to deny them is to deny Christianity : Schopenhauerianism is no more esoteric Christianity than is Hegelianism (unless indeed the latter's meaning is transmuted out of all recognition). As Kierkegaard saw very clearly, Hegelianism, professing to give the ' inside ', as it were, of the ' absolute

religion', is destructive of Christianity; but, while Hegel
enshrined Christianity, at least verbally, in his system,
Schopenhauer never pretended to be a Christian and never
pretended that his philosophy was a Christian philosophy,
thus evincing a greater intellectual honesty or clarity of
thought than those persons (few, one is glad to say), who
imagine that his philosophy is in some mysterious way compatible with Christianity. If Schopenhauer's philosophy were
true, then Christianity would be false : if Christianity is true,
as it is true, then Schopenhauer's philosophy is, in the main,
false.

It is idle to select some points from Schopenhauer's philosophy that agree, or appear to agree, with what Christians
hold, and dwell exclusively on them. Schopenhauer held that
human life is a vale of tears and Christian spiritual writers
have also, not infrequently perhaps, at least at certain periods,
elaborated this theme ; but in the first place, to recognize the
evil and suffering in the world requires only commonsense and
honesty and is the special prerogative neither of Schopenhauer
nor of the Christian, while in the second place no orthodox
Christian, however much he may stress the superiority of the
' hereafter ' to the ' here ', can deny the value of this world
and of human life or declare that life is evil and human history
nothing but a sorry spectacle. If he said this, he would not
be speaking as a Christian, who is not entitled to deny the
value of the natural order or of the ' profane ', in so far as
the latter, of course, is in accord with the moral law. Nor
are we justified in selecting what Schopenhauer says of holiness, comparing it with the Christian ascetic and mystical
doctrines and affirming their identity. The essence of holiness,
according to Schopenhauer, lies in negation, denial, while the
essence of Christian holiness is far more affirmation : it
involves renunciation of course, but renunciation of what leads
to less life, not of what leads to more life. In any case, how
can an atheistic philosophy possibly be an ' esoteric ' version
of a theistic creed ? Such a proposition could not be established without a strong dosage of sophistry and humbug.
Schopenhauer knew best what he meant, and he knew that
he did not believe in the truth of religion. However sympathetic he may have been towards Christian asceticism and
sanctity, he was far more sympathetic towards oriental and
non-Christian ideals, though he had little use for religious

doctrine in any form, save as a symbolic presentation of
'truth' for the herd that could not do without religion.

One of the reasons why some people are so keen to assert
an 'esoteric' Christianity is that they think that orthodox
Christianity is unduly anthropomorphic. Apart from the fact
that their esoteric versions are frequently bizarre and fanciful
to a degree that makes one wonder if their authors are not
perhaps mentally unbalanced, their notion that Christianity
is unduly anthropomorphic is often due to the fact that they
persist in using their imaginations when the use of the imagination (employing, as it does, images from the spatial world),
is quite out of place. God is, for instance, spoken of as transcendent, and, if one uses one's imagination, one will picture
God as spatially outside the world, just as an imaginative
picture of God's immanence can be little better than a phan-
tasm of God spatially extended, as it were, throughout the
cosmos. In reality spatial categories cannot be predicated
of God at all, and, though imaginative pictures have their
use, they should not be taken as expressing exact truth.
Another reason, naturally connected with the foregoing, why
some people object to orthodox Christian doctrine and, so far
as they are willing to retain Christianity at all, try to construct
an esoteric or 'philosophic' version, is that they refuse to
admit the dualism of Creator and creation and assert monism
of some sort or another : they speak of dualism as 'unphilo-
sophic', as repugnant to the philosophic mind. This objection
is, very largely at least, simply the objection to 'anthropomorphism' put in another way, since the dualism of Creator
and creation means a Personal God and the conception of a
Personal God is for them 'anthropomorphic'. Thus for
Schopenhauer (who did not indeed preach an esoteric version
of Christianity, though he allowed that some religious doctrines
might be true *sensu allegorico*, but not *sensu proprio*) ' Anthropomorphism is an essential characteristic of Theism '[1], because
it ascribes Personality to God. But these critics of theism
neglect the fact that when theists declare that God is personal,
they are not saying that God possesses *human* personality, but
that God is *not less* than the perfection we know as human
personality, that He is Intellect and Will in one Infinite Perfection. If this is anthropomorphism, then certainly theism is
' anthropomorphic ', but the theistic doctrine is based on the

[1] *Fragments of the History of Philosophy (Parerga and Paralipomena)*, V, p. 125.

valid axiom that the greater cannot proceed from the less as from its adequate cause. Impersonal monism cannot possibly account for human individual personality, and all attempts to do so must necessarily fail. How could Schopenhauer's irrational Will objectify itself in intelligent beings ? How could Marxist dynamic matter evolve into consciousness ? ' Emergent evolution ' is a term coined to cover the appearance of a factor that cannot be explained by the monist : not being able to deny the reality of mind and consciousness, he says that it ' emerges ', whereas all that he is entitled to say, from the purely empirical standpoint, is that it appears, i.e. was not before and now is : to go further and assert that it proceeds from an impersonal factor is to have recourse to myth. In no sense can impersonal monism be looked upon as esoteric Christianity, however much ethical values may be vindicated, as by Schopenhauer, for theism is an essential tenet of Christianity. Schopenhauer himself, of course, realized this quite clearly, as I have said : he did not look on himself as an ' esoteric ' Christian, but as a non-Christian.

I have dealt sharply with Schopenhauer in the foregoing pages, and indeed throughout this book ; but his philosophy, whatever its intrinsic value, will doubtless always be remembered as perhaps the most striking statement of the pessimistic *Weltanschauung* in the history of human thought. Other pessimists there have been, in ancient and modern times (one has only to think of Leopardi, whose writings won strong approval from the German philosopher) ; but what other pessimist has elaborated a philosophy of pessimism at the same time so thorough-going and so finely expressed as that of Schopenhauer ? His philosophy is an extreme statement of the problem of evil and suffering, that problem which we cannot in this life completely solve, but to the solution of which we most nearly approach at the feet of the Crucified Redeemer. Who died and rose again, that we might live.

INDEX